Business Economics in a Rapidly - Changing World

Business and Finance: Performance and Management

BUSINESS ECONOMICS IN A RAPIDLY- CHANGING WORLD

Additional books in this series can be found on Nova's website under the Series tab.

Additional E-books in this series can be found on Nova's website under the E-books tab.

BUSINESS ISSUES, COMPETITION AND ENTREPRENEURSHIP

Additional books in this series can be found on Nova's website under the Series tab.

Additional E-books in this series can be found on Nova's website under the E-books tab.

BUSINESS ECONOMICS IN A RAPIDLY-CHANGING WORLD

BUSINESS AND FINANCE: PERFORMANCE AND MANAGEMENT

RICHARD B. MORLAND
AND
ANTHONY J. GAGGLIONE
EDITORS

Nova Science Publishers, Inc.
New York

For permission to use material from this book please contact us:
Telephone 631-231-7269; Fax 631-231-8175
Web Site: http://www.novapublishers.com

Additional color graphics may be available in the e-book version of this book.

LIBRARY OF CONGRESS CATALOGING-IN-PUBLICATION DATA

Business and finance : performance and management / editors, Richard B. Morland and Anthony J. Gagglione.
p. cm. -- (Business economics in a rapidly-changing world: business issues, competition and entrepreneurship)
Includes index.
ISBN 978-1-61122-936-3 (hardcover)
1. Entrepreneurship--Case studies. 2. Economic policy--Case studies. 3. Fiscal policy--Case studies. 4. Economic development--Case studies. I. Morland, Richard B. II. Gagglione, Anthony J.
HB615.B88 2011
658--dc22
2010044705

Published by Nova Science Publishers, Inc. † New York

CONTENTS

PREFACE

This book presents and discusses information in the study of business and finance. Topics discussed include partner selection, market orientation and performances of international joint ventures in Taiwan; project management; Asian stock markets; consolidation and determinants of bank efficiency; the changing face of international HRM and business; empire-building; the link between microfinance and well-being and the Microcluster Value Chain Analysis.

Chapter 1 – The authors propose a two-stage approach for estimating Value-at-Risk (VaR) that can simultaneously reflect two stylized facts displayed by most asset return series: volatility clustering and the heavy-tailedness of conditional return distributions over short horizons. The proposed method combines the bias-corrected exponentially weighted moving average (EWMA) model for estimating the conditional volatility and the extreme value theory (EVT) for estimating the tail of the innovation distribution. In particular, for minimizing bias in the estimation procedure, the proposed method makes minimal assumptions about the underlying innovation distribution and concentrates on modeling its tail using the non-parametric Hill estimator and uses the moment-ratio Hill estimator for the shape parameter of the extreme value distribution. To validate the model, the authors conducted an empirical investigation on the daily stock market returns of eight emerging Asian markets: China, India, Indonesia, Malaysia, Philippines, South Korea, Taiwan, and Thailand. In addition, the proposed method was compared with J.P. Morgan's RiskMetrics approach. The empirical results show that the proposed method provides a more accurate forecast of VaR for lower probabilities of VaR violation from 0.1% to 1%. Furthermore, the authors demonstrate that applying the Hill estimator to estimate the tail of the innovation distribution can better capture additional downside risk faced during times of greater fluctuation than the second-order moment-ratio Hill estimator.

Chapter 2 - Having proper partners positively links with venture performances when firms attempt to leverage external organization's resources to span cross-border in a form of international joint venture. Since 1970s, partner selection criteria in the past studies centered on task requirement and partner characteristics, few if any had attempted to include customer as part of primary consideration in selection decisions. This research attempts to point out such negligence and to verify the important effects of lacking such factors in venture performance. Taking samples from international joint ventures in Taiwan, this research used questionnaire as instrument and successfully collected 321 valid responses with CEO, functional managers that individually answer different questions to avoid common method

variance. SPSS statistics package is the tool used to analyze gathered data. Major findings of this research include identifying and confirming the existence of customer related factors and its importance in the model of joint venture performance. Partner related factor is the most powerful predictors in predicting joint venture performance, followed by customer related factor, and task related factors. Key to become a market-driven management is selecting partner with customer related factors. There are several academic and managerial implications associated with the research finding.

Chapter 3 - Traditionally projects are considered means for getting things done, simultaneously striving for efficient and accurate methods – that is, doing more in less time. A consequence, not often discussed, is that doing more things in less time with a closer focus on cost, will inevitably lead to a more complex and tightly connected project execution system which is more sensitive to deviations. Following a "project-as-practice" perspective this paper explores and analyses how deviations are managed. The findings suggest that even though the company under consideration manages about 120 projects per year deviations cannot be avoided. The deviations were found initially to decouple (a process of creating loosely coupled activities) from the overall project process and later on to recouple (a process of tightly coupling activities) when the deviation was resolved. The paper suggests that the management of deviations is dynamic and changing and that the concept of coupling is a fruitful way of exploring the process.

Chapter 4 - Despite the importance of the art restoration sector in Italy, as well as in many other European countries, this industry has often been ignored by management studies. For these reasons this study focused on Italian art restoration firms, with particular reference to their adoption of innovative technologies such as laser technology.

The literature has widely emphasized the influence of external agents in the processes of adopting new technologies, above all in the case of small or medium-sized firms, and for those particularly linked to external forces such as suppliers and clients due to economic, regulatory and structural reasons. The study, supported by a qualitative analysis and a comparison with previously acquired quantitative data, contributes to a more comprehensive description of the art restoration sector and, analysing the role of suppliers and clients, completes the adoption model of technology innovation developed in previous research on laser technology (Verbano, Venturini, Nosella, Petroni, 2008).

The results identify the factors related to restoration firms, suppliers and clients that influence the adoption of laser and outline some suggestions to encourage its adoption in the particularly complex sector of art conservation.

Chapter 5 - The present paper examines the impact of mergers and acquisitions on the cost efficiency of the Malaysian banking sector. The analysis consists of three stages. Firstly, by using the non-parametric Data Envelopment Analysis (DEA) approach, the authors calculate the cost, allocative, and technical efficiency of individual banks during the period 1997-2003. Secondly, the authors examine changes in the efficiency of the Malaysian banking sector during the pre and post merger periods by using a series of parametric and non-parametric univariate tests. Finally, the authors employ the multivariate Tobit regression analysis to examine factors that influence the efficiency of the Malaysian banking sector during the pre and post merger periods. The empirical findings suggest that the merger has resulted in a higher mean cost efficiency of the Malaysian banking sector post merger. The authors find that the acquirers have been relatively more cost efficient in all of the seven merger cases analyzed. The results from the multivariate regression analysis suggest that

loans intensity, size, income diversification, and capitalization exhibits positive relationship with bank efficiency. On the other hand, market share and expense preference behaviour are negatively related to bank efficiency levels. The empirical findings suggest that banks in the control group have been relatively more cost efficient than those that were involved in mergers. The results suggest that the variations in Malaysian bank cost efficiency are not significantly related to economic conditions and concentration.

Chapter 6 - Under the influence of globalization, different international business strategies require the support of unique international human resource management (HRM) policies and practices in order to make the business successful. A critical challenge is how to integrate international business strategies and international HRM. The increasing debate on this topic highlights the problems in balancing the policies of HQ control, global integration and localization. However, the difficulty is how to achieve a balanced approach between these policies in reality.

This chapter looks at the integration between international business strategies and international HRM by carrying out case studies of Japanese and Taiwanese companies operating in China. There are several reasons for carrying out this research: 1. China is one of the most dynamic economies in East Asia. It has both huge amounts of FDI and many multinational enterprises (MNEs) operating within its borders. This research will have general implications of MNEs operating in one of the largest emerging economies in East Asia. 2. Japanese and Taiwanese MNEs have been the leaders in terms of offshore investment and production in East Asia. In fact, both Japanese and Taiwanese MNEs are the leading groups of foreign investors in China and other parts of Asia. By investigating these two types of MNEs, the authors will have a better understanding of their strategic considerations regarding offshore investment and business operations as well as their approach towards the integration of international business strategies and international HRM. The feedback from of this project will benefit Japanese and Taiwanese MNEs as well as other MNEs for future successful operation in China.

Following the central theme of this research project, the authors are most interested in the following perspectives of these cases: 1. their international business strategies, vision and goals; 2. their different international staffing strategies, such as using parent country nationals (PCN), third country nationals (TCN) and host country nationals (HCN); 3. the roles of headquarters (HQ) vs. subsidiary in terms of business strategy formulation, control and evaluation; 4. the detailed policies and practices of global integration and localization; 5. the future direction for improvement.

In order to have a comprehensive understanding of the relevant issues, the authors have set out this chapter as follows: Section 2 reviews the relevant literature that is related to a balanced approach of global integration and localization. Section 3 details the case studies and the investigation of the detailed policies and practices in relation to the five perspectives identified above. Section 4 discusses their findings and Section 5 concludes the chapter by highlighting the authors' major findings and implications for both theoretical understanding as well as for empirical practice. Section 5 concludes the chapter by identifying the unique research outcomes of this project, the limitation as well as future research direction.

Chapter 7 - This paper tries to study the particular workings of clusters, proposing a tool that helps with the empowerment and development of inter-organisational networks that might exist in them. It is a new tool for territorial strategic analysis focused in clustering policy based on the innovation; the microcluster value chain analysis.

Territorial competitiveness should be looked for by starting from the generation of external economies, from strategic decisions taken by those responsible for the interrelated networks, and from the identification and the empowerment of the key relationships among the agent leaders. These are the objectives that the tool proposed will try to resolve.

To achieve this, the most important thing will be to know how to locate and to diffuse the necessary knowledge to be able to identify the opportunities or key success factors that can motivate the creation of concrete inter-organisational networks in the heart of a microcluster.

Chapter 8 - Income-generating work for women is one of many attempts of the international community and national governments of developing countries to improve well-being of rural households, and empower women. While people draw their interpretation and indicators of well-being from their subjective cultural contexts, many development interventions lack reference to the perceptions of beneficiaries on what advances their well-being. This article presents an investigation of how rural women and men in the Bogoso area of Ghana perceived well-being and the impact of women's microfinance work on their perceived well-being indicators. Findings show that living within a peaceful household environment is the most important well-being indicator to the people, and that microfinance contributed significantly to reducing household conflicts, as household's and children's needs were frequently met. Thus, this article recommends attention to interventions that enhance the ability of rural households to be more engaged in economic activities to promote peace within their households. It also encourages efforts to conscientize and build capacities of household members to be affected by women's work in mitigating potential conflict triggers.

Chapter 9 - Manpower planning is a fundamental aspect of Human Resource Management which is to a great extent based on statistical techniques and focused on quantitative models for workforce systems. Aggregated Markov models are defined by transition probabilities between homogeneous subgroups of personnel of the workforce system. The analytical Markovian approach in manpower planning allows identifying interesting characteristics of the workforce system, allows predicting the evolution of the workforce and controlling it by setting the organization's human resource policies (e.g. recruitment, promotion, training). There is a rich variety of publications on Markov manpower models, in which properties of workforce systems are investigated under very specific assumptions. This paper offers a review of the different types of Markov manpower models. Hereby attention has been paid to the successive stages of the Markov manpower planning methodology in real-world applications, from model building and selection, parameter estimation, model validation to prediction and control. The paper covers the latest advances in the field.

Chapter 10 – The authors consider a model where wealth-constrained entrepreneurs have private information about the qualities of available investment projects. The authors show that some "high risk-high return" projects will receive external financing even if they are not socially profitable. Some "low risk-low return" projects will not be funded even if they are socially profitable. Government interventions can improve equilibrium. Optimal government policy may include corporate taxation, subsidies or other instruments. A universal tax on all entrepreneurs with limited liability is not optimal.

Chapter 11 - This note provides an explanation for why tax rates on capital gains are usually lower than ordinary income tax rates based on manager's agency problem related to "empire-building" and the underinvestment problem.

Chapter 12 - This paper analyzes the out-of-sample ability of different parametric and semi-parametric GARCH-type models to forecast the conditional variance and the conditional and unconditional kurtosis of three types of financial assets (stock index, exchange rate and Treasury Note). For this purpose, the authors consider the Gaussian and Student-t GARCH models by Bollerslev (1986, 1987), and two different time-varying conditional kurtosis GARCH models based on the Student-t and a transformed Gram-Charlier density.

Chapter 13 - Despite extensive corporate responsibility research into both *what* products firm produce and *how* they produce them, research is lacking in one product category in which the *what* and *how* linkage create questionable corporate practice – luxury products. Luxury is in some cases created by companies controlling the so-called user imagery of their customers, i.e., by companies encouraging 'desirable' individuals to consume their products and obstructing 'undesirable' individuals from consumption. This chapter critically analyses the implications of this corporate practice based on a study of Sweden's most luxurious nightclub. The study's results show that the nightclub has organised its activities to allow categorisations of individuals into 'desirable' and 'undesirable' customers. Furthermore, the study shows that a creation of 'misery' for the vast majority of individuals (the 'undesirable') is essential for creating 'enjoyment' for the selected few (the 'desirable'). The chapter concludes by discussing implications for practitioners interesting in altering this situation.

Versions of these chapters were also published in *Journal of Current Issues in Finance, Business and Economics,* Volume 2, Numbers 1-4, published by Nova Science Publishers, Inc. They were submitted for appropriate modifications in an effort to encourage wider dissemination of research.

In: Business and Finance: Performance and Management
Editors: R. Morland and A. Gagglione
ISBN: 978-1-61122-936-3

Chapter 1

ESTIMATION OF VALUE AT RISK FOR HETEROSCEDASTIC AND HEAVY-TAILED ASSET TIME SERIES: EVIDENCE FROM EMERGING ASIAN STOCK MARKETS

***Tzu-Chuan Kao*[1] *and Chu-Hsiung Lin*[2,*]**

[1] Department of Finance and Banking, Kun Shan University, Taiwan

[2] Department of Risk Management and Insurance, National Kaohsiung First University of Science and Technology, Taiwan

ABSTRACT

We propose a two-stage approach for estimating Value-at-Risk (VaR) that can simultaneously reflect two stylized facts displayed by most asset return series: volatility clustering and the heavy-tailedness of conditional return distributions over short horizons. The proposed method combines the bias-corrected exponentially weighted moving average (EWMA) model for estimating the conditional volatility and the extreme value theory (EVT) for estimating the tail of the innovation distribution. In particular, for minimizing bias in the estimation procedure, the proposed method makes minimal assumptions about the underlying innovation distribution and concentrates on modeling its tail using the non-parametric Hill estimator and uses the moment-ratio Hill estimator for the shape parameter of the extreme value distribution. To validate the model, we conducted an empirical investigation on the daily stock market returns of eight emerging Asian markets: China, India, Indonesia, Malaysia, Philippines, South Korea, Taiwan, and Thailand. In addition, the proposed method was compared with J.P. Morgan's RiskMetrics approach. The empirical results show that the proposed method provides a more accurate forecast of VaR for lower probabilities of VaR violation from 0.1% to 1%. Furthermore, we demonstrate that applying the Hill estimator to estimate the tail of the innovation distribution can better capture additional downside risk faced during times of greater fluctuation than the second-order moment-ratio Hill estimator.

[*] E-mail addresses: chusiung@ccms.nkfust.edu.tw; Tel.:886-7-6011000~4015; fax: 886-7-6011041. (Corresponding author)

Keywords: Value-at-Risk, bias-corrected EWMA estimator, Extreme value theory, Hill estimator, Moment-ratio Hill estimator

1. Introduction

Value-at-Risk (VaR) is a very popular measure of market risk that has been widely implemented by financial institutions. According to the Capital Adequacy Directive produced by the Bank of International Settlement in Basle (Basle Committee, 1996), the risk capital of a bank must be sufficient to cover losses on the bank's trading portfolio over a 10-day holding period on 99% of occasions. The value of risk capital is referred to as VaR. From a statistical standpoint, VaR is defined as the possible maximum loss over a given holding period with a fixed confidence level. Hence, the VaR at the $100(1-\alpha)$ percent confidence level is the lower 100α percentile of the return distribution. Thus, the VaR is estimated on the basis of the distribution of the expected returns. This entails that one needs to make assumptions concerning the form of the expected return distribution. However, ad-hoc assumptions about the form of return distribution will generate a biased estimate of the VaR. To provide the investment community and risk managers with a more accurate VaR model, this study provides a two-stage approach for reducing the estimation bias that may result from a misspecified model and applies it to the stock market returns of eight emerging Asian markets.

In the existing literature, we find three approaches to estimating the return distribution (McNeil and Frey, 2000). First, there is the non-parametric historical simulation method, in which the actual empirical distribution is considered using observations of past returns as a basis. The method is easy to implement and avoids misspecifications of the form of the return distribution. However, when using it, it is difficult to estimate the extreme VaR quantiles (Beder, 1995; Pritisker, 1997; Danielsson and de Vries, 1997). Second, there are fully parametric methods that are based on an econometric model of time varying volatility and that assume conditional normality for the returns. Examples of these methods are J.P. Morgan's RiskMetrics[1], and GARCH-type models. GARCH-type models capture the effects of volatility clustering in the returns, but have the weakness that the assumption of conditional normality does not seem to hold for actual return distributions (Baillie and DeGennaro, 1990; Poon and Taylor, 1992; Danielsson and de Vries, 1997). Third, there are methods based on extreme value theory (EVT). EVT-based models model the tails of the return distribution directly and thus have the potential to yield better estimates and forecasts of extreme VaR. However, given the conditional heteroscedasticity of asset return data, EVT-based models cannot reflect the conditional volatility (McNeil and Frey, 2000; Cotter, 2001). A number of authors have attempted to alleviate the weaknesses of each of the above approaches. Barone-Adesi et al. (1998) combine the GARCH model with an historical simulation method to estimate the VaR. They fit a GARCH model to a return series and then apply an historical simulation to infer the distribution of the innovations. McNeil and Frey (2000) estimate the VaR by filtering return series with a GARCH model and then apply

[1] The RiskMetrics approach uses a EWMA model to forecast conditional volatility. Notice that the EWMA model can be viewed as a special case of the simple GARCH model. See the JP Morgan Bank RiskMetrics Technical (1996).

threshold methods from EVT to fit the innovations distribution. McNeil and Frey's (2000) study indicates that the method proposed by Barone-Adesi et al. (1998) may work well for large data sets, but for smaller data sets, threshold methods from EVT can give better estimates of the tails of the residuals. Recently, Gencay et al. (2003), Byström (2004), and Kuester et al. (2006) have demonstrated that McNeil and Frey's (2000) method can yield accurate estimates of the VaR.

In practice, the most widely used approach estimating the VaR is J.P. Morgan's RiskMetrics (Deloitte Touche Tohmatsu, 2002). The RiskMetrics approach to calculating the VaR assumes that returns are conditional normal and uses an exponentially weighted moving average (EWMA) model to forecast conditional volatility. The main advantage of the EWMA model is the simplicity of the estimation procedure with a small number of available observations. However, Harris and Shen (2004) indicate that the EWMA model implicitly assumes that the conditional distribution of real returns is normal, if as is suggested by empirical evidence, the conditional distribution is heavy-tailed, the EWMA estimator will be inefficient.

Taking into account the foregoing, the study presented herein extends the work of McNeil and Frey (2000) and proposes a two-stage approach for estimating the VaR. The proposed method combines the bias-corrected EWMA model proposed by Harris and Shen (2004) for estimating the conditional volatility and EVT for estimating the tail of the innovation distribution. Unlike the methods of J.P. Morgan's RiskMetrics and McNeil and Frey (2000), the two-stage approach presented here possesses two advantages: (a) it can simultaneously reflect two stylized facts that are displayed by most asset return series, namely, volatility clustering and the heavy-tailedness of conditional return distributions over short horizons; and (b) it can minimize the bias in the estimation procedure. These advantages are gained because the proposed method makes minimal assumptions about the underlying innovation distribution and concentrates on modeling its tail using a non-parametric Hill estimator (Hill, 1975) and uses a moment-ratio Hill estimator (Danielsson et al., 1996) for the shape parameter of the extreme value distribution.

In an empirical investigation, the proposed two-stage approach was used to measure the downside risk for daily stock market returns of eight emerging Asian markets: China, India, Indonesia, Malaysia, Philippines, South Korea, Taiwan, and Thailand. In addition, the proposed method was compared with the RiskMetrics approach from J.P. Morgan. To assess the predictive performance of the different methods, the study employed a backtesting procedure, which included the test of predictive versus theoretical violation probability, Kupiec's (1995) unconditional coverage testing, and Christofferson's (1998) conditional coverage testing.

The remainder of this paper is organized as follows. Section 2 presents the theoretical foundations used to estimate the downside risk. Section 3 describes the stylized fact of the empirical data. Section 4 presents the empirical results. Section 5 concludes.

2. Methodology

The following subsections (i) describe the bias-corrected EWMA model proposed by Harris and Shen (2004), which was used to measure the conditional volatility; (ii) describe the non-parametric Hill estimator (Hill, 1975) and moment-ratio Hill estimator (Danielsson et al.,

1996) based on EVT for estimating the tail index of the innovations distribution; and (iii) present the backtesting procedure.

2.1. An Alternative VaR Model

Let ($X_t, t \in Z$) be a stationary time series that presents daily observations of the log return on a financial asset price. This study assumes that the dynamics of X are given by:

$$X_t = \mu_t + \sigma_t Z_t \tag{1}$$

where the innovations Z_t are a white noise process with zero mean and unit variance and are independent and identical according to a distribution function $F_Z(z)$ (i.e. iid). This study assumes that the conditional mean μ_t and the conditional standard deviation σ_t are measurable with respect to I_{t-1}, where I_{t-1} is the set of all information through time *t-1*. From Equation (1), the time *t* quantile, x_q^t, can be derived for a given probability level *q*. Therefore, x_q^t is defined such that $q = P(X_t \le x_q | I_{t-1}) = F_{X_t|I_{t-1}}(x_q)$, where $F_X(x)$ denotes the cumulative probability distribution of X_t. Using Equation (1) the probability level *q* can be rewritten as

$$\begin{aligned} q &= P\{\mu_t + \sigma_t Z_t \le x_q | I_{t-1}\} \\ &= P\{Z_t \le (x_q - \mu_t)/\sigma_t | I_{t-1}\} \\ &= F_Z\{(x_q - \mu_t)/\sigma_t\} \end{aligned} \tag{2}$$

If the quantile associated with the distribution $F_Z(z)$ is denoted as z_q, namely $z_q = (x_q - \mu_t)/\sigma_t$, the time *t* quantile (or the time *t* VaR at the $100(1-q)$ % confidence level), x_q^t, can be calculated as

$$x_q^t = \mu_t + \sigma_t z_q \tag{3}$$

Via Equation (3), x_q^t is obtained and must estimate μ_t, σ_t, and z_q. To measure x_q^t this study proposes a two-stage approach. The first stage uses the equal-weight moving-average approach to estimate μ_t and applies the bias-corrected EWMA estimator to estimate σ_t. The second stage uses the Hill estimator (Hill, 1975) and moment-ratio Hill estimator based on EVT to estimate z_q. The following subsections detail the proposed two-stage approach.

2.1.1. First Stage: Estimating μ_t and σ_t

For predictive purposes, a rolling window of 500 observations was used to dynamically estimate conditional mean μ_t and conditional standard deviation σ_t. First, this study considers using the equal-weight moving-average approach to estimate the conditional mean μ_t.

$$\mu_t = \sum_{n=1}^{500} x_{t-n} \Big/ 500 \tag{4}$$

Sequentially, this study considers that the conditional variance σ_t^2 follows the bias-corrected EWMA model proposed by Harris and Shen (2004). The EWMA model, known as an integrated GARCH or IGARCH model, is used to estimate the conditional variance σ_t^2 because it relies on one parameter only and thus facilitates estimation. The EWMA estimator is given by:

$$\sigma_t^2 = \lambda\sigma_{t-1}^2 + (1-\lambda)X_{t-1}^2 \tag{5}$$

where the parameter λ is called the decay factor and must be less than unity. The empirical study set $\lambda = 0.94$, which is the value used by RiskMetrics to estimate daily volatility. The EWMA estimator is based on the maximum likelihood estimator of the variance of the normal distribution; hence, if the EWMA model is misspecified, it will generate biased conditional variance forecasts. To generate bias-corrected conditional variance forecasts, Harris and Shen (2004) first estimate the conditional bias in the EWMA model using a realized volatility regression with squared returns, and then apply the estimated regression parameters to obtain new bias-corrected conditional variance forecasts. The theoretical framework for the estimation is detailed in Theil (1966), Mincer and Zarnovitz (1969), and Harris and Shen (2004). The estimation process is summarized as follows:

Step 1: Use Equation (5) to obtain the forecasts of conditional variance $\hat{\sigma}_t^2$.

Step 2: Use the realized volatility measured by the squared returns (X_t^2) and the conditional variance forecasts ($\hat{\sigma}_t^2$) to construct a regression model, as follows:

$$X_t^2 = a + b\hat{\sigma}_t^2 + v_t \tag{6}$$

where v_t denotes the error term. Equation (6) is widely used in the literature on volatility modeling to evaluate the explanatory power of a particular conditional variance model and to correct conditional variance forecasts (Theil, 1966; Mincer and Zarnovitz, 1969). In order to correct the bias of conditional variance forecasts that are generated by the EWMA model, we need to estimate the parameters *a* and *b*.

Step 3: Once we have estimated parameter $\hat{a}$ and $\hat{b}$, we can define a new bias-corrected conditional variance forecasts, $\hat{\hat{\sigma}}_t^2$ given by

$$\hat{\hat{\sigma}}_t^2 = \hat{a} + \hat{b}\hat{\sigma}_t^2 \tag{7}$$

2.1.2. Second Stage: Estimating z_q

Following McNeil and Frey (2000), this study assumes that the residuals distribution is not normal and that perhaps it has heavy tails or is leptokurtic. Therefore this study used EVT to model the tail of the residuals distribution and applied this EVT model to estimate z_q. EVT investigates the distribution of tail observations in large samples. In the limit, the shape of the tail follows a Pareto law for a general class of heavy-tailed distributions. The tail fatness of the distribution is characterized by the tail index. As indicated by Dewachter and Gielens (1999) and Cotter (2001), for minimizing model risk, the Hill non-parametric method for estimating the tail index is superior to parametric procedures that require assumptions about the exact distribution type of extreme values. Consequently, this study applies a non-parametric Hill estimator (Hill, 1975) and moment-ratio Hill estimator (Danielsson et al., 1996) to estimate the tail index of residuals distribution and z_q. The process used to estimate z_q is presented below.

This study assumes that the standardized residuals series $(z_{t-n}, z_{t-n+1}, \ldots, z_{t-1}) = \left(\frac{x_{t-n} - \hat{\mu}_{t-n}}{\hat{\sigma}_{t-n}}, \ldots, \frac{x_{t-1} - \hat{\mu}_{t-1}}{\hat{\sigma}_{t-1}}\right)$ follow an extreme value distribution with a tail-index parameter γ and applies the Hill estimator to estimate γ, the desired quantile z_q can be estimated by:

$$\hat{z}_q = z_{(m+1)}\left(\frac{1-q}{m/n}\right)^{-\gamma}. \tag{8}$$

Let $z_{(i)}$ denote the i th decreasing order statistic of the absolute standardized residuals such that $z_{(i)} \geq z_{(i+1)}$ for $i = 2,\ldots,n$. Specifying m as the number of tail observations, the tail estimator γ proposed by Hill (1975) is obtained as follows:

$$\gamma = \frac{1}{m}\sum_{i=1}^{m} \ln z_{(i)} - \ln z_{(m)} \tag{9}$$

For simplicity, we follow Quintos et al. (2001) and set the threshold m to be 10% of the sample size.

In addition, Danielsson et al. (1996) propose a generalization of the Hill estimator, the so-called k-order moment-ratio Hill estimator, to estimate the tail index of the distribution. They point out that the moment-ratio Hill estimator has a lower asymptotic bias than the Hill

estimator. Moreover, Wagner and Marsh (2004) demonstrate that a second-order moment-ratio Hill estimator performs better. Therefore this study also uses a second-order moment-ratio Hill estimator, ω_2, to estimate the tail-index parameter γ .The *k*-order moment-ratio Hill estimator is given by

$$\omega_k(z_{(m)}) = \frac{\phi_k(z_{(m)})}{k\phi_{k-1}(z_{(m)})} \qquad k = 1,2,... \tag{10}$$

where $\phi_0(z_{(m)}) = 1$, $\phi_k(z_{(m)}) = \frac{1}{m}\sum_{i=1}^{k}(\ln z_{(i)} - \ln z_{(m)})^k$. When k=1, the first-order moment-ratio Hill estimator ω_1 is equal to the Hill estimator (Hill, 1975).

Finally, we substitute $\hat{\mu}_t$, $\hat{\sigma}_t$ and $\hat{z}_q$ into Equation (3). Then, the forecasted time *t* VaR at $100(1-q)\%$ condition level, $\hat{x}_q^t$, is given by $\hat{x}_q^t = \hat{\mu}_t + \hat{\sigma}_t \hat{z}_q$ (11)

2.2. Backtesting VaRs

To assess the predictive performance of the different risk models and obtain a robust evaluation result, this study employed three backtesting methods, as follows:

- First, this study used the test of predictive versus theoretical probability that a VaR violation will occur that is recommended by the Basle Committee of Banking Supervision. Using each of risk models for estimating VaR, given different probabilities that a VaR violation[2] q^* will occur, this study forecasts the daily VaR. These forecasts of the VaR are then compared with the actual returns on the days in question and the number of days on which the actual returns exceed the forecasted VaR is counted. The number of such days, *N*, is called the number of exceedences. The predictive probability that a VaR violation will occur can then be obtained using the number of exceedences divided by the total number of observed returns, *T*. If the predictive probability that a VaR violation will occur that is estimated by a particular risk model is close to the theoretical probability, the risk model in question may be said to perform well for estimating VaRs.
- Second, this study used the unconditional coverage test developed by Kupiec (1995). The unconditional coverage hypothesis states that the probability that a VaR violation will occur that is obtained for a particular risk model, call it q, is significantly different from the given probability that a VaR violation q^* will occur. Namely, $H_0 : q = q^*$. The likelihood ratio (LR) statistic is

  $$LR_{uc} = -2\ln\left[(1-q^*)^{T-N}(q^*)^N\right] + 2\ln\left\{[1-(N/T)]^{T-N}(N/T)^N\right\} \sim \chi^2(1) \tag{12}$$

  The LR_{uc} test statistic has a chi-squared distribution with one degree of freedom.

[2] A VaR violation occurs when the actual returns exceed the forecasted VaR.

- Third, this study used the conditional coverage test developed by Christofferson (1998). The conditional coverage hypothesis is to simultaneously test whether the VaR violations are independent and the average number of violations is correct. Namely, $H_0 : \pi_{01} = \pi_{11} = q^*$. The LR statistic is

$$LR_{cc} = -2\ln(L_A - L_I) \sim \chi^2(2) \tag{13}$$

$$L_A = (1-q^*)^{T-N}(q^*)^N$$

$$L_I = (1-\pi_{01})^{T_{00}}(\pi_{01})^{T_{01}}(1-\pi_{11})^{T_{10}}(\pi_{11})^{T_{11}}$$

$$\pi_{ij} = T_{ij}/(T_{i0} + T_{i1})$$

where T_{ij}, $i, j = 0, 1$ is the number of times state j follows state i, state 0 denotes an actual return less than the forecasted VaR, and state 1 denotes an actual return that exceeds the forecasted VaR. The LR_{cc} test statistic has a chi-squared distribution with two degrees of freedom.

3. Data Description

To verify the performance of the proposed approach, we conducted an empirical investigation that examined the daily stock market indices of eight emerging Asian markets (China, India, Indonesia, Malaysia, Philippines, South Korea, Taiwan, and Thailand[3]) for the period August 23, 1991 to August 23, 2007. The daily returns were measured by the first difference of the natural logarithm of the stock market index. The dataset was downloaded from Datastream.

Table 1 lists the preliminary statistics of the returns for the eight stock markets. The mean returns for the entire period are almost zero. According to the standard deviation for the returns, investing in firms that are listed on the Chinese stock market carries with it a higher risk than for the stock markets of other countries. The returns distributions are heavy-tailed or leptokurtic, as demonstrated by high kurtosis and highly significant Jargue-Bera statistics. The returns distributions for the South Korean and Taiwanese stock markets display a negative skewness, and for the stock markets of other countries they display a positive skewness. This implies that negative extreme returns are more likely to occur than the normal distribution forecasts in the stock markets of South Korea and Taiwan, while in other countries positive extreme returns are more likely to occur than the normal distribution forecasts. These findings indicate that the returns distributions for the eight emerging Asian stock markets can be characterized by fat-tailed distributions and that the left (or negative)

[3] The names of the eight emerging Asian stock market indices are as follows: (1) China: Shanghai SE Composite Price Index (2) India: India BSE National Price Index (3) Indonesia: Jakarta SE Composite Price Index (4) Malaysia: KLCI Composite Price Index (5) Philippines: Philippine SE Price Index (6) South Korea: Korea SE Composite Price Index (7) Taiwan: TSEC Weighted Index (8) Thailand: Bangkok S.E.T. Price Index.

and right (or positive) tails should be treated, respectively[4]. In addition, this investigation also reports the ADF statistics, which indicate that the eight emerging Asian stock market return series are stationary. Ljung-Box statistics for the returns themselves and for the squared returns are also presented. These statistics confirm that the empirical return series contains autocorrelation and volatility clustering, which suggests that the conditional modeling of short run returns is beneficial.

Table 1. Summary statistics of the daily returns for eight emerging Asian stock markets

Statistics	China	India	Indonesia	Malaysia	Philippines	South Korea	Taiwan	Thailand
Mean	0.0004	0.0005	0.0005	0.0002	0.0003	0.0002	0.0002	0.0000
Maximum	0.1522	0.1664	0.1313	0.1492	0.1618	0.0898	0.0617	0.1135
Minimum	-0.1401	-0.1194	-0.1273	-0.1424	-0.0974	-0.1280	-0.0698	-0.1606
Std. Dev.	0.0221	0.0162	0.0152	0.0138	0.0147	0.0182	0.0151	0.0167
Skewness	0.0378	0.0473	0.0114	0.3799	0.5894	-0.1578	-0.1017	0.1949
Kurtosis	10.5611	10.7223	12.5916	19.1659	13.2976	6.5508	5.0820	9.8330
Jarque-Bera [a]	9550.72*	10375.36*	15494.22*	44317.97*	18267.50*	2230.79*	778.79*	7918.29*
ADF [b]	-34.14	-58.48	-53.14	-53.75	-53.87	-60.68	-62.06	-57.45
Ljung-Box Q(6) [c]	43.94*	62.73*	131.59*	66.96*	120.76*	131.59*	30.02*	52.42*
Ljung-Box $Q^2(6)$ [d]	1078*	497.24*	630.63*	1913.80*	2044.6*	871.09*	558.60*	592.84*
Observations	4009	4175	4042	4061	4081	4213	4271	4057

Note: * significant at 1% level

[a] Jarque-Bera is a test statistic for testing whether the series is normally distributed.

[b] ADF indicates augmented Dickey and Fuller (1979,1981) unit root tests for whether the series is stationary.

[c] Ljung-Box $Q(6)$ indicates the Ljung-Box Q-statistics at lag 6 by log return series, it is a test statistic for the null hypothesis that there is no autocorrelation up to order 6.

[d] Ljung-Box $Q^2(6)$ indicates the Ljung-Box Q-statistic at lag 6 by squared log return series, it is a test statistic for the null hypothesis that there is no autocorrelation up to order 6.

4. Empirical Results

To implement Equation (11), we used a moving window of 500 observations to measure dynamically the forecasts of the VaR given different probabilities of VaR violation, which range from 0.1% to 5%. The proposed two-stage approaches, the B-EWMA-Hill method and B-EWMA-moment-Hill method, were compared with RiskMetrics approach (named EWMA). The B-EWMA-Hill method combines the bias-corrected EWMA model with the Hill estimator, while the B-EWMA-moment-Hill method combines the bias-corrected EWMA model with the second-order moment-ratio Hill estimator. To assess the predictive performance of different VaR models, we used a backtesting procedure that included the test

[4] Although both the left and right tails of the return distributions are interesting from the perspective of risk management, we chose to focus solely on estimating the left tails of the return distributions to measure the downside risk for the eight emerging Asian stock markets.

of predictive versus theoretical violation probability, Kupiec's (1995) unconditional coverage test and Christofferson's (1998) conditional coverage test.

Table 2 lists the empirical results for predictive versus theoretical probability that a VaR violation will occur. For all the emerging Asian stock markets, the B-EWMA-Hill method outperformed the other methods when the violation probabilities were below 1%. Furthermore, for violation probabilities of from 0.1% to 1%, the predictive probabilities that a VaR violation will occur that computed by RiskMetrics and the B-EWMA-moment-Hill method exceeded the theoretical probabilities and the predictive probabilities that a VaR violation will occur that were calculated using the B-EWMA-Hill method conditional were equal to or slight higher than the theoretical probabilities. As a result, the forecasts of VaR estimated by RiskMetrics and B-EWMA-moment-Hill methods have an underestimation bias and those estimated by the B-EWMA-Hill method have a slight underestimation bias. Consequently, using the B-EWMA-Hill method to measure VaR can capture the additional downside risk that is faced during times of greater fluctuation.

To demonstrate that the proposed two-stage approach is reasonably accurate for estimating VaR, we also checked its validity systematically by backtesting, according to the procedures proposed by Kupiec (1995) and Christoffersen (1998). Kupiec's (1995) methodology is an unconditional coverage testing and Christoffersen's (1998) methodology is a conditional coverage testing. Their null hypothesis is that the risk model is correct. Thus, if the test statistics reject the null hypothesis, the proposed risk model is not adequate. The empirical results are presented in Tables 3 and 4. For all emerging Asian stock markets (the Indian and South Korean stock markets excepted), the B-EWMA-Hill method exhibit excellent results given probabilities of VaR violation from 0.1% to 1% because the unconditional and conditional coverage test statistics (i.e. LR_{uc} and LR_{cc}) fail to reject the null hypothesis in almost all cases. However, for the Indian and South Korean stock markets, the use of RiskMetrics, the B-EWMA-Hill method and the B-EWMA-moment-Hill method could not provide more accurate VaR forecasts. Given that the problem of estimating VaR is still related to the estimation of conditional volatility, the results suggest that the decay factor λ in the EWMA and bias-corrected EWMA models may vary across returns series and that the choice of decay factor may lead to variations in performance[5].

Summarizing the above findings, given lower probabilities of VaR violation, the B-EWMA-Hill method for measuring VaR is more accurate than the RiskMetrics and B-EWMA-moment-Hill methods. Furthermore, the results show that using the Hill estimator to estimate the tail of the innovation distribution can better capture the nature of downside risk than can the second-order moment-ratio Hill estimator.

[5] We set $\lambda = 0.94$.

Table 2. Backtesting results: predictive vs. theoretical VaR violation probability

Country	Method	Theoretical VaR violation probability							
		0.05	**0.025**	**0.01**	**0.005**	**0.004**	**0.003**	**0.002**	**0.001**
China	EWMA	0.0568#	0.0369#	0.0202#	0.0127	0.0099	0.0091	0.0075	0.0067
	B-EWMA-Hill	0.0742	0.0472	0.0218	0.0115#	0.0075#	0.0060#	0.0044#	0.0024#
	B-EWMA-moment-Hill	0.0798	0.0580	0.0306	0.0187	0.0171	0.0147	0.0099	0.0060
India	EWMA	0.0557#	0.0347#	0.0232	0.0183	0.0157	0.0146	0.0101	0.0090
	B-EWMA-Hill	0.0706	0.0388	0.0198#	0.0086#	0.0078#	0.0064#	0.0045#	0.0026#
	B-EWMA-moment-Hill	0.0740	0.0489	0.0258	0.0157	0.0127	0.0112	0.0075	0.0034
Indonesia	EWMA	0.0535#	0.0366#	0.0228	0.0185	0.0161	0.0149	0.0138	0.0106
	B-EWMA-Hill	0.0704	0.0444	0.0200#	0.0106#	0.0079#	0.0059#	0.0031#	0.0016#
	B-EWMA-moment-Hill	0.0755	0.0507	0.0283	0.0145	0.0122	0.0102	0.0079	0.0028
Malaysia	EWMA	0.0503#	0.0355	0.0226	0.0191	0.0179	0.0152	0.0117	0.0097
	B-EWMA-Hill	0.0659	0.0339#	0.0160#	0.0074#	0.0051#	0.0039#	0.0023#	0.0012#
	B-EWMA-moment-Hill	0.0748	0.0452	0.0269	0.0144	0.0117	0.0105	0.0066	0.0035
Philippines	EWMA	0.0538#	0.0348#	0.0232	0.0151	0.0139	0.0124	0.0108	0.0085
	B-EWMA-Hill	0.0712	0.0418	0.0186#	0.0077#	0.0062#	0.0039#	0.0027#	0.0008#
	B-EWMA-moment-Hill	0.0763	0.0534	0.0294	0.0186	0.0143	0.0108	0.0077	0.0035
South Korea	EWMA	0.0622#	0.0350#	0.0206#	0.0125#	0.0099#	0.0092	0.0070	0.0044
	B-EWMA-Hill	0.0685	0.0468	0.0265	0.0133	0.0099#	0.0081#	0.0055#	0.0022#
	B-EWMA-moment-Hill	0.0700	0.0534	0.0343	0.0210	0.0177	0.0147	0.0118	0.0070
Taiwan	EWMA	0.0552#	0.0386#	0.0216	0.0155	0.0148	0.0133	0.0105	0.0076
	B-EWMA-Hill	0.0700	0.0433	0.0180#	0.0087#	0.0065#	0.0032#	0.0022#	0.0007#
	B-EWMA-moment-Hill	0.0765	0.0523	0.0296	0.0180	0.0141	0.0115	0.0069	0.0040
Thailand	EWMA	0.0449#	0.0297#	0.0156#	0.0106	0.0086	0.0078	0.0066	0.0051
	B-EWMA-Hill	0.0598	0.0344	0.0164	0.0074#	0.0047#	0.0039#	0.0031#	0.0012#
	B-EWMA-moment-Hill	0.0641	0.0426	0.0215	0.0117	0.0109	0.0078	0.0051	0.0035

Note: “ # “ indicates the predictive VaR violation probability is close to theoretical VaR violation probability.

Table 3. Backtesting results: unconditional coverage test statistics (LR_{uc})

Country	Method	Theoretical VaR violation probability							
		0.05	**0.025**	**0.01**	**0.005**	**0.004**	**0.003**	**0.002**	**0.001**
China	EWMA	2.3322#	12.8328	20.5967	21.0165	15.6769	20.4081	22.5960	36.0394
	B-EWMA-Hill	27.2845	40.6976	26.6352	15.6694	6.2865#	5.7034#	5.2696#	3.4576#
	B-EWMA-moment-Hill	40.1815	82.3225	69.5371	55.4481	59.3757	59.0054	40.3283	28.6257
India	EWMA	1.7439#	9.3104	34.1521	56.4215	52.5857	61.6824	44.2555	62.8056
	B-EWMA-Hill	21.3250	18.0694	20.1995	5.7073*	7.7441	7.5889	6.0941#	4.8180#
	B-EWMA-moment-Hill	28.3847	49.4017	46.8783	39.1355	32.1852	35.3166	23.5040	9.1945
Indonesia	EWMA	0.6273#	12.2273	30.9007	54.7617	52.9988	61.6270	75.5222	78.8775
	B-EWMA-Hill	19.8201	32.0895	20.0816	12.1644	7.4181	5.5564#	1.4202#	0.7093#
	B-EWMA-moment-Hill	30.2593	53.3971	57.5555	30.6866	27.5888	27.1362	25.0177	5.2662*
Malaysia	EWMA	0.0040#	10.2228	30.3326	59.4982	67.0299	64.3435	56.4484	69.1553
	B-EWMA-Hill	12.4116	7.5244	7.8412	2.5957#	0.6749#	0.6306#	0.1395#	0.0697#
	B-EWMA-moment-Hill	29.0789	34.8110	50.5695	30.2653	25.0341	29.3053	17.0415	9.7359
Philippines	EWMA	0.7724#	9.1644	33.2556	34.2991	38.7966	42.4901	49.1808	99.7529
	B-EWMA-Hill	21.7930	24.9928	15.3405	3.3433#	2.6715#	0.6004#	0.5867#	4.1445#
	B-EWMA-moment-Hill	32.5519	64.9135	64.6887	56.3411	41.3411	31.5975	24.5629	27.6823
South Korea	EWMA	7.9808	9.9086	23.6959	21.7377	16.9971	22.4688	20.5231	17.1286
	B-EWMA-Hill	17.6400	42.2164	51.4942	25.5575	16.9971	16.0811	11.3772	2.9496#
	B-EWMA-moment-Hill	20.4086	68.1483	98.9340	77.4215	68.8995	63.9844	60.6444	41.4626
Taiwan	EWMA	1.5148#	18.0584	28.4604	39.3763	47.7116	53.3724	49.2360	48.6991
	B-EWMA-Hill	20.8025	31.2905	14.5920	6.1042#	3.6306#	0.0545#	0.0363#	0.2391#
	B-EWMA-moment-Hill	35.4062	64.7873	70.3495	56.4709	42.5393	39.0618	19.9493	13.8857
Thailand	EWMA	1.4262#	2.1887	6.9963	11.9956	10.1922	13.7138	17.1067	21.4194
	B-EWMA-Hill	4.8713	8.2987	8.9058	2.6297#	0.2891#	0.6432#	1.3861#	0.0721#
	B-EWMA-moment-Hill	9.8557	26.9299	25.6872	16.8351	20.9485	13.7138	8.4972	9.7712

Note: The critical value of the LR_{uc} statistics at 1% significant level is 6.6349. "#" indicates test results not reject null hypothesis at 1% significant level.

Table 4. Backtesting results: conditional coverage test statistics (LR_{cc})

Country	Method	Theoretical VaR violation probability							
		0.05	**0.025**	**0.01**	**0.005**	**0.004**	**0.003**	**0.002**	**0.001**
China	EWMA	10.9224	22.0800	21.3435	21.6519	17.0067	22.0044	24.8468	38.6934
	B-EWMA-Hill	42.5895	42.6171	26.6726	16.3452	6.5754#	5.8831#	5.3662#	3.4862#
	B-EWMA-moment-Hill	52.0718	88.4909	69.7111	55.4652	59.4654	59.3231	41.6580	28.8054
India	EWMA	30.5209	25.0596	42.8937	62.5868	57.2685	67.1173	53.7739	73.7257
	B-EWMA-Hill	51.2713	38.0375	36.2947	23.5123	27.1014	22.8058	17.3364	4.8547#
	B-EWMA-moment-Hill	55.7928	73.6935	67.0903	51.6681	43.6462	48.7470	36.6623	14.4683
Indonesia	EWMA	20.8270	15.4334	37.3363	61.1549	61.2960	67.0755	81.8390	79.9883
	B-EWMA-Hill	47.9754	38.0748	22.7437	13.2753	7.7352#	5.7344#	1.4707#	0.7219#
	B-EWMA-moment-Hill	58.3914	66.8305	65.6353	36.4131	31.1858	28.3601	25.3347	5.3049*
Malaysia	EWMA	26.9185	39.8781	51.8354	77.1518	86.4028	82.9127	75.2672	85.2367
	B-EWMA-Hill	36.5472	28.5272	25.2184	4.8787#	4.3849#	5.3897#	7.0446#	0.0767#
	B-EWMA-moment-Hill	60.0595	51.1958	74.0748	40.1318	28.8857	33.9049	19.7286	14.9271
Philippines	EWMA	28.1307	28.7716	45.7548	43.4304	49.1232	54.6324	58.0770	101.5379
	B-EWMA-Hill	45.6153	51.5482	16.4065	10.2407	5.5964#	0.6782#	0.6247#	4.1476#
	B-EWMA-moment-Hill	58.7291	89.9826	77.5188	59.5942	41.6828	32.6242	26.6757	27.7453
South Korea	EWMA	7.9808#	9.9086	23.6959	21.7377	16.9971	22.4688	20.5231	17.1286
	B-EWMA-Hill	19.1412	46.0865	57.5430	31.9085	26.5940	22.4210	20.7926	2.9762#
	B-EWMA-moment-Hill	21.5149	72.8063	106.7779	84.6469	75.4326	73.0936	73.1556	48.9540
Taiwan	EWMA	19.2337	26.8263	30.1819	39.5255	47.9325	53.7853	49.8492	49.0197
	B-EWMA-Hill	36.7875	50.5594	15.6314	6.5234#	3.8659#	0.1131#	0.0623#	0.2420#
	B-EWMA-moment-Hill	50.0684	83.5100	76.5823	57.5103	42.8478	39.8093	20.2115	13.9733
Thailand	EWMA	5.4015#	4.8638#	11.9489	21.2636	21.9125	26.6115	25.2672	25.1242
	B-EWMA-Hill	12.6733	12.4725	13.3721	9.8975	4.3096#	5.3971#	7.0615#	0.0791#
	B-EWMA-moment-Hill	15.0062	33.9947	30.1047	24.8886	29.7933	26.6115	12.2021	14.9570

Note: The critical value of the LR_{cc} statistics at 1% significant level is 9.2103. "#" indicates test results not reject null hypothesis at 1% significance level.

5. Conclusion

The main contribution of the study reported herein is to provide a two-stage approach that incorporates the non-parametric Hill estimator and the moment-ratio Hill estimator based on EVT into a bias-corrected EWMA model for estimating VaR. This approach is especially appealing because it makes minimal assumptions about the underlying innovation distribution and concentrates on modeling its tail using the non-parametric Hill estimator and use the moment-ratio Hill estimator for the shape parameter of the extreme value distribution. Moreover, rather than using the RiskMetrics approach developed by J.P. Morgan, applying the bias-corrected EWMA model to estimate conditional volatility, as we have done, can reduce the misspecified model risk. The empirical study that involved the eight emerging Asian stock markets demonstrated the accuracy of the proposed approach.

For lower probabilities of VaR violation from 0.1% to 1%, the backtesting showed that the proposed B-EWMA-Hill method produces more accurate forecasts of VaR than the RiskMetrics and B-EWMA-moment-Hill methods. Thus, the proposed B-EWMA-Hill method can ensure adequate prudence for the setting of risk capital. Furthermore, we demonstrate that using the Hill estimator to estimate the tail of the innovation distribution can better capture the additional downside risk faced during times of greater fluctuation than the second-order moment-ratio Hill estimator.

References

Baillie, R. & DeGennaro, R. (1990). Stock Returns and Volatility. *Journal of financial and Quantitative Analysis*, 25, 203-214.

Barone-Adesi, G., Boutgoin, F., & Giannopoulos, K. (1998). Don't Look Back. *Risk*, 11(8).

Base Committee on Banking Supervision (1996). Ammendment to the Capital Accord to Incorporate Market Risks. *Basle Report* (24), BIS.

Beder, T, S. (1995). Seductive but Dangerous. *Financial Analysis Journal*, September-October, 12-24.

Byström, H.N.E. (2004). Managing Extreme Risks in Tranquil and Volatile Markets Using Conditional Extreme Value Theory. *International Review of Financial Analysis*, 13, 133-152.

Christoffersen, P. (1998). Evaluating Interval Forecasts. *International Economic Review*, 39, 841-862.

Cotter, J. (2001). Margin Exceedences for European Stock Index Futures Using Extreme Value Theory. *Journal of Banking & Finance*, 25, 1475-1502.

Danielsson, J., Jansen, D.W., & de Vries, C.G. (1996). The Method of Moments Ratio Estimator for the Tail Shape Parameter. *Communication in Statistics Theory and Methods*, 25(4), 711-720.

Danielsson, J. & De Vires, C. G. (1997). Tail Index and Quantile Estimation with Very High Frequency Data. *Journal of Empirical Finance*, 4, 241-257.

Dewachter , H. & Gielens, G. (1999). Setting Futures Margins: the Extremes Approach. *Applied Financial Economics*, 9, 173-181.

Deloitte Touche Tohmatsu. (2002). *Global Risk Management Survey*.

Gencay, R., Selcuk, F., & Ulugülyağci, A. (2003). High Volatility, Thick Tails and Extreme Value Theory in Value-at-Risk Estimation. *Insurance: Mathematics and Economics*, 33, 337-356.

Harris, R.D.F. & Shen, J. (2004). Estimation of VaR with Bias-Corrected Forecasts of Conditional Volatility. *Journal of Derivatives*, 11(4), 10-20.

Hill, B.M. (1975). A Simple Approach to Inference About The Tail of A Distribution. *The Annals of Mathematical Statistics*, 3, 1163-1174.

JP Morgan. (1996). Riskmetrics *TM* Technical Document. (4th ed), New York.

Kuester, K., Mittnik, S., & Paolella, M. S. (2006). Value-at Risk Prediction: A Comparison of Alternative Strategies. *Journal of Financial Econometrics*, 4, 53-89.

Kupiec, P. (1995). Technique for Verifying the Accuracy of Risk Management Models. *Journal of Derivative*, 3, 73-84.

McNeil, A. & Frey, R. (2000). Estimation of Tail-Related Risk Measure for Heteroscedastic Financial Time Series: An Extreme Value Approach. *Journal of Empirical finance*, 7, 271-300.

Mincer, J., & Zarnovitz, V. (1969). The Valuation of Economic Forecasts. In J. Mincer, ed., *Economic Forecasts and Expectations*. Cambridge: National Bureau of Economic Research.

Poon, S. H. & Taylor, S. J. (1992). Stock Returns and Volatility: An Empirical study of the UK Stock Market. *Journal of Banking and Finance*, 16, 37-59.

Pritsker, M. (1997). Evaluating Value at Risk Methodologies: Accury versus Computational Time. *Journal of Financial Services Research*, 12(3), 201-243.

Theil, H. (1966). Applied Economic Forecasting. Amsterdam: North Holland.

Quintos, C., Fan, Z., & Phillips, P. C. B. (2001). Structural Change Tests in Tail Behavior and the Asian Crisis. *Review of Economic Studies*, 68, 633-663.

Wanger, N., & Marsh, T. A. (2004). Tail Index Estimation in Small Samples Simulation Results for Independent and ARCH-type Financial Return Models. *Statistical Paper*, 45, 545-562.

In: Business and Finance: Performance and Management
Editors: R. Morland and A. Gagglione
ISBN: 978-1-61122-936-3

Chapter 2

CUSTOMER RELATED FACTORS IN PARTNER SELECTION, MARKET ORIENTATION, AND PERFORMANCES OF INTERNATIONAL JOINT VENTURES IN TAIWAN

***Frank F.C. Pan*[1,*] *and Tsuen-Ho Hsu*[2,°]**
[1] Healthcare Administration Dept., Tajen University, Taiwan
[2] Marketing and Distribution Management,
National Kaohsiung First University of Science and Technology, Taiwan

ABSTRACT

Having proper partners positively links with venture performances when firms attempt to leverage external organization's resources to span cross-border in a form of international joint venture. Since 1970s, partner selection criteria in the past studies centered on task requirement and partner characteristics, few if any had attempted to include customer as part of primary consideration in selection decisions. This research attempts to point out such negligence and to verify the important effects of lacking such factors in venture performance. Taking samples from international joint ventures in Taiwan, this research used questionnaire as instrument and successfully collected 321 valid responses with CEO, functional managers that individually answer different questions to avoid common method variance. SPSS statistics package is the tool used to analyze gathered data. Major findings of this research include identifying and confirming the existence of customer related factors and its importance in the model of joint venture performance. Partner related factor is the most powerful predictors in predicting joint venture performance, followed by customer related factor, and task related factors. Key to become a market-driven management is selecting partner with customer related factors. There are several academic and managerial implications associated with the research finding.

---

* E-mail address: frankpan@mail.tajen.edu.tw, Healthcare Administration Dept., Tajen University, 20 Wei-Hsin Road, Yenpu, Pingtung, Taiwan 907.
° E-mail address: thhsu@ccms.nkfust.edu.tw, Professor of Marketing and Distribution Management, National Kaohsiung First University of Science and Technology, No. 2, Jhuoyue Rd., Nanzih District, Kaohsiung City 811, Taiwan, R.O.C..

Keywords: International Joint Venture, Partner selection factors, Market orientation, Taiwan, Knowledge-based view, Customer capital

1. INTRODUCTION

Resource-based theories scholars describe firm's cooperating activities as seeking complementary resources and capabilities that currently absent in its resource stock for competition (e.g. Wernerfelt, 1995; Eisenhardt & Martin , 2000 etc.). Compare to resource internalizing, leveraging such external resources is preferable in terms of cost-effectiveness (Coviello & Munro, 1997). Contrast to foreign direct investment (FDI), international joint ventures (IJV) provides multinational enterprises (MNE) opportunities to gain local expertise and market access as well as local knowledge in a relative lower costs (Makino & Delios, 1996), thus has become one of major strategic alternatives for international expansion (Osland & Cavusgil, 1996; Hennart & Reddy, 1997). The literature generally agree that proper venturing partner is the key to the success of cross-border venture (Littler & Leverick, 1995; Dacin, Hitt & Levitas, 1997), and formal and rigorous partner selection has positive effects in finding appropriate partner as well as fostering better performance (Njissen, Douglas & Galis, 1999).

Extant studies on partner selection factors can roughly be categorized into Geringer (1991)'s typology. The partner related factor (PRF) concern more on what partner's characteristics will benefit the joint business, thus focuses on criteria that relate with potential partners' capabilities or complement abilities. For example, strategic fit (Lasserre, 1984; Harrigan, 1988) for mutual value creation that was unable to achieve by conventional trading (Kanter, 1994; Brouthers, Brouthers & Wilkinson, 1995). The task related factors (TRF) concern mainly on partner's capabilities toward specific tasks (Geringer, 1991; Al-Khalifa & Peterson, 1998), and focus on capabilities and competences for specific tasks the MNE seeks in that market. For example, specific local asset (Tomlinson, 1970), complementary technology and marketing system (Adler & Hlavacek, 1976), financial related factors (Luo, 1998), human and physical asset resources (Hitt, Levitas, Arregle & Borza, 2000), and other resources that contributable to the specific ventures (Awadzi, 1987).

Spanning business cross-border, MNE in most cases appreciates the importance of customers, yet numerous industrial cases that experienced fail are ascribed to ignoring this vital element (Deloitte Haskins & Sells International, 1989; Stickler, 2001). Accordingly, there are numerous calls in the academics to include customer into management studies (Brief & Bazerman, 2003). In the other hand, marketing scholars have evidenced linkages between market oriented operation and market performance are strong and positive (Slater & Narver, 1994a; Slater & Narver, 1994b; Kohli, Jaworski & Kumar, 1993; Pelham, 1997; Hurley & Hult, 1998; Cano, Carrillat & Jaramillo, 2004; Kirca, Jayachandran & Bearden, 2005). Ironically, few studies place customer as primary consideration in the studies on international cooperative activities. Taking the works collected in the Social Science Citation Index (SSCI) as example. There are 28 articles or less than 2 % of 1,528 works on alliance or cooperation between years of 1999 and 2003 had included customer or consumer as part of their studies (Pan, 2004). Apparently, the academicians did not substantially embrace importance of customers in their studies on international joint efforts, thus leave the role customers play as a puzzle.

Knowledge-based view advocates that human, structural, and customer capital are the three core resources firms needed for mission accomplishment (Petrash, 1996). Past studies on partner selection have extensively explored the first two groups, and few if any on the third. Base on the customer-based knowledge perspective, this research attempts to reveal the importance of customer factors in the partner selection by exploring its effects on joint venture performance. Research is conducted in Taiwan, in which has attracted tremendous foreign investments from the TRIAD (Ohmae, 1985) in the past decades.

2. Literature Review and Hypotheses

We review the literature in the following sections by covering theories used for, past studies in the partner selection, as well as studies on customer-based knowledge. We discuss them in later sections along with several hypotheses.

2.1. Theories for Partner Selection

Theories appropriate to explain partner selection may include transactional cost theory, resource-based view, organizational learning perspective, resource dependency theory, and knowledge-based view. Transaction cost theory advocates that firm is directly resulting from asset specificity (Williamson, 1979). The economic rationality confines the decisions associated with asset internalizations (Hoskisson, Eden, Lau & Wright, 2000) or externalizations (i.e. cooperatives including joint ventures) by assessing the level of transactional costs (Coase, 1937). Transactional cost theory emphasizes solely on the cost, ignores the value creation that one of the major outcomes joint venture aim to achieve (Alexander & Young, 1996; Lin, 2006).

Resource-based theories suggest firms possessing tangible and intangible resources (Wernerfelt, 1995) to build core competences through fostering sustainable and hardly copiable capbilities (Barney, 1991). Linking external organizations for those heterogeneous resources (Eisenhardt & Martin, 2000) to stay compettiive becomes primary rationale behind partner selection. Thus, partner selection criteria vary along with task-specific environment, of which makes needed context-specific resources for joint-ventured firm. Core to this problem is that venture partners should be identified prior to such contextual difficulties appear. Accumulation and integration of customer-related knowledge is the most notably heterogeneous resources for MNE in host country. Firms that not purposefully include customer-based knowledge in selecting partner may expose to the risks of losing local acceptance (Jaworski, Kohli & Sahay, 2000; Harris & Cai, 2002). This means merely seeking complentary physical and human resources is not sufficient as partner selection criteria (Lyles & Salk, 1996; Gibbert, Leibold & Probst, 2002), yet it might be useful to shorten the list of partner candidates.

Organizational learning perspective proposes single loop learning within roganization and double loop learning from external organizations for valuable knowledge to direct high-performance operation (Argyris, 1977 ; Powell, Koput & Smith-Doerr, 1996). Key to this perspective is the organization's learning capability toward new knowledge that partners brought to the venture (Shenkar & Li, 1999 ; Parise & Henderson, 2001), and the level of

knowledge givers' 'learnability' (Brush & Licata, 1983; Turbin, 1993). Codifiable or explicit knowledge could be easily trasnferred and learned between partners, yet customer knowledge that context-specifically pertians to consumer behaviors such as personal relationship, reputation, experience is not one of them (Ruigrok & Wagner 2003; Uhlenbruck, Meyer & Hitt, 2003). Unfortunately, knowledge on how customer will react and behave in particular scenarios is nothing but vital to the success of any cross-cultural ventures (Rodriguez, Perez & del Val, 2003).

Resource dependency theorists identified that organizations can survive becuase they are able to access and maintain linkages with needed resources from the network the organizations embedded (Pfeffer & Salancik, 1978). Continegnt to the context, management of the firm shall continuously modify decisions regarding potential parties to collaborate and commitment to such collaboration. This implicitly means the management is more concern on the enviornment monitoring (Pfeffer & Salancik, 1977). In the cases of global management, commitment to the partners is an integral part of the top management of the jointed venture business. Applying resource dependence theory in partner selection may not be appropriate for this decision should be made before cross-border joint venture bring into existence.

Knowledge-based viewed (KBV) suggests that effective exploring and exploiting current and new knowledge jointly contribute to firm's comptitiveness by creating value for customers (Nonaka, 1994). Contrast to property-based resource, knowledge-based resource is more intangible and tacit in nature (Das & Teng, 2000), of which is unique and is highly isolated from competitor's imitating intent (Barney, 1991; Miller & Shamsie, 1996). As important capital to firm, knowledge resources include human, structual, and customer (Petrash, 1996; Edvinsson & Sullivan, 1996; Reid, Bussiere & Greenaway, 2001). Human capital refers to individual employee's techniques, experiences, routines, and instincts; whereas structural capital refers to those organization-based technologies, data, patents, innovations, and processes etc. Past studies on partner selection limit thier concerns on the need of these two kinds of capital. As a result, the literature categorized selection criteria as task and partner related factors, and ignored the customer related factors that pertain to customer capital.

Few if any studies on partner selection factors studies have involved market knowledge as part of selection criteria. Knowledge-based view is one of the first theories identifies market and customer knowledge as independent and critical factors in helping company's competitive advantage. Petrash (1996) is one of the scholars that first remind us our ignorance toward customers in knowledge studies, though customer capital in this study is confined as perceived value after transaction (Petrash, 1996, p.366) and even not other factors that affecting such perception. As a matetr of fact, customer knowledge shall include those information that affecting or shaping customer's purchasing behaviors, of which could hardly access through market or market agency (i.e. advertising agencies). For MNEs, as outsiders of a market, the best approach to tune with such information is to explore and exploit immensely within institution they embed (Simonin, 1997; Parise & Henderson, 2001).

2.2. Literature on IJV Partner Selection

Partner selection study may be found in the very early literature, yet Tomlinson (1970)'s study in India and Pakistan would be the pioneer in systematic approach with a conclusion of six major factors associated with the subsidiary's tasks as selection criteria. Diverse studies emerged later focus on the potential contribution of each partner could benefit the joint venture as major attributes of an ideal partner (e.g. Adler & Hlavacek, 1976; Lasserre, 1984; Harrigan, 1988). Geringer (1991) then summarizes these studies and simplifies the selection criteria as partner-related and task-related factors, of which later becomes one of major guidelines for IJV partner selection process (Glaister & Buckley, 1997; Al-Khalifa & Peterson, 1998). Majority of the literature agreed that a good joint venture would bring firms unique values that individual firm alone could not achieve (Bleeke & Ernst, 1991). Proper partners who possessed strengths that complementary to firm's capabilities (Devlin & Bleakley, 1988), especially to the core market or core techniques (Hoffmann & Schlosser, 2001), will significantly strengthen performance (Tomlinson, 1970; Cavusgil & Evirgen, 1997). Although a good partner may not guarantee success (Inkpen & Ross, 2001), improper decisions of this kind will jeopardize a venture (Deloitte Haskins & Sells International, 1989). Making good decision on partner decision is vital, though not almighty.

Although two-factor typology prevails as common wisdom, we believe one important element is missing. Although partners could contribute strengths in any stages of value chain, the ultimate goal of any value chain is to supply value to customers (Porter, 1985), and then value for company emerge. Seeking values from joint venturing with external organizations, firms need to offset or exceed additional transactional costs and power sharing (Harrigan, 1988) that accompanied with joint venture (Gulati & Singh, 1998). Partner who provides task-related resources or fit for particular competences may just be beneficial for company values, not for customer. Task oriented partner selection could hardly result in customer value. In sum, partners' potentiality of becoming venture partner will be judged by assessing its contribution potential to customer value instead of firm's value (Madhok & Tallman, 1998).

Partner related factors are organization-specific (Geringer, 1991; Al-Khalifa & Peterson, 1997). Criteria of PRF tend to contingent with organizational characteristics, cultures, and probably other emotional background. In the other hand, task related factors are task-specific. Criteria are more subjective and may contingent with emerging tasks and missions. It is thus possible to present an endless list of factors for an ideal partner, yet brings no academic or managerial implications (Geringer, 1991; Varis & Conn, 2002). By identifying the serious absence of customer in the partner selection studies, we raise customer related factors as additional and critical factor beyond conventional partner and task factors. This is not to add the length of the list but to remind the importance of customer and to bridge the gap between current studies and reality in this market–oriented or customer-centered age (Brief & Bazerman, 2003; Ricci, 2003; Kirca et al., 2005). We believe more attention on customer will bring international joint venture more successes in either jointed business or for parent firms. Figure 1 shows the conceptual framework as follow.

2.3. Customer-Based Knowledge

We illustrate the importance of customer-based knowledge in business operations and argue later in subsequent sections how such knowledge could help identifying a proper partner for customer values.

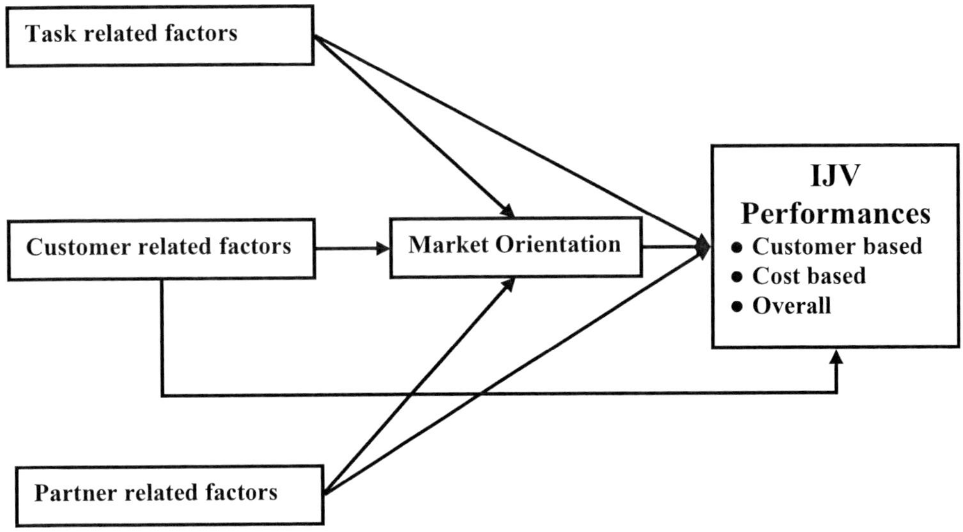

Figure 1. Conceptual framework for selection factors and IJV performances.

Customer satisfaction generates company's profits (Blackwell, Milliard & Engel, 2006). A customer-centric organization would make endless efforts to explore, design, develop, and provide products and services in response to customers' preference (Esteban, Millan, Molina & Martin-Consuegra, 2002). To meet what customers need comprehensively represents an everlasting challenges despite that technology converges, income parity emerges, and media and advertising converges to unify consumer behavior (de Mooji & Hofstede, 2002). For example, there are manifested impacts of national features on conusmers' perception of quality, image, and preference of imported products in varied way (Lastovica, Bettencourt, Hughner & Kuntze, 1999; Kaynak & Kara, 2002). As a result, firms in attempt to penetrate into foreign market generally encounter dual difficulties. One is the difficulty in understanding the consumer behavior, of which is context-specific and hardly generalizable between distinctive cultures (e.g. Laroche, Kalamas & Cleveland, 2005). Another distinctive yet related problem is the need of applying such knowledge into operational strategies. The literature in marketing and business have long reported similar findings (e.g. Balabanis & Diamantopoulos, 2004). Compare to tangible inputs, customer and consumer related elements are mostly intangible, tacit, and frequently market-specific. Except codifiable customer information that could be obtained from the market, customer related knowledge is normally generated from purposefully interactions with rivalries and customers and thus highly possible to be unique and inimitable (Prahalad & Hamel, 1990; Barney, 1991). This means customer-based knowledge is extremely valuable input to the firm (Duncan & Moriarty, 1998). Lacking support of long-term customer relationship, venture parties' subjective considerations can hardly sufficiently receive and later properly transform it into valuable

knowledge (Wulf, Odekerken-Schroder & Iacobucci, 2001). Strategic actions based on customer knowledge drive firms stay fine tune with target customers, from which obtain good level of customer preference and satisfaction (Sheth, Sisodia & Sharma, 2000; Selden & MacMillan, 2006). Joint venturing with customer-oriented partners provides optimal alternative for MNE's entry difficulties.

2.4. Hypotheses

2.4.1. Customer Related Factors and IJV Performance

Companies obtain satisfactory return and subsequent sustainable competence by satisfying target customers' need from time to time (Levitt, 1960; Porter, 1980). This makes customer as the center of company activities, no matter how MNE enter a market. Entering a market under integration strategy is likely to erect task or mission as primary consideration in partner decision to achieve parents' goals. In reality, this task-oriented joint venture becomes an agent of parent firms, thus are likely to direct resources to foster the principal's benefit. Task oriented in mind and long for customer loyalty in hand would be a hallucination. Similarly, determining a partner simply centered on partner's trustability and competence rather than on capabilities of satisfying expected customers will again have no influence on customers' preference.

No matter what factors were applied to determine a partner, cross-border joint venture needs to involve its target customers as major consideration for survival. This means customers will be eventually included in the new venture business. Taking customer related factors well in advance in the partner seeking stage may not only guarantee a market-oriented subsidiary but also a highly motivated team (Kirca et al., 2005). Team that collectively market-oriented will be more prone to customer demands, of which in turn attract preference and loyalty. We thus propose a positive correlation between customer-related factors and IJV performance.

H_1 : As the task related factors and partner related factors remain as partner selection criteria, using customer related factors in selecting venture partner positively affects the performance of international joint venture.

2.4.2. Customer Related Factors and Market Orientation

Starting from resources available, alternatives of market development may vary from totally non-market oriented to fully market-oriented (Day & Nedungadi, 1994). The literature suggests that market-oriented strategy that simultaneously caring competition and customers is superior to other approaches in terms of both customer-based and cost-based performances. Task related factors implicitly require the partner to jointly accomplishing the parent's corporate goals, of which act as the primary criteria in guiding partner seeking. As to the partner related factors, the literature alternatively prescribes it as trustable and strategically 'fit' to corporate mission (Lasserre, 1984; Harrigan, 1988; Geringer, 1991; Barclay & Smith, 1997). Both of task and partner related factors underlying partner selection inevitably ignore the importance of customer factors, and thus the jointed business is unlikely to be market oriented but competition oriented or self-centered (Day & Nedungadi, 1994).

List of possible complementary resources may endlessly ranges from functional to supportive factors (Geringer, 1991; Hitt et al., 2000; 2004; Gale & Luo, 2004). Since

'foreignness' is the fatal for firms to gain legitimacy in the host market, MNE needs most the tacit information centered on target customers. Conspicuous physical and psychological distance from host market cultures prevent MNE from factually apprehending those behaviors that embedded in culture-specific contexts. Obtaining such customer-based knowledge is unlikely to accomplish as those functional elements. Heterogeneous knowledge at this kind needs long-term customer service experience (Eisenhardt & Martin, 2000; Wulf et al., 2001) or alternatively allies with, or relies on customer-oriented partners.

Adding customer related factors into partner decision beyond conventional PRF and TRF will have positive effects on venture's market-oriented potentials, for this will integrate organization's resources as a whole in response to both of customers' requirement and rivalries' competition (Lorange & Roos, 1990). We therefore hypothesize the relationship between customer related factors and market orientation as follow.

H_2 : As the task related factors and partner related factors remain the partner selection criteria of cross-border venture, selecting joint venture partner with customer related factors positively affect the extent of company's market orientation.

2.4.3. Market Orientation and IJV Performance

Market-oriented organizations receive superior image on customer perceived quality and satisfaction (Saxe & Weitz, 1982). The literature has proved positively affect of market orientation at organizational level on organizational performance, profit, revenue, and market share (Cano et al., 2004; Kirca et al., 2005). In the other hand, market orientation also internally benefit the organization by increasing organizational commitment, employee's morality, job satisfaction, reducing role conflict (Kirca, et al., 2005), of which in turn facilitate a favorable loop of service profit chain (Lovelock, 2003). Although debates regarding the linkage between market orientation and organizational performances remain that some criticize the strength of such linkage and some conclude a negative relation or not significant (See detail in Nakata & Sivakumar, 2001), there are even more evidences for positive effects across various industries and contexts. For example, in businesses of hospital (Wrenn, 1997), hotel (Sargeant & Mohamad, 1999), educational services (Qureshi, 1993), and manufacturing (Kohli et al., 1993) as well as in the contexts of firm scale (Pelham, 1997), value chain stages (Siguaw, Simpson & Baker, 1998), and cross-country study (Ward, Girardi & Lewandowska, 2006) are some of notable studies that provide evidences for a positive linkage. We thus hypothesize the higher the market orientation of an international joint venture business will positively result in a better performance.

H_3 : Performance of an international joint venture in host market positively correlates with the extent of market orientation of this venture business.

3. METHODS

3.1. Measurement

We use Likert scale to measure the respondents' perception, of which '1' as 'not important', and '5' as 'very important'. We illustrate measurements of each construct in the following sections.

Task related factors. *Task related factors*, as defined by Geringer (1991), are those technical or resource factors that are expected to be required for the accomplishment of particular task. Geringer (1991) interviewed corporate managers with a list of critical success factors that summarized from studies of Steiner (1968), Tomlinson (1970), Stopford & Wells (1972), Renforth (1974), Tomlinson & Thompson (1977) and conclude a fifteen-items list as *task related factors*. Studies conducted by Khan & Suh (2005) and Wang & Kess (2006) in the context of China provide that scale developed by Geringer (1991) is cross-culturally generalizable. We adopt this scale since Taiwan and China have long shared same culture heritage as similar Chinese community. We deleted three items after the pilot test. Nine items were kept for use after exploratory factor analysis and expert validation with $\alpha = 0.9429$.

Partner related factors. Evidence shows that IJV performance directly links with partner related factor (Robson, 2002). Unfortunately, *partner related factors* were not like task factors that were well defined in Geringer (1991). From the transactional cost perspective, any partner that assumes lower uncertainty and costs would be an ideal partner (Geringer & Hebert, 1989; Gulati & Singh, 1998; Madhok & Tallman, 1998). Local partner in host country could also be viewed as an agent to the firm, thus criteria of determining a qualified agent, such as level of opportunism or trustable (Hoffmann & Schlosser, 2001) from this candidate's records are good indicators for IJV partner. In order to create value that could not achieve by traditional transactions, factors related to potential partner may include operational efficiency and effectiveness, free of opportunism, trustable, and optimally is strategically fit or are resource complementary (Harrigan, 1988; Kanter, 1994; Littler & Leverick, 1995; Barclay & Smith, 1997; Douma, Bilderbeek, Idenburg, & Looise, 2000; Insch & Steensma, 2006). Six items retained for the *partner related factors* with $\alpha = 0.9145$.

Customer related factors. This factor group refers to possible influencing factors associated directly with customers purchasing behavior. Factors at this kind bring its influences into full play in the market, and are core part to the market knowledge, in which composed by market-based resources and marketing support resource (Hooley, Greenley, Cadogan & Fahy, 2005). In this sense, we include acquiring, interpreting, and integrating knowledge that associated with customers and competitors as *Customer related factors* in this research. Some scholars argued a market-driven organization should be capable of market sensing, customer linking, channel bonding, and technology monitoring (Day, 1994). Channel bonding is highly task related, customer bonding is customer related, and the rest are closely associated with competitors. We summarized literature and use a five item scale to capture the construct of customer related factor with $\alpha = 0.8773$. These are capabilities of acquiring customer knowledge toward product and services, acquiring competitors' information, and a structural information system for receiving, analyzing, and distributing customer-related information.

Market orientation. Although customer capital is the most important component of a firm's resource (Petrash, 1996), knowledge on rivalries is also critical for both may impose dual impacts on firm's production behaviors and outcomes (Porter, 1980; Hunt & Morgan, 1995; Blackwell et al., 2006). Taking both customer and competitor into account seems to be a prevailing wisdom in marketing research. Most market orientation related scales substantially follow this concept, for example, MARKOR (Kohli et al., 1993), MKTOR (Narver & Slater, 1990), and the one proposed by Deshpande, Farley, & Webster (1993) (DFW). Deshpande and colleagues modify MARKOR and MKTOR as a simplified version but involve all major considerations in the original scales. As industrial experts also suggest,

we adopt DFW to measure the level of market orientation. Alpha for *market orientation* is satisfactory at 0.8414.

Joint venture performances. Measuring company performance by either objective or subjective approach has no major differences, for these two are closely associated. Studies on market orientation are more likely to measure the performance by customer loyalty, customer satisfaction, innovation, and product quality (Kirca et al., 2005). Rationale for using these measurements is that customer satisfaction fosters customer's trust and commitment, of which in turn create a reliable long-term relationship and subsequently revenue growth (Morgan & Hunt, 1994). In the other hand, customer loyalty increases repetitive purchasing, reduce complain, lower operating and service costs, and accordingly enrich organizational performance (Szymanski & Henard, 2001). Similar logic appears true to customer's perception on firm's innovation and product quality, and will have positive relationship with market orientation (Day & Nedungadi, 1994). Relative cost and relative profit are another two inquiries to examine the outcomes of the firm's commitment to the customers, in which relative profit is in reverse form. Share of the market is a reflection of the firm's position in a market. This construct has seven items with $\alpha = 0.9293$.

3.2. Validity and Common Method Variance

Content validity is confirmed by two actions. Items of the questionnaire are all drawn from literature is the first to assure a content validity. We have also invited several scholars from international business as well as marketing to review the draft, and then consult with industrial experts for the appropriateness of each question. The questionnaire has three language editions, Chinese, English, and Japanese. All three editions have been edited through back-translation procedures (Kerlinger & Lee, 2000). Construct validities, convergent and discriminant, are confirmed by examining the p value of pair correlations, in which correlations and p values of related items in the same construct are high and significant and those for different constructs are low or not significant.

Common method variance. To avoid common method variance (CMV) that is highly possible causing bias in research outcomes with incorrect correlation between independent and dependent variables. We invite CEOs or high rank executives of each individual company to answer the first part of questionnaire, the independent variables. Functional managers, as assigned or further invited by the CEO, answer the second part of questions, dependent and control variables. Since respondents to the questionnaire are different and answer questions in different places, data collected could be highly reliable that no CMV bias may appear.

3.3. Samples

Unit of analysis for this research is the joint venture company that established in Taiwan, includes companies in both manufacturing and service sectors that at least 15% foreign capital and no single party owned 75% shares of equity. Samples are purposefully taken from several business groups. The first group is the companies in the synergy production system (*Keirestsu*), of which represents typical supply chain in Taiwan. Companies in the export

processing zone are included in the second group of companies for these firms were expected to aim rather on foreign than local markets. Members of trading association in different regions are the third group, for these companies involved certain levels of import or export business. Traditional manufacturers across major industrial parks, and service and retailing giants are the fourth and the fifth groups.

4. Results and Analyses

We collected 353 questionnaires, of which have ignored 32 questionnaires for fatal absence of either independent or dependent variables. The overall response rate is high at 64.2% of 500 dispatched.

4.1. Sample Description

Table 1. Descriptive statistics

History	N	%	Accu. %
< 1 year	56	17.45	18.69
2-3 years	86	26.79	45.48
4-5 years	115	35.83	80.06
> 5 years	64	19.94	100
Region			
Japan	130	40.5	40.5
N. America	95	29.6	70.09
W. Europe	47	14.64	84.74
Others	49	15.26	100
Cultural Distance			
Similar	132	41.12	41.12
Some	144	44.86	85.98
Large	45	14.02	100
Industry			
Service	153	47.66	47.66
Retailing	73	22.74	70.4
Manufacturing	88	27.41	97.82
Trading	7	2.18	100
Customers			
Industrial	65	20.25	20.25
Reseller	91	28.35	48.6
Consumer	119	37.07	85.67
Varied	46	14.33	100

Firms in the data were mostly established more than two years (80%), as shown in table 1. Japan and USA (include Canada) are the two major home countries of foreign investor, 80% of respondents perceived similar or few if any cultural distance between partners, service and retailing industries are the major contributors of data and serve varied customers.

4.2. Partner Selection Factors and IJV Performance

The literature tends to hypothesize partner selection factors with the level of the subsidiary's performance (Geringer, 1991; Ellis, 2006). In the marketing literature, as suggested by Day & Wensley (1988, 1994), performance could be categorized as customer-based performance (CUP) and competitor/cost-based performance (COP) to fully reflect the outcomes of company's effort in attracting customers as well as in competing with rivalries. Beyond CUP and COP, scholars generally agreed consolidating these two indexes as a single one in order to reflect the reality of corporate performance (Narver & Slater, 1990; Kohli et al., 1993; Day & Nedungadi, 1994). This is the overall performance (OP) in this study.

Customer-based performance. The model feature the regression of TRF and PRF on CUP, as shown in table 2, indicates a low level of explanation for customer-based performance with R^2=0.015, of which reveals PRF and TRF are not sufficient in explain the variance of the firm's performance in attracting customers. By adding CRF into the model, variance explained up to an acceptable level at 0.293, in which CRF represent the major source of impacts (0.463), much higher than PRF and TRF, as shown in table 2. This reveals the importance of customer related factors as a role in better generating customer satisfaction and customer loyalty.

Competition-based performance. Alternative set of performance concerned is the competition-based performance, of which the most often indicator particularly in those strategically important markets. Model 4 in table 2 indicates that PRF and TRF explained 63.4% of COP variance. This means TRF and PRF could be used together in successful predicting a firm's COP.

Table 2. Partner selection factors and performances

	CUP		COP		OP	
Models	1	2	3	4	5	6
Constant	3.311*	2.217*	0.350*	0.383*	1.830*	1.300*
TRF	0.068	-0.075	0.243*	0.248*	0.156*	0.087
PRF	0.065	0.063	0.644*	0.644*	0.354*	0.353*
CRF		0.463*		-0.014		0.225*
R	0.121	0.541	0.797	0.797	0.645	0.716
R^2	0.015	0.293	0.635	0.644	0.416	0.513
Adj. R^2	0.008	0.286	0.632	0.631	0.412	0.508
F	2.353	43.72	276.015	183.577	113.107	111.35

CUP, customer-based performance; COP, competition-based performance; OP, Overall performance TRF, Task related factors; PRF, Partner related factors; CRF, Customer related factors

Adding CRF as the third predictors in the model, variance to be explained raise to a higher level of R^2= 0.644. PRF is the major predictors in both two models of COP with high coefficient relation (0.644), and CRF in the model has negative impact on COP. This explicitly indicates that selecting potential partner base on PRF would be effective and efficient as long as the subsidiary is designed solely for competition-based performance. Negative impacts of CRF on COP may implicitly advise us that too much pro-customer may jeopardize COP.

Overall performance. The literature generally advocates to simultaneously aware both CUP and COP for short and long term returns (Narver & Slater, 1990; Day & Wensley, 1988; Kohli & Jaworski, 1990). PRF and TRF, as shown in table 2, together explain 41.6% of variance of OP. PRF is again the major predictors (0.354) of overall performance. In the model 6, we add CRF with PRF and PRF in predicting OP. Although variance explained is lower than that in model 4, this seems to be a satisfactory model for OP as the dependent variable is closer to the reality, and R^2= 0.513 is sufficient in most management studies. In sum, PRF remains the major predictor in this model, CRF as the second, and TRF as the least and may be better to be replaced by CRF. Figure 2 shows the effects of CRF adding.

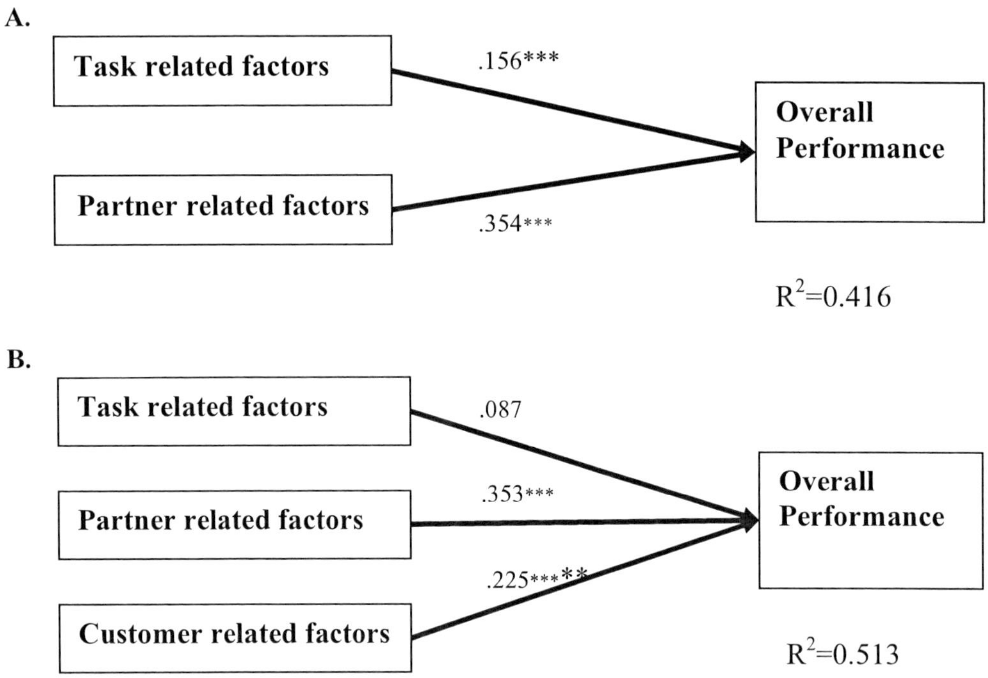

Figure 2. Partner selection factors and overall performance of IJV.

4.3. Market Orientation

Two sets of relationship associated with market orientation are interesting to determine. One is how partner selection factors affect a firm's market orientation, and the other how such market orientation is in turn affecting overall performance. Model 1 of table 3 shows predicting power of TRF and PRF as 0.052 (n. s.) and 0.295 respectively with R^2=0.224. PRF

is better a performance predictor in this relationship. Adding CRF as the third predictor, R^2 of the model 2 up to 0.459, where CRF appears as the best predictor, followed by PRF. This means adding CRF in partner selection, firms are more likely to be market oriented, from which supports H_2. Previous studies generally advocate that market orientation directly link with firm's performances in many different terms (Kirca et al., 2005). We analyze the relationship of these two constructs and receive similar results. Shown as in the right column of table 3, R^2=0.445, the effect of market orientation on overall performance is high as 0.673. Market orientation is a powerful predictor of overall performance.

Table 3. Partner selection factors, market orientation, and performance

D. V.	Market orientation (MO)		O. P.
Models	1	2	3
Constant	2.534*	1.432*	1.311*
TRF	0.052	0.015	
PRF	0.295*	0.249*	
CRF		0.381*	
M. O.			0.673*
R	0.474	0.677	0.667
R^2	0.224	0.459	0.445
Adj. R^2	0.208	0.441	0.440
F	13.606	26.293	76.301

* $p<0.05$

5. Conclusions

5.1. Conclusion

This research explores and confirms the importance of the role customer-related factors play in selecting an ideal international joint venture partner for International joint venture performances. This research first reveals that adding CRF into partner selection has substantially improved the variance explained of IJV overall performance (Pan, 2004; Levitt, 1960; 1983; Lenskold, 2004), and by which supports Hypothesis 1. This research has also confirmed that an IJV with higher level of market orientation will gain better customer-based and overall performances (Klein & Chekitan, 1997).

Types of factors applied in selecting partner tend to affect the JV's marketing strategies (Geringer, 1990; Arino & Abramov, 1997; Al-Khalifa & Peterson, 1998). Seeking partners under task related factors in mind, firms incline to have lower level of market orientation, whereas firms that seeking partners under customer related factors appear to have higher level of market orientation. Noteworthy is the additive of CRF into original model of PRF and TRF has substantial and positive effects on IJV's market orientation, and eventually helpful to overall performance of the joint-ventured business (Day & Nedungadi, 1994; Ricci, 2003). Hypothesis 2 is supported.

Consistent to previous studies, the model that linking market orientation and customer-based performance has best level of variance explained, followed by the model that predicting overall performance. This provides evidence regarding the predicting value of marketing orientation, and support the hypothesis 3. Adding the construct of customer related factors into the model not only further strengthens the level of explanation power on IJV performance but also affects predicting ability of task related factor. Noteworthy is that these two constructs have very low collinearity.

5.2. Theoretical Implications

Beyond traditional PRF and TRF in international joint venture partner selection, this research further addresses the importance of customer related factors. Taking customer capital of knowledge-based view, we proof the importance of customer related factors as critical partner criteria other than PRF and TRF. This has some important academic implications.

Knowledge on customers' purchasing behavior is an integral part of resources that firm required in building competitive advantage. Scholars from knowledge-based view may have confined customer capital within customer value perception, thus prevent the customer related factors emerging in this kind of studies. Recently, academicians urge to learn from customers, to explore more into customers' mind (Garcia-Murillo & Annabi, 2002). Evidence provided in this research indicates that factors affecting purchasing behavior in each stage, from external environment factors to consumer internal factors, shall be included in firm's customer information system. Availability of such information system is an integral part of customer related factors for the decisions of IJV partner.

Regression analysis shows that task related factors has limited predicting ability on IJV's competitor-based performance, and not on customer-based performance. This reveals that task factors alone without help of market orientation may be not sufficient in explaining IJV performance. Customer related factor is important in predicting customer-based performance as well as overall performance, but not competitor-based performance. Compare to CRF and TRF, PRF is a powerful predictor for every kind of performances. Finding of this research finding has confirmed the perspectives hold by resource-based view.

5.3. Managerial Implications

MNE's attempt to leverage partner's resources in geographical spanning, shall first find proper partner under CRF consideration instead of TRF, or to the minimum add PRF as part of primary criteria. In the past two decades, plethoras of Taiwanese firms seek overseas development in a wide variety of markets. However, many of them recruiting partners under task related factors have experienced failures. Alternatively, those collaborate with partners who are pro-customers have secured abundant growth and competitive advantages. For example, Tingyi (Master Kang instant noodle), I-Land Foods (Want Want snacks), and China Motor Corporation (CMC vehicles) are those cases that expanding with the help of market oriented partners.

Customer related factors can also applicable to local firms that seeking foreign investments. In doing so, firms will be easier to attract and locate market-oriented prospective

for the consensus of market orientation strategies, and consequently favorable customer acceptance and performance in local venture (Day & Nedungadi, 1994; Littler & Leverick, 1995; Kaynak & Kara, 2002). The most notable success of market-oriented example is the joint venture between Carrefour (France) and President Enterprise (Taiwan), this joint venture proofed to itself by gaining biggest market share and growing branches. In the other hand, Taiwan automakers could be good example for not failures because of seeking partners based on task related factors. Half century after the first joint venture project in early 1960s, today's Taiwan automobile industry hardly stands on its own feet.

Market orientation as a strategic approach starts from learning from customers, and exploring determinants of customer purchasing decision to performing in a customer-centric way. In other words, firms shall move from product-centric concept to customer-centric (Selden & MacMillan, 2006), Customer-centric organizations view customers as business partners (Ricci, 2003), and thus incline to commit themselves to understand customers, from which accumulate customer capital and upgrade customer knowledge exploiting techniques. As numerous empirical studies confirmed, these customers will reward good level of preference and loyalty to this customer-centric company.

REFERENCES

Adler, L., & Hlavacek, J. D. (1976). Joint Ventures for Product Innovation. New York: American Management Association.

Alexander, M., & Young, D. (1996). Outsourcing: Where's the value? *Long Range Planning*, 29 (5), 728-730.

Al-Khalifa, A. K., & Peterson, S. E. (1998). The partner selection process in international joint ventures. *European Journal of Marketing*, 33 (11/12), 1064-1081.

Argyris, C. (1977). Double loop learning in organizations. *Harvard Business Review*, 55 (5), 115-125.

Arino, A. & Abramov, M. (1997). Partner selection and trust building in West European—Russian joint ventures. International Studies of Management & Organization, *Spring*, 27 (1), 19-37.

Awadzi, W. (1987). Determinants of joint venture performance: A study of international joint ventures in the United States. Unpublished PhD dissertation, Louisiana State University.

Balabanis, G., & Diamantopoulos, A. (2004). Domestic country bias, country-of-origin effects, and consumer ethnocentrism: A multidimensional unfolding approach. *Journal of the Academy of Marketing Science*, 32 (1), 80

Barclay, D. W., & Smith, J. B. (1997). The effects of organizational differences and trust on the effectiveness of selling partner relationships. *Journal of Marketing*, 61 (1), 3-20.

Barney, J.B. (1991). Firm resources and sustained competitive advantage. *Journal of Management*, 17 (1), 99-120.

Blackwell, R. D., Miniard, P. W., & Engel, J. F. (2006). Consumer Behavior 10th e, Mason, Ohio: Thomson Southwestern.

Bleeke, J. and Ernst, D., (1991). The Way to Win in Cross-border Alliances. *Harvard Business Review*, 69 (6), 127-135.

Brief, A. P., & Bazerman, M. (2003). Editor's Comments: Bringing in consumers. *Academy of Management Review*, 28 (2), 187-189.

Brouthers, K. D., Brouthers, L. E., & Wilkinson, T. J. (1995). Strategic alliances: Choose your partner. *Long Range Planning*, 28(3), 18-25.

Brush, D., & Licata, B. J. (1983). The impact of skill learnability on the effectiveness of managerial training and development. *Journal of Management*, 9 (1), 27-39.

Cano, C. R., Carrillat, F. A., & Jaramillo, F. (2004). A meta-analysis of the relationship between market orientation and business performance. *International Journal of Research in Marketing*, 21 (2), 179-200.

Cavusgil, T., & Evirgen, C. (1997). Use of expert system in international marketing. *European Journal of Marketing*, 31 (1), 73-86.

Coase, R. H. (1937). The nature of the firm. Economica, 4, 386-405.

Coviello, N, & Munro, H. (1997). Network relationship and the international process of small software firms. *International Business Review*, 6 (4): 361-386.

Dacin, M. T., Hitt, M. A., & Levitas E. (1997). Selecting partners for successful international alliances: Examination of U.S. and Korean firms. *Journal of World Business*, 32 (1), 3-16

Das, T. K., & Teng, B. S. (2000). A resource-based theory of strategic alliance. *Journal of Management*, 26(1), 31-61.

Day, G. S., & Nedungadi, P. (1994). Managerial representations of competitive advantage. *Journal of Marketing*, 58 (2), 31-44.

Day, G. S., & Wensley, R. (1988). Assessing advantage: A framework for diagnosing competitive superiority. *Journal of Marketing*, 51 (1), 1-10.

De Mooji, M., & Hofstede, G. (2002). Convergence and divergence in consumer behavior: Implications for international retailing. *Journal of Retailing*, 78 (1), 61-69.

Deloitte, Haskins & Sells International. (1989). Team Up for the Nineties – Can You Survive without a Partner? New York: Deloitte, Haskins & Sells.

Deshpande, R., Farley, J. U., & Webster, F. E. (1993). Corporate culture, customer orientation, and innovativeness in Japanese firms. *Journal of Marketing*, 57, 23-37.

Devlin, G..., & Bleakley, M. (1988). Strategic alliances: Guidelines for success. *Long Rang Planning*, 21 (5), 18-23.

Douma, M., Bilderbeek, J., Idenburg, P., & Looise, J. (2000). Strategic alliances: Managing the dynamic of fit. *Long Range Planning*, 33, 579-598.

Duncan, T. & Moriarty S. E. (1998). A communication-based marketing model for managing relationship. *Journal of Marketing*, 62(1), 1-13.

Edvinsson, L., & Sullivan, P. (1996). Developing a model for managing intellectual capital. *European Management Journal*, 14 (4), 356-364.

Eisenhardt, K. M., & Martin, J. A. (2000). Dynamic capabilities – What are they? *Strategic Management Journal*, 21, 1105-1121.

Ellis, P. D. (2006). Market orientation and performance: A meta-analysis and cross-national comparison. *Journal of Management Studies*, 43 (5), 1089-1107.

Eric, W. K., & Tsang. E. W. K. (1999). A preliminary typology of learning in international strategic alliances. *Journal of World Business*, 34 (3), 211-229.

Esteban, A., Millan, A., Molina, A., & Martin-Consuegra, D. (2002). Market orientation in service: A review and analysis. *European Journal of Marketing*, 36 (9/10), 1003-1021.

Gale, A., & Luo, J. (2004). Factors affecting construction joint venture in China. *International Journal of Project Management*, 22 (1), 33-42.

Garcia-Murillo, M. & Annabi, H. (2002). Customer knowledge management. *Journal of the Operational Research Society,* 53, 875-884.

Geringer, J. M. (1991). Strategic determinants of partner selection criteria in international joint ventures. *Journal of International Business Studies*, 22 (1), 41-62.

Geringer, J. M., & Hebert, C. A. (1989). Measuring performance of international joint venture. *Journal of International Business Studies*, 22(2), 249-263.

Gibbert, M, Leibold, M., & Probst, G. (2002). Five styles of customer knowledge management, and how smart companies use them to create value. *European Management Journal*, 20 (5), 459-485.

Glaister, K. W., & Buckley, P. J. (1997). Task-related and partner-related selection criteria in UK international joint ventures. *British Journal of Management*, 8 (3), 199-222.

Gulati, R., & Singh, H. (1998). The architecture of cooperation: Managing coordination costs and appropriation concerns in strategic alliances. *Administrative Science Quarterly*, 43 (4), 781-815.

Harrigan, K. R. (1988). Joint ventures and competitive strategy. *Strategic Management Journal,* 9,141-158.

Harris, L. C., & Cai, K. Y. (2002). Exploring market driving: A case study of DeBeers in China. *Journal of Market - Focused Management*, 5 (3), 171-196.

Hennart, J. F., & Reddy, S. (1997). The choice between merger/acquisitions and joint venture: The case of Japanese investors in the United States. *Strategic Management Journal*, 18(1), 1-12.

Hitt, M. A., Levitas, E., Arregle, J-L., & Borza, A. (2000). Partner selection in emerging and developed market contexts: Resource-based and organizational learning perspectives. *Academy of Management Journal*, 43 (3), 449-467.

Hoffmann, W., & Schlosser, R. (2001). Success factors of strategic alliances in small and medium-sized enterprises: An empirical survey. *Long Range Planning*, 34, 357-381.

Hooley, G. J., Greenley, G. E., Cadogan, J. W., & Fahy, J. (2005). The performance impact of marketing resources. *Journal of Business Research*, 58 (1), 18-27.

Hoskisson, R. E., Eden, L., Lau, C-M., & Wright, M. (2000). Strategy in emerging economies. *Strategic Management Journal*, 43 (3), 249-267.

Hunt, S. & Morgan, R. M. (1995). The comparative advantage theory of competition. *Journal of Marketing*, 59 (2), 1-15.

Hurley, R. F., & Hult G. T. M. (1998). Innovation, market orientation, and organizational learning: An Integration and Empirical Examination. Journal of Marketing, 62 (3), 42-54.

Inkpen, A., & Ross, J. (2001). Why do some strategic alliances persist beyond their useful life?' *California Management Review*, 44 (1), 132-148.

Insch, G. S., & Steensma, H. K. (2006). The relationship between firm strategic profile and alliance partners' characteristics. *Journal of Managerial Issues*, 18 (3), 321-341.

Jaworski, B. J., Kohli, A. K., & Sahay, A. (2000). Market driven versus driving market. *Journal of the Academy of Marketing Science*, 28 (1), 45-54.

Jo, M. S. (1998). Contingency and contextual issues of ethnocentrism-pitched advertisements: A cross-national comparison. *International Marketing Review*, 15 (6), 447-457.

Kanter, R. M., (1994). Collaborative advantage: The art of alliances. *Harvard Business Review,* 72 (4), 96-108.

Kaynak, E. & Kara, A. (2002). Consumer perceptions of foreign products: An analysis of product-country images and ethnocentrism. *European Journal of Marketing*, 36 (7/8), 928-949.

Khan, O.J., & Suh, T. (2005). A multi-group analysis between developed and emerging markets on societal liberalization attracting foreign investment. *Journal of Global Marketing*, 19 (2), 77-94.

Kirca, A. H., Jayachandran, S., & Bearden, W. O. (2005). Market orientation: A meta-analytic review and assessment of its antecedents and impact on performance. *Journal of Marketing*, 69 (4), 24-41.

Klein, J. G., Ettenson, R., & Morris, M. D. (1998). The animosity model of foreign product purchase: An empirical test in the People's Republic of China', *Journal of Marketing*, 62(1), 89-100.

Klein, S. & Chekitan D. (1997). Partner selection in market–driven strategic alliance. *South African Journal of Business Management*, 28 (3), 97-106.

Kohli, A. K., & Jaworski, B. J. (1990). Market orientation: The constructs, research propositions, and managerial implications. *Journal of Marketing*, 54 (1), 1-18.

Kohli, A. K., Jaworski, B. J., & Kumar, A. (1993). MARKOR: A measure of market orientation. *Journal of Marketing Research*, 30 (4), 467-477.

Laroche, M. L., Kalamas, M., & Cleveland, M. (2005). "I" versus "We": How individualists and collectivists use information sources to formulate their service expectations. *International Marketing Review*, 22 (3), 279-308.

Lasserre, P. (1984). Selecting a foreign partner for technology transfer. *Long Range Planning*, 17 (6), 43 - 49.

Lastovica, J. L., Bettencourt, L. A., Hughner, R. S., & Kuntze, R.J. (1999). Lifestyle of tight and frugal: Theory and measurement. *Journal of Consumer Research*, 36 (2), 85-98.

Lenskold, J. D. (2004). Customer-centric marketing ROI. *Marketing Management*, 13 (1), 26.

Levitt, T. (1960). Marketing myopia. *Harvard Business Review*, 38 (4), 45-56.

Levitt, T. (1983). The globalization of markets. *Harvard Business Review*. 61 (3), 92-102.

Lin, H. M. (2006). Interorganizational collaboration, social embeddedness, and value creation: A theoretical analysis. *International Journal of Management*, 23 (1), 548-558.

Littler, d., & Leverick, F. (1995). Joint ventures for product development: Learning from experience. *Long Range Planning*, 28 (3), 37-45.

Lorange, P. & Roos, J. (1990). Formation of cooperative ventures: Competence mix of the management teams. *Management International Review*, 30, 69-86.

Luo, Y. (1998). Joint venture success in China: How should we select a good partner? *Journal of World Business*, 33(2), 145-166.

Lyles, M., & Salk, J. (1996). Knowledge acquisition from foreign parents in international joint ventures: An empirical examination in the Hungarian context. *Journal of International Business Studies*, 27 (5), 877-903.

Ma, H. (2004). Toward global competitive advantage: Creation, competition, cooperation, and co-option. *Management Decision*, 42 (7/8), 907-925.

Madhok, A., & Tallman, S. B. (1998). Resources, transactions and rents: Managing value through interfirm collaborative relationships. *Organization Science*, 9 (3), 326-339.

Makino, S., & Delios, A. (1996). Local knowledge and performance: Implications for alliance formation in Asia. *Journal of International Business Studies*, 27 (5), 905-928.

Miller, D. & Shamsie, J. (1996). The resource-based view of the firm in two environments: The Hollywood film studios from 1936 to 1965. *Academy of Management Journal*, 39 (3), 519-543.

Morgan, R. M., & Hunt, S.D. (1994). The commitment-trust theory of relationship marketing, *Journal of Marketing*, 58 (3), 20-38.

Nakata, C., & Sivakumar, K. (2001). Instituting the marketing concept in a multinational setting: The role of country culture. *Journal of the Academy of Marketing Science*, 29 (summer), 255-275.

Narver, J. C., & Slater, S. F. (1990). The effect of market orientation on business profitability. *Journal of Marketing*, 54 (4), 20-35.

Njissen, E. J, Douglas, S. P., & Galis, G. (1999). Gathering and using information for the selection of trading partners. *European Journal of Marketing*, 33 (1/2), 143-162.

Nonaka, I. (1994). A dynamic theory of organizational knowledge creation. *Organization Science*, 5, 14-37.

Ohmae, K. (1985). Triad Power: The Coming Shape of Global Competition. New York: Free Press.

Osland, G. E., & Cavusgil, S. T. (1996). Performance issues in U.S.-China joint ventures. *California Management Review*, 38(2), 106-130.

Pan, F-C. (2004). Ally strategic alliance with consumers? Who care? *Journal of American Academy of Business*, 4 (1), 323-329.

Parise, S., & Henderson, J. C. (2001). Knowledge resource exchange in strategic alliances. *IBM Systems Journal*, 40 (4), 908-924.

Pelham, A. M. (1997). Mediating influences on the relationship between market orientation and profitability in small industrial firms. *Journal of Marketing Theory and Practice*, 5 (summer), 55-76.

Petrash, G. (1996). Dow's journey to a knowledge value management culture. *European Management Journal*, 14 (4), 365-373.

Pfeffer, J. & Salancik, G. R. (1977). Organization design-The case for a coalitional model of organizations. *Organizational Dynamics*, 6 (2), 15-30.

Pfeffer, J., & Salancik, G. R. (1978). The External control of Organizations: A Resource Dependence Perspectives, New York: Harper and Row Publishers

Porter, M. E. (1980). Competitive Strategy. New York: Free Press.

Porter, M. E. (1985). Competitive Advantage. New York: Free Press.

Powell, W., Kogut, K., & Smith-Doerr, L. (1996). Interorganizational collaboration and the locus of innovation: Networks of learning in biotechnology. *Administrative Science Quarterly*, 41 (1), 116-145.

Prahalad, C. K., & Hamel, G. (1990). The core competence of the corporation. *Harvard Business Review*, 68 (3): 79-91.

Qureshi, S. (1993). Market-driven public institutions attract stress. *Journal of Professional Service Marketing*, 9 (2), 83-92.

Rawwas, M. Y. A. (2001). Culture, personality and morality: A typology of international consumers' ethical beliefs. *International Marketing Review*, 18 (2), 188-211.

Reid, D., Bussiere, D., & Greenaway, K. (2001). Alliance formations for knowledge-based enterprises. *International Journal of Management Reviews*, 13 (1), 79-100.

Renforth, W. E. (1974). A comparative study of joint international business ventures with family or non-family firm partners: The Caribbean community experience. Doctoral dissertation, Indiana University, Indiana.

Ricci, R. (2003). Move from product to customer centric. *Quality Progress*, 36 (11), 22.

Robson, M. J. (2002). Partner selection in successful international strategic alliances: The role of co-operation. *Journal of General Management*, 28 (1), 1.

Rodriguez, S. D., Perez, J. F. M., & del Val., M. P. (2003). An empirical study about the effect of cultural problematic on organizational learning in alliances. *The Learning Organization*, 10 (2/3), 38-48.

Ruigrok, W., & Wagner, H. (2003). Internationalization and performance: An organizational learning perspective. *Management International Review*, 43 (1), 63-84.

Sargeant, A., & Mohamad, M. (1999).Business performance in the UK hotel sector- does it pay to be market-oriented? *The Services Industries Journal*, 19 (3), 42-59.

Saxe, R. & Weitz, B. A. (1982). The SOCO scale: A measure of the customer orientation of sales people. *Journal of Marketing Research*, 19 (3), 343-351.

Selden, L, & MacMillan, I. C. (2006). Manage customer-centric innovation systematically. *Harvard Business Review*, 84 (4), 108-123.

Shenkar, O., & Li, J. (1999). Knowledge search in international cooperative ventures. *Organization Science*, 10, 134-143.

Sheth, J. N. Sisodia, R. S., & Sharma, A. (2000). The antecedents and consequences of customer-centric marketing. *Journal of the Academy of Marketing Science*, 28 (1), 55-66.

Siguaw, J. A., Simpson, P. M., & Baker, T. L. (1998). Effects of supplier market orientation on distribution market orientation and the channel relationship: The distributor perspective. *Journal of Marketing*, 62 (3), 99-111.

Simonin, B. L. (1997). Transfer of marketing know-how in international strategic alliance: An empirical investigation of the role and antecedents of knowledge ambiguity. *Journal of International Business Studies*, 30 (3), 463-490.

Slater, S. F., & Narver, J. C. (1994a). Market orientation, customer value, and superior performance. *Business Horizons*, 37 (2), 22-28.

Slater, S. F., & Narver, J. C. (1994b). Does competitive environment moderate the market orientation – performance relationship? *Journal of Marketing*, 58 (1), 46-55.

Stickler, J. (2001). Viewpoint: Building successful strategic alliances. *Strategic Direction*, 17 (8), 3-4.

Szymanski, D. M. & Henard, D. H. (2001). Customer satisfaction: A meta-analysis of the empirical evidence. *Journal of the Academy of Marketing Science*, 29 (4), 16-35.

Tomlinson, J. W. C. (1970). The Joint Venture Process in International Business: India and Pakistan, Cambridge, MA: MIT Press.

Uhlenbruck, K., Meyer, K. E., & Hitt, M. A. (2003). Organizational transformation in transition economies: Resource-based and organizational learning perspectives. *Journal of Management Studies*, 40 (2), 257-283.

Varis, J, & Conn, S. (2002). Alliance partner selection – A literature review. Telecom Business Research Center Lappeenranta, working papers 14, Lappeenranta University of Technology, Finland.

Wang, L., & Kess, P. (2006). Partnering motives and partner selection: Case studies of Finnish distributor relationships in China. *International Journal of Physical Distribution & Logistics Management*, 36 (6), 466-478.

Ward, S., Girardi, A., & Lewandowska, A. (2006). A cross-national validation of the Narver and Slater market orientation scale. *Journal of Marketing Theory and Practice*, 14 (2), 155-167.

Wernerfelt, B. (1995). The resource-based view of the firm: Ten years after. *Strategic Management Journal*, 16 (3), 171-174.

Williamson, O. E., (1979). Transaction cost economics: The governance of contractual relationships. *Journal of Law and Economics*, 22(2), 233-261.

Wrenn, B. (1997). The market orientation construct: Measurement and scaling issues. *Journal of Marketing Theory and Practice*, 5 (3), 31-54.

Wulf, K. D., Odekerken-Schroder, G. & Iacobucci, D. (2001). Investments in consumer relationship: A cross-country and cross-industry exploration. *Journal of Marketing*, 65 (4), 33-50.

In: Business and Finance: Performance and Management ISBN: 978-1-61122-936-3
Editors: R. Morland and A. Gagglione

Chapter 3

On Managing the Uncertain: Observations of Project Management

Markus Hällgren*

Umeå School of Business, 901 87 Umeå, Sweden

Abstract

Traditionally projects are considered means for getting things done, simultaneously striving for efficient and accurate methods – that is, doing more in less time. A consequence, not often discussed, is that doing more things in less time with a closer focus on cost, will inevitably lead to a more complex and tightly connected project execution system which is more sensitive to deviations. Following a "project-as-practice" perspective this paper explores and analyses how deviations are managed. The findings suggest that even though the company under consideration manages about 120 projects per year deviations cannot be avoided. The deviations were found initially to decouple (a process of creating loosely coupled activities) from the overall project process and later on to recouple (a process of tightly coupling activities) when the deviation was resolved. The paper suggests that the management of deviations is dynamic and changing and that the concept of coupling is a fruitful way of exploring the process.

Introduction

Traditionally, projects are considered means for getting things done, an issue that is highlighted in the contemporary project management literature (c.f. Ekstedt *et al.*, 1999; Engwall and Westling, 2004) where a key ingredient in the development of project management tools and techniques is using methods that are more time and cost efficient. (Lindkvist *et al.*, 1998). Thus, the need for simultaneous speed and accuracy is emphasized, creating a demand for more elaborate planning and control methods. A consequence, not often discussed, is that doing more things in less time with a closer focus on cost will inevitably lead to a more complex and tightly connected project execution system (compare

---

* Corresponding author: (phone) + 46 90 786 58 85; (fax) + 46 90 786 66 74; markus.hallgren@usbe.umu.se; www.markushaellgren.com

Perrow, 1984), which is more sensitive to deviations. To put it differently, planned activities in a project are doomed to be interrupted by deviations having various impacts (Hällgren and Maaninen - Olsson, 2005). Surprisingly, , as a research and practitioner community, we do not know how unexpected events (deviations) are managed in practice – away from theoretical constructs and suggestions on how to handle them (Cicmil, 2006). Equally disturbing is that we do not know much about the mechanisms and the deviation management logics. Therefore, the question that will be given focus in this paper is:

How Are Deviations Managed in Practice in Tightly Coupled Projects?

Some organizations experience very few major deviations despite functioning in tightly coupled and complex environments (Roberts, 1990b; Weick, 2004). Interestingly, these organizations recognize that they rely on both tight and loose coupling in their activities – contrary to what is described in the literature. In the contemporary literature on projects and coupling processes, projects are generally described as loosely coupled organizations with planned, tightly coupled activities (Christensen and Kreiner, 1991; Dubois and Gadde, 2002). Although these insights are useful and valid, they neglect the micro-activities - the practice - of managing projects. Therefore the question of coupling is elaborated upon through a project-as-practice approach which implies that the activities of the practitioners are taken seriously (Johnson *et al.*, 2003). In this context, this means how practitioners make use of their abilities to manage the unexpected in tightly coupled power plant projects. (c.f. Whittington, 2003; Jarzabkowski, 2005; Whittington, 2006). The aim of this paper is to examine the logic of coupling processes with regard to deviations. This will shed some light on what makes projects able to handle a simultaneous need for flexibility and stability which for a long time have interested scholars of organizational theory (Burns and Stalker, 1961; Thompson, 1967; Weick, 1976). The conclusion ties the analytical pieces together and shows that the sum is larger than its parts. The paper is structured accordingly.

BACKGROUND

Organizing Verbs

The struggle to stamp out the nouns and replace them with verbs is attributed to Karl Weick (1979:44). He suggests than any organizing process is achieved by ecological change, enactment, selection and retention. Enactment is about bracketing parts of the overall organizing process, or dividing it into events which assembled make up the "organizing"; selection about sorting out meaningful understandings and finally preserving them (Weick, 1979; Weick *et al.*, 2005:414). This bracketing process (which projects are argued to be a result of (Lundin and Söderholm, 1995)) is *not an outcome* of organizing but a sensitizing device in the shape of practices influencing what is, or is not bracketed (Weick, 1979:166). Using the word "practices" is intentional, it highlights the connection to the practice idea (Weick uses "previous events") and that is useful for the next part of the argument. The overall process which Weick describes as "enactment, selection and retention" could also be

described as how the situated praxis influences the shape of the practitioners' practices and how these concepts merge in episodes of organizing. (There is more about the Practice Turn in for example, Whittington (2006) or Schatzki *et al* (2001)).

Hendry and Seidl (2003), drawing on Luhmann (1995) (who have the same interest in social systems as Weick) argue that the overall processes of an organization can be divided into streams of interrelated episodes of communication (as part of organizing). From a more general organizing viewpoint these episodes can be meetings, planning sessions, informal talks, going-away days (Whittington, 2006). Essentially the episodes are parts of the processes which are singled out from other organizing processes and are comparable with the enactment part of Weick's model.

When an episode is singled out (as part of previous experiences, and compared once again) a certain situated praxis follows, (again compared to the selection part of the model) and later on are either retained or not into the overall behavior (compared to practices). Thus what we have is a process of bracketing, acting and re-connecting. Hendry and Seidl suggest that it can be described as a process of coupling which we need to understand better in order to understand practice. However, as Weick (1976) and Orton and Weick (1990) argue, to say that something is loosely coupled (when it is given an identity and requires a response) is only the beginning as what is really interesting happens *within* the process., – that is, what happens when such a mechanism kicks in. This would support the ideas of Hendry and Seidl, but also the more general views from an "as-practice" perspective.

Loosely Coupled Systems

The core of the organizing argument is one of loosely coupled systems (Weick, 1979:236) The concept of coupling was formally introduced to organization theory by Professor Karl Weick in (1976) drawing of arguments from Glassman (1973). In the literature, loose coupling is commonly argued to be a barrier to change and learning and a facilitator of innovation on an organizational level (e.g. Dubois and Gadde, 2002). In projects, this is recognized not only in how projects are used for producing novel solutions when it is not necessary for the entire organization to change, but also the problem of learning between projects. Initially, loose coupling was seen as an enabler and a feature which explained the organizing of local practices, in turn admitting novel solutions in a limited context (Weick, 1976; Snook, 2002). The strength of coupling is that it allows the researcher to examine the rationality and indeterminacy of organizations simultaneously, as well as organizations which are open and closed at the same time (c.f. Orton and Weick, 1990:205; Scott, 2003:271-272). "[Loosely] coupled events are responsive, *but* [...] each event also preserves its own identity and some evidence of its physical or logical separateness. [...] Their attachment may be circumscribed, infrequent, weak in its mutual effects, unimportant, and/or slow to respond. [...] [Loose coupling] also carries connotations of impermanence, dissolvability, and tacitness all of which are potentially crucial properties of the "glue" that holds organizations together." (Weick, 1976:3) (For a comprehensive exposition of the subject and the literature see Orton and Weick (1990) On the other hand, tightly coupled activities are those that are directly responsive -ones in which a change spreads rapidly like rings on the water such as in a concurrent engineering project where a plan commonly specifies what each party is expected to do and the activities are both tightly coupled and dependent on each other.

Upset with how the coupling concept was being used, Orton and Weick subsequently made a critical literature review of the various applications. They started their critique with the claim that the concept "is widely used and diversely understood"(Orton and Weick, 1990:203). Five voices of loose coupling emerged; Causation, Typology, Direct Effects, Compensations and Organizational Outcomes. (see Orton and Weick, 1990) The voices all struggle with the issue of choosing between a dialectical and a uni-dimensional approach to coupling. The dialectical approach is the good one according to Orton and Weick. Being dialectic means that tight and loose coupling is present at the same time. Being uni-dimensional on the other hand is bad. It is bad because it drifts away from the original meaning in the sense of putting tight and loose coupling at the end of a scale without acknowledging their parallelism and mutual influence. To aid understanding Orton and Weick essentially broke down the coupling concept into distinctiveness and responsiveness describing them thus: "If there is neither responsiveness nor distinctiveness, the system is not really a system, and it can be defined as a non-coupled system [1]. If there is responsiveness without distinctiveness, the system is tightly coupled [2]. If there is distinctiveness without responsiveness, the system is decoupled [3]. If there is both distinctiveness and responsiveness, the system is loosely coupled [4]." The idea is that these concepts are dialectic, thus not mutually exhaustive and uni-dimensional. (Orton and Weick, 1990:205) The differences are illustrated in exhibit 1 below, the numbers corresponds to the numbers above.

		Responsiveness	
		No	Yes
Distinctiveness	Yes	[3] Decoupled system	[4] Loosely coupled system
	No	[1] Non-coupled system	[2] Tightly coupled system

Exhibit 1. Types of coupling (compare Orton and Weick, 1990).

"If a person selectively attends to the openness, independence and indeterminate links among some elements, he or she will describe what amounts to a decoupled system. That characterization, too, is incomplete and inaccurate because parts of the system remain coupled and closed". That said, the research does not become less powerful but it could benefit from a more uni-dimensional approach, possibly meaning that the micro-perspective of "The Practice Turn" (Schatzki *et al.*, 2001; Jarzabkowski *et al.*, 2007; Whittington, 2007) could be a fruitful development as suggested by Hallet and Ventresca (2006) in association with institutional theory development.

From an institutional perspective, construction industry projects are loosely coupled to their organizations. The projects are loosely coupled because there is a focus on the single project rather than the continuous business, a need for local adjustments at the building site, utilization of standardized parts, competitive tendering, market-based exchange, and self-determination; features which are met by the loose coupling mechanisms of localized adaptation, buffering, sensing, generation of variation and self-determination. (Dubois and Gadde, 2002) Even though project literature commonly treats coupling on an institutional level (c.f. Christensen and Kreiner, 1991; Kreiner, 1995; Lindkvist et al., 1998; Dubois and Gadde, 2002) the concept of coupling could also be brought down to a task management level where the prerequisites of the hierarchically higher levels are created, e.g. knowledge processes (Brusoni *et al.*, 2001) and where it contributes to the understanding of how different parts of an organization interact (Andersen, 2006:22).

Further down, within the project, the activities seems to be tightly coupled when examining them on the surface (Hällgren, 2007) even though they appear to be loosely coupled from the level above (Dubois and Gadde, 2002). The reason is that It would not be efficient (efficiency being a hallmark of projects) to carry around slack; there is commonly one accepted way of reaching the goal (the plan); a strong reliance on coordination; the project is centralized, not very delegated there is causal dependence between activities and so forth - all hallmarks of tight coupling (Weick, 1976:5-6). Loose coupling is generally considered to be a kind of local practice which is not necessarily according to the initial intentions of the planner (compare Snook, 2002). Thus it is fruitful to depart on a journey exploring the intricate meanings of coupling in a project context.

To put it differently, the micro-processes found on the task level commonly influence the levels above, or they are sedimented throughout the organization (Giddens, 1979:55). The problem with coupling is that the possibility that what seems to be loosely coupled from one perspective is not necessarily so when the context and the situation is examined from another point of view. (Weick, 1976:9-11) The importance of "perspective" is thus once again brought to our attention. In addition, what is coupled in one way at one occurrence is not necessarily so in a similar future situation. Coupling is thus a changing process which needs to be captured in the actions of the practitioners. These transitions from loose coupling to tight coupling are facilitated by the unexpected as this forces the organization to change its logic of activities. Thus deviations are essential to an understanding of the micro-patterns of loosely coupled projects.

Project Management in the Face of Deviations

Traditionally projects are considered means for getting things done. (Ekstedt et al., 1999). The reason that projects are efficient is that they are limited which makes it possible to initiate action and to pay attention to deviations. From this perspective the unexpected is regarded as unnatural (Tsoukas and Chia, 2002:567) - something that should be avoided and managed accordingly - although it is recognized that there different types of projects (c.f. Turner and Cochrane, 1993; Shenhar and Dvir, 1996; Crawford and Pollack, 2004) and that some will experience more deviations than others.

Following the line of argument deviations are defined as unexpected events which are identified (given distinctiveness) and requiring attention (given responsiveness). which

conforms with the idea that it is not a deviation until someone has said so in a social setting beyond the individuals' own reasoning (Weick, 1979; Engeström, 2000). The first step is thus that someone recognizes a deviation and announces it, or in other words, that someone `brackets and labels the event′ (Weick, 1979; Weick *et al.*, 2005). These deviations obviously constitute an important part of the project manager's work. Loose coupling of the organization (Dubois and Gadde, 2002) or the activities (Weick, 1976) is however seen as a feature which limits the impact of deviations and has therefore been given extra scrutiny (c.f. Weick and Roberts, 1993).

In project management literature this local practice is a neglected field of research as most literature focuses on plans, methods and tools or what Clegg et al (2005) call "synoptic" accounts. Such accounts are generally brief and general However, some studies – most unintentionally, some intentionally - take a project-as-practice approach. For example, Simon (2006) studied the role of the project manager in the computer industry based on the actions performed; Nilsson (2005) found that a project manager's day in the software industry was highly fragmented and meeting-intensive; Hällgren and Maaninen-Olsson (2005) researched deviations and their handling in a rolling-mill project. Pitsis, *et al* (2003) on the other hand, studied project management meetings during the "Sydney 2000 Olympic infrastructure project" where a chase for "future perfect" experienced several deviations and obstacles but still reached the goal. The above-mentioned studies reveal a local practice that departs from the make-believe constructs of the traditional literature. Thus,: "*[G]etting more involved with analytical and mostly rational theoretical models of projects will only provide more make-believe statements on project management issues.*" (Blomquist *et al.*, 2006:3-4)

Planning for Deviations

Whether they reflect local practice or not, plans are assumed to be means for specifying what tasks should be done, by whom and when, in endeavors that are complex in the sense that many interrelated activities are conducted in parallel, involving many people. Plans are thus instrumental. Diesel power plants which consist of literally thousands of activities and hundreds of people and apply a severely compressed concurrent engineering approach are a case in point. (Alsakini *et al.*, 2004; Lindahl, 2005). By means of plans, otherwise complex activities are broken down to allow more tightly coupled and efficient systems (systems in the sense of interacting activities (Simon, 1996:183-185)). This has made plans one of the most important features of project management (Dvir and Lechler, 2004).

Tools for planning are rational and straightforward. Through knowledge of the goal and the context and the application of past knowledge, they try to find the stabilizing features of the development. Whenever an event that challenges the plan occurs, it is expected that it receive a structured response (c.f. Nicholas, 2001; Gray and Larson, 2006). These are change and risk management procedures which commonly rely on quantitative measurements, reports, negotiations and formal decisions (Barkley, 2004). Such procedures serve to keep the plan and the tasks tightly coupled to the overall goal.

On a detailed level a plan describes the execution of the task, even the task broken down to a single afternoon. On this level a plan can be sequential, that is when the tasks come after each other. The tasks can also be arranged, as in this case, in a parallel pattern. If intentionally and heavily used this is addressed by concurrent engineering or fast tracking. That is, the

delivery time in the project is deliberately shortened as much as possible which decreases the amount of available slack in the project and increases the complexity (defined as the number of activities (Simon, 1996)) and tight coupling (responsiveness but not distinctiveness) between tasks (Weick, 1976; Orton and Weick, 1990) and need for coordination and adjustment (Thompson, 1967:55). Applying concurrent engineering thus puts an extra challenge to the neglected project execution (Love *et al.*, 1998; Kloppenborg and Opfer, 2002) when it produces more deviations that require attention.

METHOD

Recent developments in academia have taken on the task of capturing the practice of the practitioners and bringing back what is relevant not only to education but also academia as well as providing the practitioners themselves with the possibility of reflecting upon their own actions.

The research is based on Geertz's (1973:6) argument that in order to build strong theories and understanding of an organizing phenomenon, there is a need to focus on the actions of the individuals in the specific context. The ethnographic approach is believed to capture these actions. As Geertz (1973:6) put it "If you want to understand what science is, you should look first to what its practitioners do: anthropologists do ethnography." It is important to note however that there are other methodological means that may achieve practice-based results-interviews, for example, but also quantitative methods – but for the question and aimed posed observations are the obvious choice.

The empirical findings, on which this paper reports, comprise a twelve week long ethnographic observational study of two project teams in the independent power solutions business. In addition, triangulating the findings of the observations, there are 60 interviews, reports, contracts, minutes-of-meetings, more than 5000 emails, two week-long on-site project implementation visits and innumerable informal discussions related to the projects and their context.

So far, project management and temporary organizing have focused primarily on tools and methods but they also adopt a process approach to the developments (Söderlund, 2004). The practice approach is believed to provide additional unique insights to the findings by giving them content. Practice is thus examined as the actions of the practitioners which could be further elaborated and transformed into, or become part of, a process. This brings us to a question of what practice is. Practice can be defined in, and by, three broad concepts. These are the Praxis (situated actions) of the Practitioners (the men and women in project management) and their Practices (tools, methods, norms, values) (see Jarzabkowski, 2000; Johnson et al., 2003 for a review). These three concepts cannot be separated but rather they co-exist as they shape each other. The strength of the practice approach can also be found in this co-existence. Capturing the praxis of the practitioners will, if implemented correctly, bring organizing mechanisms to the surface rather than make-believe statements found in many "theories", tools and methods. Thus, the practice turn provides the foundation upon which statements can be elaborated.

This particular research has been analyzed in a number of steps using the project-as-practice perspective and Nvivo 8.0 software. First of all, let us be clear on the fact that the choice of the particular deviations that are addressed in the paper is important. The deviations

that are addressed all had significant impact upon the projects where they occurred. They also show intricate relations among individuals, actions and organizational entities. More importantly, the deviations are representative of the other 12 found in table 1. Secondly, during the course of the research, there were a number of weeks for reflection which provided the possibility of thinking about the developments (compare Yin, 1994). Thirdly, directly after the observations, the three chosen projects were written down as summary descriptions and sent for validation by the project managers. The fourth step was to write articles and present it in various forms and occasions (presentations, conferences etc.). This provided theoretical, empirical and analytical tools for further development. Fifthly, in this specific paper, the knowledge that has been accumulated during the course of the research breaks down the deviations into behaviors and analysis that address the issues in a broader sense. Sixthly, the analysis was brought together to form a somewhat unified theory of deviation related practice. The last stage was possible by using the multiple perspectives that emerged earlier in the research and is believed to answer to the relevance challenge of practice research.

Observations

The Company

The company is a company with global businesses, divided into several departments. One of them - the land based power plant department – has at any time during the year an average of 120 simultaneous projects, ranging from delivery to turnkey type projects to be delivered over periods from 3 - 24 months. An average project runs for 12 months. As a company that has been utilizing deliberate project management techniques in many projects for about 20 years, they are used to managing projects. The main weapon of competition is their concurrent engineering and ability to help the customer to benefit from their window of opportunity.

At the department there are about 30 project teams. One team consists of one project manager and a mechanical and electrical senior engineer. When the teams manage a turnkey project a senior civil engineer joins the team. When applicable, mainly for turnkey projects, a site team is associated with the project team. The site team manages the execution in the foreign country while the project team is responsible for planning, reporting, and customer contacts. This research has focused on the project team at the corporate office.

All in all, 15 deviations are presented in this article. They are summarized in exhibit 2 Two of the deviations are given extra scrutiny to aid the subsequent discussion.

Deviation 1 – Damaged Equipment

Damaged equipment was the cause of a deviation in a project with a twelve month schedule. The problem was discovered at a rather late stage of the project, partly because of the delay in the logistics. The damaged equipment consisted of a number of charge air

silencers and switchgear cubicles. The deviation threatened to delay the entire project by three months, which would shred the budget to pieces.

The first thing the project team tried to understand was the extent of the damage through phone calls, photos, emails and by sending a junior engineer from the sister project to the project with the damaged equipment.

NO	DEVIATION	DESCRIPTION	MANAGEMENT
1	Damaged equipment	Equipment found to be damaged, with a two month replacement process	Dummy pieces, rearrangement of tasks
2	Logistics delay	Equipment delayed by a month, including some critical equipment	Rearrangement of tasks, inform involved parties
3	Payment	The client did not pay according to an agreed schedule	Careful negotiations, involving support services and sales
4	Negotiations	Sensitive negotiations with a shipyard which were prolonged	Break down and discuss details
5	Demobilization of personnel	Personnel demobilized from construction site	Contact and force subcontractor to re-mobilize
6	Tank erection progress	Tank construction progress too slow	Contact and force subcontractor to increase speed
7	Pipe rack	Critical equipment within the client's scope was not finished in time	Careful reminders to customer, rearrangement of activities and demobilization
8	Switch gear delay	Critical equipment within the client's scope was not finished in time	Careful reminders to customer, rearrangement of activities and demobilization
9	Missing blueprint	Instructions for blueprint were missing when they should have been designed	Design parts around the specific blueprint and account for its features
10	Failing breaker	Breaker kept going of due to technical malfunction	Trial and Error problem solving, finally replaced failing equipment
11	Engine variance	Engine had a variance because the client had not finished some tasks of his	Contact expert, look into issue and explain to the customer
12	Language incompatibility	The entire contract including instructions in a foreign language. Demand for all documentation in that language	Appoint language support service to project and translate important parts of the contract. Try to renegotiate
13	Engine positioning	Engine positioning tools not present	Make use of alternative lifting arrangements
14	Change order	Various change orders from sub-contractors	Consider and decide
15	Heat recovery	Heat recovery did not function due to site conditions	Contact expert and explain the conditions

Exhibit 2. Deviations and their management.

Parallel to these developments, the project manager started to try to contact the logistics company, which later made their own flawed investigation. In the end the insurance company had to be notified. Developments continued for ten weeks and during this time the project manager felt forced to order the material without full knowledge about the extent of the problem, although he made a probable calculation of it. He told one of his engineers in an

email: "I understand that the two switchgear cubicles are so badly damaged that we need to supply new ones. Please act accordingly to not lose more time." While waiting for the ordered material to arrive, the site team continued with the construction of the project plan using the damaged parts as dummy equipment which they could build around and replace later.

In the later stages of the developments the equipment deviation and the logistics deviation (see exhibit 1, deviation 2) became the subject of numerous reports, discussions and emails. The reason for the deviation emerged as a mishap during pre-loading which the logistics company was aware of – and had even photographed - but which was not reported to the project team. The logistics company eventually needed to meet the project manager to discuss reimbursement. It was clear to every one that there were no contracts stating the responsibilities in the case. Even though there had been organizational routines for reimbursement, everybody knew that they could not be implemented. Instead, any settlement had to be made by drawing on the goodwill between the companies. At the end, the company was reimbursed, and the reimbursement was acceptable to all parties even though it was about a tenth of the initial demands.

Deviation 2 – Payment

This deviation occurred in a quite novel project where the previous project had been done ten years earlier. The customer's contract specified that the first and major payment was due two weeks after signing and if not then, after an additional two weeks. In the latter case, a daily extension would apply.

Problems with the payment were associated with the inability of the customer to make the initial payment on both the first and second opportunities. At the same time as the payment negotiations were proceeding, the project team had to negotiate with a number of shipyards, and choose one (see exhibit 1, deviation 4). The problem was that these negotiations were dependent upon the customer's ability to pay. The dates that were negotiated with the shipyard were thus dependent on the dates of the payment. The payment negotiations were on the other hand dependent on the outcomes of the shipyard negotiations. Adding to the problem the missing payment threatened to delay the entire project which had very tight time and budget limitations. The solution to the problem was to set a date on which the customer had to make the payment. If it was not made, the shipyard would receive a small payment which could be regained, albeit with deductions, with certain percentage intervals and dates. Provided that the payment was not prolonged too long, this solution would provide the company with some money from an earlier smaller payment. The negotiations and the payment finally worked out but it was not until the last possible date that the money arrived.

Exhibit 2 represents mechanisms of loose coupling during the decoupling process (when a deviation is becoming responsive and distinctive) and mechanisms of tight coupling during the recoupling process (when a deviation is losing its distinctiveness but remains responsive). Three loose coupling mechanisms were identified and eight tight coupling mechanisms. The process where these mechanisms were found was not sequential but parallel and intertwined.

Loose Coupling Mechanisms

The findings from table 2 suggest that the decoupling process is achieved through three general mechanisms of loose coupling (number of occurrences within parenthesis);

1. Alternative path (15/15)
2. Responsibility (15/15)
3. Slack (1/15)

The first pattern refers to processes where alternative paths are created for activities, equipment and time. That is, the expected path is interrupted and work arounds are created to fit the situational need. The responsibility patterns refer to how the responsibility for a certain issue was transferred, embraced or argued for. *Transferring* the responsibility, (for example for the. logistics delay), implies that someone else will cover whatever the costs are or they will manage the situation.

#	Deviation	Loose Coupling Mechanisms During Decoupling	Tight Coupling Mechanisms During Recoupling
1	Damaged equipment	Alternative path (activities, equipment), Transfer (responsibility)	Reassume original path, Coordination, Negotiation, Acceptance (responsibility)
2	Payment	Alternative path (activities, time), Transfer (responsibility)	Create new path, Acceptance (responsibility)
3	Logistics delay	Alternative path (activities), Slack, Transfer (responsibility)	Reassume original path, Coordination, Negotiation, Acceptance (responsibility, decision)
4	Negotiations	Alternative path (activities), Embracing (responsibility)	Reassume original path
5	Demobilization of personnel	Transfer (responsibility)	Reassume original path
6	Tank erection progress	Alternative path (time, activities), Pushing (responsibility)	Reassume original path, Coordination, Acceptance (responsibility)
7	Pipe rack	Alternative path (time), Transfer (responsibility)	Create new path, Non-acceptance (responsibility)
8	Switch gear delay	Alternative path (time), Transfer (responsibility)	Create new path, Non-acceptance (responsibility)
9	Missing blueprint	Alternative path (equipment)	Reassume original path, Coordination
10	Failing breaker	Alternative path (time), Transfer (responsibility)	Acquire resources, Acceptance (responsibility)
11	Engine variance	Alternative path (time), Transfer (responsibility)	Coordination, Negotiation, Acceptance (responsibility)
12	Language incompatibility	Alternative path (activities), Embracing (responsibility)	Acquire resources, Create path
13	Engine positioning	Alternative path (equipment), Transfer (responsibility)	Reassume original path, Coordination, Negotiations, Acceptance (responsibility)
14	Change order	Embracing or Transfer (responsibility)	Acceptance (decision)
15	Heat recovery	Transfer (responsibility)	Acceptance (responsibility)

Exhibit 3. Deviations and mechanisms of coupling.

Embracing the responsibility, (for example for the negotiations) on the other hand, means that no one else is to blame and the problem belongs to the organization. *Arguing for* responsibility, (for example, tank construction) means that it is not clear cut who is to blame or carry responsibility and the situation has to be worked out and managed by mutual

agreement. The creation and use of slack occurred, for example, when the logistics were delayed. The reason for using this buffer was basically that it was available and the issue was well-known. However, what made it distinctive was that the slack exceeded the intended buffer.

Tight Coupling Mechanisms

The findings from Table 2 suggest that the recoupling process is achieved through eight general mechanisms of tight coupling (number of occurrences within parenthesis);

1. Reassume original path (7/15)
2. Create path (4/15)
3. Coordination (6/15)
4. Negotiation (4/15)
5. Acceptance (10/15)
6. Non-acceptance (2/15)
7. Acquire resources (1/15)
8. Replacement (1/15)

Reassuming the original path meant that the project continued on the same path as before the deviation (e.g. the damaged equipment) in contrast to *creating an additional path* (e.g. payment). *Coordination* meant that activities were coordinated in such a way that all changes in the project were aligned (e.g. tank construction). *Negotiations* were less determined as the solution was dependent on a mutual understanding between several actors (e.g. the engine variance). *Acceptance* of responsibility or for a decision (e.g. engine positioning) and *non-acceptance* of responsibility (e.g. pipe rack) determined whatever path the responsibility and subsequent activities would take. *Acquire resources* (language incompatibility) has to do with creating more resources for the resolution. It basically means capitulating and buying a way out of the deviation and thus is connected to returning to the original path.

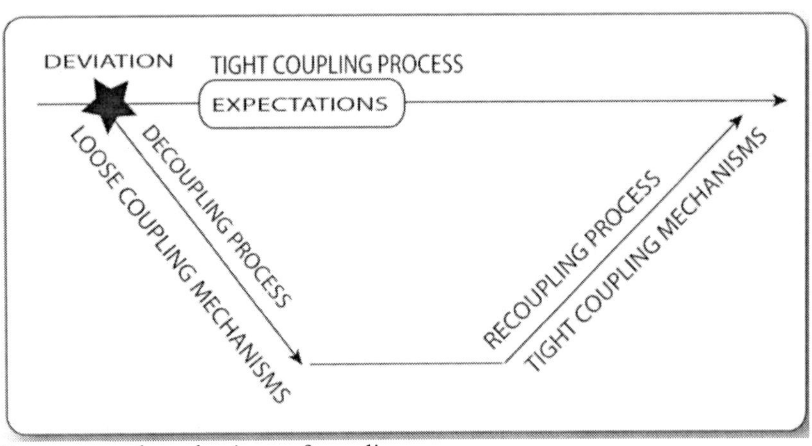

Exhibit 4. Processes and mechanisms of coupling.

The decoupling process is not mutually exhaustive meaning that one deviation can carry several loose coupling mechanisms whilst being tightly coupled to other activities within the project. Similarly, recoupling requires tight as well as loose coupling mechanisms. In addition, a deviation is not necessarily entirely decoupled before the recoupling process commences and this concurs with the basic arguments of Orton and Weicks (1990). The general patterns are found in exhibit 4 above.

DISCUSSION

Traditionally projects are considered means for getting things done simultaneously striving for efficient and accurate methods – that is, doing more in less time. A consequence, which has been given extra scrutiny in this paper, is that doing more things in less time with a closer focus on cost, will inevitably lead to a more complex and tightly connected project execution system which is more sensitive to deviations and require more attention from the management.

Following that basic argument, since projects are a tool for managing change and unstable conditions (Lundin and Söderholm, 1995), they experience deviations more often than not as the context and task changes. (Dvir and Lechler, 2004). In the project it is vital that deviations are managed swiftly (Hällgren, 2007) That is why risk and change management together with the plan are essential to the execution of the project (compare Nicholas, 2001). It is apparent that even for companies such as the one in this paper used to managing projects over many years deviations are a problem. However, contemporary project management literature is quite limited in how it describes what is done during the implementation process (Kloppenborg and Opfer, 2002) on the "floor" , or - to paraphrase Geertz (1973) - how it describes the situated praxis of practitioners regarding to deviations. Therefore, the aim of this paper was to examine the logic of coupling processes in regard to deviations. (Orton and Weick, 1990), establishing that something is loosely or tightly coupled is trivial but it becomes interesting when the detailed processes are investigated Therefore, within the boundaries of their argument the following is put forward:

Decoupling is achieved through the recognition of the deviation as a responsive and distinctive situation that needs to be managed. Once decoupled and governed by loosely coupled mechanisms, recoupling commences and tightly coupled mechanisms bring the deviation back on track so that they display a uni-dimensional behavior. From a management point of view, deviations are not mutually exhaustive and managing them needs to be sensitive to whatever changes are put in place as those changes will have an influence beyond the original deviation. The first logic that is displayed is thus one where old practices (norms, values, rules and routines (Whittington, 2006) are applied to bracket the deviation and decouple it through loose coupling mechanisms. The second logic is one where these old practices are applied to solve the problems generated by the deviation but also contribute to the stock of practices which can be utilized in future situations. From a management point of view this understanding means that in order to achieve a change in behavior or add new knowledge one should focus on what is coupled to what and in accordance with what logic.

Therefore, through the analysis I outline a practice associated with the effective management of deviations.

Processes and Mechanisms of Coupling

It has been suggested that loosely coupled behavior is not loosely coupled for a long time (Roberts, 1990a; Snook, 2002). Upon decoupling, loose coupling follows. Loose coupling is achieved when something displays distinctiveness and responsiveness (Orton and Weick, 1990) which conforms with the idea that it is not a deviation until someone has said so in a social setting beyond the individuals' own reasoning (Weick, 1979; Engeström, 2000). The first step is thus that someone recognizes a deviation and announces it, or in other words, that someone `brackets and labels the event′ (Weick, 1979; Weick *et al.*, 2005). This process is referred to as the decoupling process of a deviation. It is necessary in order to protect the project as a common system. The deviation is separated from the organizing process as that allows for the project to continue relatively uninterrupted. Being identified as something that is different and requiring attention gives the issue responsiveness and contributes to a decoupling process making it loosely coupled.

Loose coupling seems to be achieved through responsibility being transferred (11/15), embraced (3/15) or argued for (1/15) in combination with creating alternative paths in activities (7/15), equipment (2/15) or time (6/15). Uni-dimensionality is achieved when the recoupling process and tightly coupling mechanisms are accepted as simultaneously present. That is, tight coupling mechanisms are present at the same time and coupled to other expectations of the project. These expectations are diverse but have to do with time, cost and quality and the goal of the project. Non-compliance may turn out to be expensive. Tight coupling seems not only to be more diverse but to follow one general pattern. The tendency for acceptance of responsibility is more common in combination with reassuming the original path. This seems to be likely as accepting responsibility creates less interference from other sources.

Coupling Processes and Deviation Solutions

Decoupling begins with bracketing and labeling the deviation (giving it distinctiveness) in a process of enactment and selection in response to "ecological change" (Weick, 1979). The logic that is displayed is one where the situated praxis is used to assess the situation and select a plausible explanation and a solution, followed by adding and preserving whatever knowledge that is created. This is the retention part of Weick's (1979) model. Thus, there are two processes, one of situated praxis (actions dependent on the situation) and one of practices preserved in a shared social system between several practitioners (Whittington, 2006) following the idea that the process by necessity is started.

The two processes have different features. Situated praxis can be mostly individual and/or mostly social dependent on whatever the case and need is (keeping in mind that it is framed against a social setting). Practices on the other hand are only shared between several practitioners and can be drawn upon later when the praxis is applied to another future deviation – or situation. The point is that the management of a deviation is both an individual and a social process that needs to be managed diligently in order to be successful.

Implications

Mechanisms of loose and tight coupling can probably be found in various combinations. The aim of this paper is not to delve into such issues but such an investigation may add to the understanding of the management process. A word of caution though, these investigations should be done by context-sensitive methods, such as observations (Weick, 1976; Orton and Weick, 1990).

Research has neglected the lion's share of Weick's (1979) work when it stops at saying that nouns are bad. Based on the findings in this paper it seems fruitful to take a closer look on the enactment, selection and retention process. The consequences of not having mutually exhaustive deviations are that the management needs to be sensitive to whatever changes are done to the expectations surrounding the path of the project. As some parts will be tightly coupled they will be influenced by even minor changes, while other parts (and sometimes desired ones) may hardly be influenced at all. Likewise, created knowledge is dependent on what is connected to what. To utilize whatever knowledge is created one should take a closer look at where in the process it is created, what it is connected to, and what logic it follows, whether that is an individual or social logic.

Conclusions

Whittington *et al* (2004) warned us about taking practice perspective too lightly. He argued that the practice perspective needs to be connected to aggregated levels of analysis. Through the analysis of 15 deviations this paper has showed that coupling is not a steady state but rather is dependent on the solution that is sought and its impact. Based on a limited number of deviations, one should of course be cautious about generalization but being a general organizing phenomenon some observations seem in order. Two major arguments were made. The management of deviations carries processes of decoupling and recoupling with loose and tight coupling mechanisms, displaying a uni-dimensional behavior. Secondly, a logic of individual and/or social praxis is followed by a social preservation of the knowledge that is created and used.

References

Alsakini, W. and Wikstrom, K. and Kiiras, J. (2004) Proactive schedule management of industrial turnkey projects in developing countries. *International Journal of Project Management,* 22 (1 SU -), 75-85.

Andersen, E. S. (2006) Toward A Project Management Theory For Renewal Projects. *Project Management Journal,* 37 (4), 15.

Barkley, B., T. (2004) *Project Risk Management,* New York, McGraw-Hill.

Blomquist, T. and Gällstedt, M. and Hällgren, M. and Nilsson, A. and Söderholm, A. (2006) Project as practice: Making project research matter. *IRNOP VII.* Xian, China.

Brusoni, S. and Prencipe, A. and Pavitt, K. (2001) Knowledge Specialization, Organizational Coupling, and the Boundaries of the Firm: Why Do Firms Know More Than They Make? *Administrative Science Quarterly,* 46 (4), 597-621.

Burns, T. and Stalker, G. M. (1961) *The management of innovation*, Tavistock.

Christensen, S. and Kreiner, C. (1991) *Projektledning, att leda och lära i en ofullkomlig värld,* Lund, Academia Adacta.

Cicmil, S. (2006) Understanding project management practice through interpretive and critical research perspectives. *Project Management Journal,* 37 (2), 27-37.

Clegg, S. and Kornberger, M. and Rhodes, C. (2005) Learning/Becoming/Organizing. *Organization,* 12 (2), 147-167.

Crawford, L. and Pollack, J. (2004) Hard and soft projects: a framework for analysis. *International Journal of Project Management,* 22 (8), 645-653.

Dubois, A. and Gadde, L.-E. (2002) The construction industry as a loosely coupled system: implications for productivity and innovation. *Construction Management and Economics,* 20 (7), 621-632.

Dvir, D. and Lechler, T. (2004) Plans are nothing, changing plans is everything: the impact of changes on project success. *Research Policy,* 33 (1), 1-15.

Ekstedt, E. and Lundin, R. A. and Söderholm, A. and Wirdenius, H. (1999) *Neo-Industrial Organising, renewal by action and knowledge formation in a project-intensive economy,* London, Routledge.

Engeström, Y. (2000) Activity Theory and the Social Construction of Knowledge: a Story of Four Umpires. *Organization,* 7 (2), 301-310.

Engwall, M. and Westling, G. (2004) Peripety in an RandD Drama: Capturing a Turnaround in Project Dynamics. *Organization Studies,* 25 (9), 1557-1578.

Geertz, C. (1973) *The Interpretation of Cultures,* New York, Basic Books.

Giddens, A. (1979) *Central problems in social theory: Action, structure, and contradiction in social analysis,* London, Macmillan.

Glassman, R. B. (1973) Persistence and loose coupling in living systems. *Behavioral Science,* 18 (2), 83–98.

Gray, C. F. and Larson, E. W. (2006) *Project Management: The managerial process,* New York, McGraw - Hill.

Hallett, T. and Ventresca, M. J. (2006) How Institutions Form: Loose Coupling as Mechanism in Gouldner's Patterns of Industrial Bureaucracy. *American Behavioral Scientist,* 49 (7), 908-924.

Hendry, J. and Seidl, D. (2003) The structure and significance of strategic episodes: Social systems theory and the routine practices of strategic change. *Journal of Management Studies,* 40 (1), 175-197.

Hällgren, M. (2007) Beyond the point of no return: On the management of deviations. *International Journal of Project Management,* 25 (8), 773-780.

Hällgren, M. and Maaninen - Olsson, E. (2005) Deviations, uncertainty and ambiguity in a project intensive organization. *EURAM,* Munich

Jarzabkowski, P. (2000) *Top management teams in action in three UK universities*, Doctoral Thesis, Warwick University, Warwick: UK

Jarzabkowski, P. (2005) *Strategy as Practice,* London, Sage Publishers.

Jarzabkowski, P. and Balogun, J. and Seidl, D. (2007) Strategizing: The challenges of a practice perspective. *Human Relations,* 60 (1), 5-27.

Johnson, G. and Melin, L. and Whittington, R. (2003) Micro Strategy and Strategizing: Towards an Activity-Based view. *Journal of Management Studies,* 40 (1), 3-22.

Kloppenborg, T. and Opfer, W., A. (2002) Forty years of Project Management Research: Trends, Interpretations, and predictions. IN Slevin, D., P. and Cleland, D., I. and Pinto, J. K. (Eds.) *The Frontiers of Project Management Research.* Newton Square, Project Management Institute.

Kreiner, C. (1995) In Search of Relevance: Project Management in Drifting Environments. *Scandinavian Journal of Management,* 11 (4), 335-346.

Lindahl, M. (2005) The little engine that could. On the "managing" qualities. On the managing qualities of technology. IN Czarniawska, B. and Hernes, T. (Eds.) *Actor-Network Theory and Organizing.* Malmö, Liber.

Lindkvist, L. and Söderlund, J. and Tell, F. (1998) Managing Product Development Projects: On the Significance of Fountains and Deadlines. *Organization Studies,* 19 (6), 931.

Love, P. and Gunasekaran, A. and Li, H. (1998) Concurrent engineering: a strategy for procuring construction projects. *International Journal of Project Management,* 16 (6), 375-383.

Luhmann, N. (1995) *Social systems,* Stanford, California, Stanford University Press.

Lundin, R. A. and Söderholm, A. (1995) A theory of the temporary organization. *Scandinavian journal of Management,* 11 (4), 437 - 455.

Nicholas, J. M. (2001) *Project Management for business and technology,* London, Prentice Hall.

Nilsson, A. (2005) The Change Masters: Project Managers in Short Duration Projects. *Project Perspectives,* 27 (1), 42-45.

Orton, D., J. and Weick, K. E. (1990) Loosely Coupled Systems: A Reconceptualization. *Academy of Management Review,* 15 (2), 203-223.

Perrow, C. (1984) *Normal Accidents: Living with High Risk Technology,* Princeton, Princeton University Press.

Pitsis, T., S. and Clegg, S. R. and Marossezeky, M. and Rura-Polley, T. (2003) Constructing the Olympic dream: A future perfect strategy of project management. *Organization Science,* 14 (5), 574 - 590.

Roberts, K., H. (1990a) Managing High Reliability Organizations. *California Management Review,* 32 (4), 101-113.

Roberts, K., H. (1990b) Some Characteristics of One Type of High Reliability Organization. *Organization Science,* 1 (2), 160-176.

Schatzki, T. R. and Knorr-Cetina, K. and Von Savigny, E. (2001) *The practice turn in contemporary theory,* New York, Routledge.

Scott, W. R. (2003) *Organizations,* New Jersey, Prentice Hall.

Shenhar, A. J. and Dvir, D. (1996) Toward a typological theory of project management. *Research Policy,* 25 (4), 607-632.

Simon, H. (1996) *The Sciences of the Artificial,* Cambridge, MA, The M.I.T Press.

Simon, L. (2006) Managing creative projects: An empirical synthesis of activities. *International Journal of Project Management,* 24 (2), 116-126.

Snook, S., A. (2002) *Friendly Fire: The Accidental Shootdown of U.S.Black Hawks Over Northern Iraq,* Princeton, Princeton University Press.

Söderlund, J. (2004) Building theories of project management: past research, questions for the future. *International Journal of Project Management,* 22 (3), 183-191.

Thompson, J. D. (1967) *Organizations in action,* New York, Mcgraw - Hill.

Tsoukas, H. and Chia, R. (2002) On Organizational Becoming: Rethinking Organizational Change. *Organization Science,* 13 (5), 567-582.

Turner, J. R. and Cochrane, R. A. (1993) Goals-and-methods matrix: coping with projects with ill defined goals and/or methods of achieving them. *International Journal of Project Management,* 11 (2), 93-102.

Weick, K. E. (1976) Educational Organizations as Loosely Coupled Systems. *Administrative Science Quarterly,* 21 (1).

Weick, K. E. (1979) *The Social Psychology of Organizing,* New York, McGraw-Hill.

Weick, K. E. (2004) Normal Accident Theory As Frame, Link, and Provocation. *Organization Environment,* 17 (1), 27-31.

Weick, K. E. and Roberts, K., H. (1993) Collective Mind in Organizations: Heedful Interrelating on Flight Decks. *Administrative Science Quarterly,* 38 (3), 357-381.

Weick, K. E. and Sutcliffe, K. M. and Obstfeld, D. (2005) Organizing and the Process of Sensemaking. *Organization Science,* 16 (4), 409-421.

Whittington, R. (2003) Practice perspectives on strategy: Unifying and developing a field. *Academy of Management Conference.* Denver, CO.

Whittington, R. (2006) Completing the Practice Turn in Strategy Research. *Organization Studies,* 27 (5), 613-634.

Whittington, R. (2007) Strategy Practice and Strategy Process: Family Differences and the Sociological Eye. *Organization Studies,* 28 (10), 1575-1586.

Whittington, R. and Johnson, G. and Melin, L. (2004) The emerging field of strategy practice: some links, a trap, a choice and a confusion. *EGOS,* Ljubljana, Slovenia

Yin, R., K. (1994) *Case study research: design and methods,* Thousand Oaks, Sage coperation.

In: Business and Finance: Performance and Management ISBN: 978-1-61122-936-3
Editors: R. Morland and A. Gagglione

Chapter 4

THE ADOPTION OF LASER TECHNOLOGY IN ITALIAN ART RESTORATION FIRMS: THE ROLE OF SUPPLIERS AND CLIENTS

Karen Venturini[1]* and Chiara Verbano[2]

[1]Department of Economics and Technology, University of San Marino, Strada della Bandirola 44, 47898 Montegiardino, Republic San Marino

[2]Department of Management and Engineering, University of Padova, Stradella San Nicola 3, 36100 Vicenza, Italy

ABSTRACT

Despite the importance of the art restoration sector in Italy, as well as in many other European countries, this industry has often been ignored by management studies. For these reasons this study focused on Italian art restoration firms, with particular reference to their adoption of innovative technologies such as laser technology.

The literature has widely emphasized the influence of external agents in the processes of adopting new technologies, above all in the case of small or medium-sized firms, and for those particularly linked to external forces such as suppliers and clients due to economic, regulatory and structural reasons. The study, supported by a qualitative analysis and a comparison with previously acquired quantitative data, contributes to a more comprehensive description of the art restoration sector and, analysing the role of suppliers and clients, completes the adoption model of technology innovation developed in previous research on laser technology (Verbano, Venturini, Nosella, Petroni, 2008).

The results identify the factors related to restoration firms, suppliers and clients that influence the adoption of laser and outline some suggestions to encourage its adoption in the particularly complex sector of art conservation.

Keywords: Laser technology, Technology adoption, Art Restoration Firms, Suppliers, Superintendencies.

* E-mail:kventurini@unirsm.sm

1. INTRODUCTION

The cultural heritage of a country is "the legacy of physical artifacts and intangible attributes of a group or society that are inherited from past generations, maintained in the present and bestowed for the benefit of future generations" (Wikipedia, 2008). The tangible cultural heritage is made up of historical, artistic, archaeological, ethno-anthropological, archival and bibliographic property worthy to be conserved. Italy can claim one of the most important historical heritage in the world with more than 4,000 museums and galleries (405 of which are State property), 2,100 archaeological sites, 85,000 churches and chapels of historical interest, 6,000 libraries (containing antique documents), 40,000 historical homes, and 20,000 citadels and castles (CENSIS, 2003). The UNESCO's World Heritage List for 2008 confirms this, attributing to Italy the largest number of "cultural sites" (43) of worldwide interest.

The valorisation of the cultural heritage of a country is a priority not only for the socio-cultural value but also for the economic value it is able to generate. It has been amply demonstrated that the cultural assets are an important lever for economic development of a territory. Initiating developing processes that rely on maximizing the cultural-artistic resources of a country involves activating the productive sectors that directly participate in the process of enhancing this type of asset; in other words, the restoration and chemical sectors and the field of information technology.

Technology plays a role in facilitating the restoration and conservation of cultural heritage as well as access to it. Numerous projects in recent years have involved the transfer of new technologies with chemical-physical origins to the art heritage sector for use in diagnostic investigation and conservation and restoration work, while IT is frequently used nowadays to organize available resources, stimulate demand, and manage cultural institutions. The adoption of technologies transferred from other sectors and adapted to the specific requirements of conserving art works can also provide firms with fresh opportunities for offering new services, qualitatively better results, and possible reductions in costs.

Despite the relevance of technological innovation, few studies have analysed the economic-organizational mechanisms governing the adoption of technologies by those in the conservation sector. Among those that exist, one study of the factors determining the adoption of lasers (Verbano, Venturini, Nosella, Petroni, 2008) has focused attention on a technology whose process of diffusion is proving particularly slow, despite the substantial benefits it offers compared with traditional restoration techniques. Indeed, in certain circumstances the laser can be used where other restoration techniques cannot, and in some cases it saves time by eliminating one stage (pre-consolidation) of restoration work. Moreover, the laser offers qualitatively better results compared to traditional techniques since it permits the operator to follow the microstratification of the modified surface (greater selectivity) and to interrupt the work at any moment (greater control). The laser also allows the removal of layers of dirt from an art work in a non-invasive manner (invasive substances such as water and chemical products are not injected), thus preserving the extremely thin patinas present on the material being cleaned (Salimbeni, 2001). The aforementioned study (Verbano, Venturini, Nosella and Petroni, 2008) examined the variables that affect restoration firms' innovative behaviour directly correlated to the firms themselves. On the other hand the literature has highlighted

the role that agents other than the restoration firms may play in the process of adopting innovation (Gatignon and Robertson, 1986; Von Hippel, 1986).

The aim of this chapter is therefore to present the adoption model previously developed and to extend it focusing attention on the role and behaviour of public sector clients as well as those of producers and distributors of lasers for restoration work. A qualitative analysis and a comparison with quantitative data from the previous research allow for a deeper understanding of these two types of agents (suppliers and public sector clients) and for the introduction into the adopted model of variables concerning supply and clients sectors identified from the literature review. Checking with suppliers and clients has in addition allowed us to give greater substance to the previously identified factors and to obtain further explanatory results related to the process of laser adoption.

The chapter is organized as follows: Paragraph 2 briefly describes the characteristics of Italian art conservation sector, the Paragraph 3 the characteristics of Italian art conservation firms as results of the previous research; Paragraph 4 refers to the literature review supporting the laser adoption model; Paragraph 5 defines the objectives and the methodology of the research; the results of the survey are presented in Paragraph 6, and lastly, the conclusion of the chapter is discussed in Paragraph 7.

2. The Characteristics of the Art Conservation Sector

The term conservation is used to refer to all activities carried out to protect, restore and maintain works of art. In particular the term restoration (from the Latin *restaurare* composed of *re* meaning again and *staurare* meaning to make solid) has acquired various meanings over time which have often been contradictory, with regard to the culture of the period and its relationship with history. According to an eminent scholar, restoration is "the methodological moment of recognition of the work of art, in its physical consistency and its aesthetic and historical double polarity, in view of transmission to the future" (Brandi, 1974).

Specifically, the sector for the conservation of artistic and cultural works (See Figure 1) is made up of:

- public and private owners of items of artistic or cultural works (Regions, Provinces and Municipalities, ecclesiastical institutions, private individuals),
- the Superintendencies (the local administrative branches of the Ministry) that have the job of authorizing and managing restoration work through receiving tenders and that can be assisted in their activities by specific public entities dedicated to research and high training (ICR; OPD e ICPL),
- public and private organizations that directly carry out conservation work (government restoration centres and restoration firms).

The sector's economic structure appears to be characterized by a clear dominance of public demand. According to current legislation the Ministry for Heritage and Cultural Activities is responsible for managing cultural and environmental heritage in order to ensure the organic preservation of artistic and cultural assets of international and national interest. Each year the Ministry chooses the intervention strategies and the amount of contributions to transfer to its operational bodies. Among the latter are the Superintendencies, peripheral

bodies that carry out the duties of protection, conservation and restoration of cultural assets (historical, artistic and ethno-anthropological, architectonic and landscape, archeological and archival). Superintendencies' activities can be briefly expounded in the following combined actions:

- identification of assets with historic and artistic interest, survey of the same and subsequent "conservation restriction" certification over the individual assets (protected assets);
- protection of the assets, or rather the control, through specific permits, over restoration works, relocations, exportation and cultural landscape projects;
- valorization of the heritage, namely the promotion and development of the cultural activities necessary to spread the value of the assets.

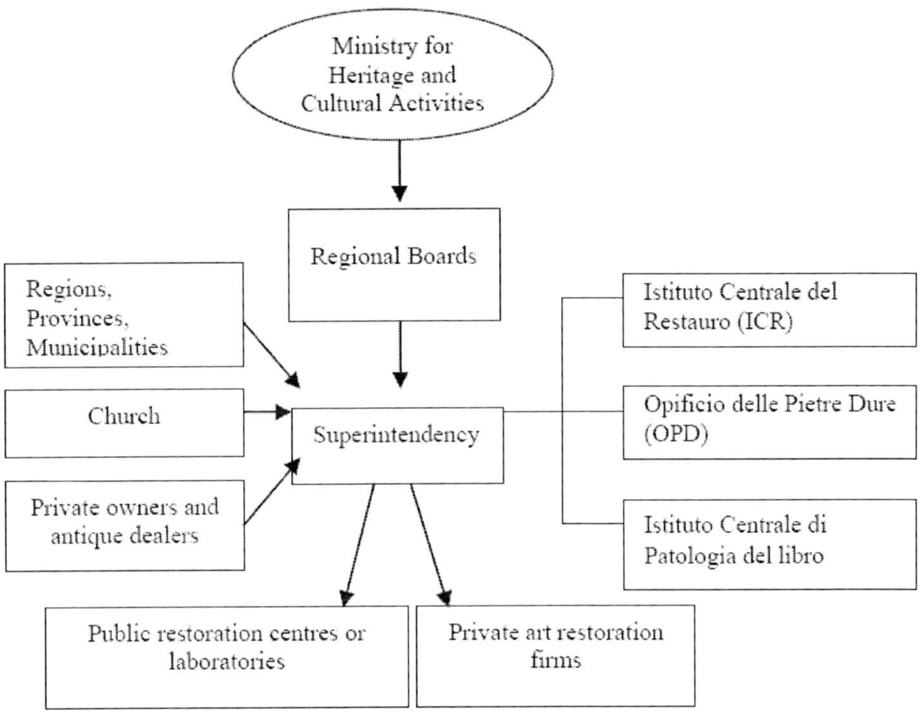

Figure 1. Main actors in the Italian art restoration industry (Source: Verbano et al, 2008).

Restoration carried out on property belonging to the public, ecclesiastical bodies or the like can be carried out directly in the public laboratories of the Superintendencies, or may be assigned, in accordance with the public tender regulations (D.P.R. 554/1999), to private enterprises. Each Superintendency has the authority to choose those enterprises it wishes to invite to bid for tenders. According to the law on public tenders, the awarding of contracts via public auction or restricted tendering is carried out using the criterion of the greatest discount. Firms also obtain restoration commissions from other subjects such as ecclesiastical bodies or private persons and organizations. The State and its bodies guide the intervention strategy and manage the most of the orders. In this action the same public organizations also define the

technical specifications of the restoration orders and these indications are, for the most part, related to traditional restoration techniques.

Lastly, an interesting structural characteristic of the sector lies in the presence of major public institutions related to the Ministry (Istituto Centrale per il Restauro, Istituto Centrale di Patologia del Libro and Opificio delle Pietre Dure). These institutions perform research activities and particularly complex restoration works, carry out the necessary surveys for the formulation of regulations and technical specifications with regard to conservation work, have high-level professional training schools and lastly provide, upon request, technical assistance to Superintendencies. Furthermore, these institutions have for years played a fundamental role in the field of research, conservation and restoration at international level. One of the most important aims pursued internationally by these institutions is the continuing training of technicians able to deal with the problems of conservation and restoration of the archeological areas, monument sites, decorated structures and works of art located in the countries to which they belong. Thus Italy has established itself as leader in the field of restoration and is called upon to export its know-how worldwide owing to the acknowledged professionalism of its technicians and the results of their restoration work.

One further point on restoration concerns the "Restoration Charter". The necessity to make uniform and standardize the restoration activity of all the public and private organizations led, in 1972, to the issuance of special regulations by the Ministry for Heritage and Cultural Activities, entitled the Restoration Charter (amended in 1987) which indicates the criteria to be adopted in order to guarantee the quality and uniformity of the restoration work carried out on artistic and cultural assets.

Table 1. Distribution of public sector contracts in 2007 in the categories concerning the restoration of cultural works

Category	Number of contracts	Percentage (%) of the total number of contracts in all the categories	Amount
OS2	54	0.30	€ 22,973,460
OG2	1,217	7.40	€ 1,087,694,119
OG1	4,940	29.90	€ 5,726,555,367

Source: Parliamentary Report 2007 – Monitoring Center on Public Tenders.

Lastly in order to understand the sector's economic aspect we can cite some significant data. According to the general summary of 2007, the amount of resources that the Ministry of Heritage and Cultural Activities dedicated to the area of cultural and landscape assets totaled € 103,884,868.50 (Ministry of Heritage and Cultural Activities, 2007). With regards to the contracts drafted by the Superintendencies with the individual firms, we cite the data published by the Monitoring Center on Public Tenders (AVCPLFS, 2007). Table 1 below

shows the distribution of the public sector contracts (in 2007) for the awarding of tenders according to the tender category[6].

3. The Italian Art Conservation Firms: Main Characteristics and Innovative Profile

Supply in the sector concerning the conservation of cultural works is however constituted by a rather atomized universe of small and very small enterprises often artisan in nature (Best, 1990). From what has emerged from the empirical analysis conducted on a sample of 100 Italian firms (Verbano, Venturini, Nosella and Petroni, 2008), restoration firms, allowed to take part in bidding for public contracts because they possess a SOA certificate[7], were found to be small, consolidated companies with, in the majority of cases, a turnover of less than one million euros. These restoration companies can be characterized, based on the SOA certification held, as follows:

- *56 firms qualified only with the OS2 category* (category for the restoration and maintenance of decorated surfaces and protected objects) are the smallest, with less than 10 employees, and are more frequently partnerships or individual artisans. These firms carry out restoration (82% of commissions) and secondarily conservation (18%), on protected immoveable assets such as buildings, frescoes and statues (71% of cases) and protected objects (24%). It must be underlined that these companies, more than the others, acquire work also as a result of their own promotion, despite the fact that the predominant method for all the companies in the sector is public tender.
- *27 firms qualified with the OS2 and OG2 categories* (category for the restoration and maintenance of objects and immoveable assets, and protected decorated surfaces), have, in 84% of cases, less than 25 employees and are mainly partnerships or limited liability companies. These companies devote themselves principally to the activity of restoration of almost exclusively protected immoveable assets, and generally acquire work by public tender (76% of cases) and subcontracting (15%).
- *17 firms qualified with the OS2, OG2 and OG1 categories* (restoration and maintenance of objects and immoveable assets, and protected decorated surfaces, as well as civil and industrial buildings) are largely joint-stock companies (70%) of various sizes, though in 62% of cases they have more than 25 employees. Since these

[6] Firms wishing to participate in public tenders for amounts greater than €150,000 must possess an SOA certificate. It is a document valid for 5 years that provides the required proof that a firm has the capacity to fulfil public contract bids. Depending on the activities they carry out, firms can be SOA certified in one or more categories. The categories pertaining to the restoration of cultural assets are: OS2 category, which includes the restoration and maintenance of historical-artistic decorated surfaces and movable artworks, OG2 category which includes the restoration and maintenance of protected fixed and movable artworks and decorated surfaces, OG1 which includes the restoration and maintenance of protected fixed and movable artworks and decorated surfaces, and civil and industrial buildings.

[7] We focused on firms in the OS2 category, which includes the restoration and maintenance of historical-artistic decorated surfaces and movable artworks, since it is the only category specialized in restoration and conservation activities (the other categories also carry out activities other than restoration such as the construction of buildings, etc). Some companies in the OS2 category are also registered in the OS2 and OG1 categories.

companies possess SOA certification in three categories, they almost exclusively work by means of public tenders (90% of commissions), favoring the construction (53% of cases) and restoration (47%) of protected immoveable assets (88%). From the interviews conducted it appears that the restoration commissions acquired are often subcontracted.

Lastly public clients widely prove to be the principal market for all the categories of companies (from 75 to 79% of work).

Examination of the data related to the proprietors and/or managing directors of restoration companies highlights that they are on average between 40 and 60 years old and have a high-school diploma or degree in a discipline that rarely concerns the restoration sector. It therefore follows that the specific training of the proprietors and/or managing directors directors is developed in the majority of cases "in the field" (51%), or by frequenting specific courses. Learning-by-doing is attested by the common previous experiences of the proprietors and/or directors (58% of cases) as children of entrepreneurs or ex-employees of companies in the sector.

Another aspect analyzed in order to understand the features of the firms in the sector is strategic policy, expressed by those factors of competitiveness which are considered the most significant. From the results one can see that in first place, in terms of importance, is the quality of the restoration, followed by the training of personnel and technological innovation; the search for new markets is not perceived as a particularly important factor for the purposes of competiveness.

To characterize the restoration firms from the innovation point of view one need observe that only half of companies invest in technological innovation for restoration and, in particular, it is those firms qualified as OS2 and OS2/OG2 that invest more widely, since the other firms, though they are larger (and therefore have greater financial resources), have concentrated their activity in civil construction rather than in restoration and conservation. As far as the level of investment is concerned, this is in most cases modest, because more frequently firms invest low percentages of turnover, and, since the turnover is rather moderate, the absolute value of these investments can be considered modest.

With regard to the object of the technological investments, approximately half the companies state that they have recently adopted alternative cleaning methods (ultrasound, laser, enzymes, solvents, specific products, etc.), but only 15% of these firms have effectively adopted laser technology. Moreover only 13 of the 100 companies surveyed have effectively borne the purchase cost, since there are two companies which, though they have the equipment, have preferred to rent it.

Among the sources of information considered important for the diffusion of the technology are: attending conferences and seminars, exchanges of information between competing companies, consultation of sector-specific journals and attending demonstrations. The informative contribution supplied by attending training courses, from promotional activities performed by the suppliers of machinery and equipment and from the Internet does not appear to be significant.

Among those factors considered the most important for the purposes of adoption of the technology are: the explicit request made by the Superintendency to utilize the technology (in this case laser), pursuit of a policy of allocating orders aimed at a more balanced ratio

Table 2. Factors affecting innovation adoption

	Organizational factors	*External factors*	*Technological factors*
Cooper and Zmud (1990)	User community (education, resistance to change) Organization structure	Organizational environment (uncertainty, inter-organizational dependence)	Complexity of technology Task to which the technology is being applied
Dholakia and Kshetri (2004)	Firm characteristics (firm size, type of business) Past experiences and attitudes Prior technology use	Perceived competitive pressure	
Tsikriktsis, Lanzolla and Frohlich (2004)	Internal barriers(rigid structure, lack of motivations and skills.) Expected access to new markets	External pressure	Expected performance benefits
Baldwin and Lin (2002)	Organization problems (education, resistance to change, poor management attitude); Labor problems (skills and training difficulties); Information problems	Institutional problems (government regulations and standard, R&D investment tax credit)	Cost and maintenance expenses
Waarts, Everdingen and Hillegersberg (2002)	Adopter characteristics (attitude towards innovation, resources) Internal environment (organizational structure)	External environment (level of competition, supplier competition, pressure from other firms)	Perceived innovation characteristics (advantages and compatibility)
Lal (1999)	Entrepreneurial characteristics (qualification, knowledge base of entrepreneur); Firm size; Workforce	International orientation factors	
Iacovou *et al.* (1995)	Perceived financial cost	Perceived industry pressure	Perceived direct benefits
Kuan and Chau (2001)	Perceived technical competence	Perceived government pressure	Perceived indirect benefits
Santarelly and D'Altri (2003) Fink (1998)	Internal resourses In-house IT expertise Organizational culture	Outside support External resources and environment	Potential advantages
Igbaria *et al.* (1998)	Demographic variables Organizational factors (internal technical experience, training)	External pressure Extra-organizational factors	
Premkumar and Roberts (1999)	Top management support; Size; Technology Expertise	Competitive pressure External support Vertical linkages	Relative advantages Cost Complexity Compatibility
Mehrtens *et al.* (2001)	Level of technology knowledge and use	Internet user expectation	Advantages Business tool
Sadowski et al. (2002)		Competitive pressure External support Incentives	
Dewar and Dutton (1986)	Depth of knowledge resources and firm size		
Damanpour (1992) Cohen (1995) Jensen (2004)	Firm size (availability of human and financial resources)		
Freel (2005)	Managerial competences	External linkages	
Kimberly and Evanisko (1981)	Educational level of the administrator Organization size and age	Competitive pressure	
Maxwell and Westerfield (2002)	Education, professional background of entrepreneur		
Dobbin et al. (1987)	Organizational size	External pressure (public visibility motivation)	
Romijn and Albaladejo (2002) Hemmert (2004)		External linkages (Universities, research institutes)	
Souitaris (2002)	Technical competences Market competences Human resource competences Organizational competences		
Leonard-Barton and Deschamps (1988)	Personal characteristics Managerial influences		
Gatignon and Robertson (1989)	Decision maker characteristics Organizational characteristics	Competitive environment Supply-side factors	

Source: Petroni, Turra, Verbano, Venturini, 2006.

between cost and quality, and the offer of monetary incentives by the State. It must be underlined that all three cases concern factors involving the State. Other factors which are considered important are economically more favorable sales conditions and collaboration with research institutes, which currently involve only 30% of companies. On the other hand the circulation of technical information originating from other sources, comparison with other companies adopting the technology and the promotional activities carried out by suppliers are not considered particularly significant.

4. The Laser Adoption Model: The Role of Suppliers and Clients

A firm's adoption of a particular technology is the response to a series of stimuli that derive from both an internal and external environment. Table 2 summarizes the main factors, found in the literature, that affect the adoption of an innovation.

The previous empirical analysis (Verbano et al. 2008) has confirmed that the difficulty of adopting lasers is due to:

- structural factors: the limited size and limited income-financing circuit, criteria based on fulfilling tenders in the public sector that depress the development of strategies focused on quality and innovation, the further development of relationships between firms, universities and research institutes;
- cultural factors: the firms' limited managerial expertise and the conservative attitude of the Superintendencies.

The study, however, has not confirmed the firm manager's lack of technical training to be among the factors hindering the adoption of lasers, while it has slightly confirmed the improvement of a firm's reputation following its adoption of this technology (with a limited level of significance due to the scant number of companies using laser in the sample considered), and its geographical proximity to research centres and laser suppliers (Table 3).

The literature has extensively emphasized the influence played by the external environment in the process of adopting new technologies, particularly with regard to small and medium-sized firms (Rothweel and Dodson, 1991; Iacovou, 1995; Freel, 2000; Tsikriktsis, Lanzolla, Frohlich, 2004).

In the external environment there are a multiplicity of agents (competitors, suppliers, clients, professional associations, research centres and universities, public administrations, local communities and others), that interact with the firm to condition its behavioural strategy to a greater or lesser degree.

Among these agents suppliers play a determining role. Indeed the primary condition for any kind of process of spreading and adopting a new technology is its distribution, and therefore availability, in the marketplace (Kohn and Husing, 2006). Furthermore, besides being physically present, the cost of the technology must be perceived as being reasonable in relation to its benefits. The cost, a determinant in the process of purchasing a technology, also depends on the level of competition among the suppliers of the technology. The first variable in the supply sector that influences the process of adopting a technology is therefore the level

of competition (Bass, 1980; Gatignon and Robertson, 1986; David and Olsen, 1992). A second variable to consider is the behaviour of suppliers assessed in terms of the pressure they put on client firms and the support they offer them.

Table 3. Driving and resistance factors affecting the adoption of laser by restoration firms

	Resistance factors		Driving factors	
	1. limited size	yes	5. improvements in firm reputation and image	probably yes
Internal	2. difficulty evaluating the economic aspects of the investment	yes	6. expected improvement in the performance of the service provided	Yes
	3. limited technical training on the part of the entrepreneur	no		
External	4. policy for assigning contracts based solely on price	yes	7. relationships with universities and research institutes	Yes
			8. request to use laser technology from public institutions	Yes
			9. proximity to laser research centers or laser producers/distributors	weak yes

Source: Verbano, Venturini, Petroni, Nosella, 2008.

Among these agents suppliers play a determining role. Indeed the primary condition for The pressure may manifest itself in the supplier's explicit request to adopt innovation (Iacovou, 1995; Premkumar and Roberts, 1999; Tsikriktsis, Lanzolla, Frohlich, 2004), and essentially it depends on two factors: the power of the partner and its influencing strategy (Provan, 1980). In their turn, these factors are correlated to the relationship between the size of the supplying firm and the size of the client firm.

The support, on the other hand, depends on the marketing policy that the supplying firm decides to develop. Empirical studies have shown how suppliers' marketing efforts have a particular weight in the decision to adopt a technology, especially in the period immediately after the technology has been introduced and before information on it is available (Dos Santos and Peffers, 1998).

The various marketing strategies that may influence the adoption of innovation can be summarized as:

- reduction of the risk of adoption: the supplier seeks to reduce the partner firm's risk through financial incentives (price reductions, payment by instalments, leasing) or by granting a trial period (Premkumar and Roberts, 1999);

- information and communication activities: the supplier communicates the features and benefits of the new technology through visits to firms, conference participation, magazine publications, internet (Clark and Staunton, 1989);
- training programmes for technicians and firm managers (Attewell, 1992, Premkumar and Roberts, 1999);
- building a good reputation in the market by convincing opinion leaders, developing an intensive promotional campaign, and publicizing new clients' names (Rogers, 1995).

A third variable in the supply sector that may influence the adoption of a new technology is the involvement of the client-user in the process of developing the technology (Rogers, 1983). In fact, the possibility of designing a technology that exactly meets users' needs is a decisive factor in its rapid diffusion and success (Geroski, 2000; Frambach et al., 1998, Harrison and Waite, 2005). Finally, it should be kept in mind that once the technology has been designed and placed on the market, the suppliers are further able to influence its adoption through their learning process. In fact, producers of new technology benefit from learning-by-doing approaches aimed at a reduction in average production costs, and offering the new technology to subsequent clients at lower prices (Geroski, 2000).

Other agents that may influence an organization in the process of adopting a new technology are its clients (Von Hippel, 1986) and professional institutions (Di Maggio and Powell, 1983; Zucker, 1987). The latter, operating within the firm's field of reference, define the social relationships and models of behaviour. In the art conservation sector the Superintendencies perform a double role as both clients commissioning restoration work (through the system of public bidding) and as reference bodies, since they are also promoters of methods and criteria for conservation (legislative decree 42/2004).

In general, the literature on innovation has shown that the practice of public tenders can be a valid instrument in stimulating innovation (Edquist et al., 2000; Rolfstam, 2005), especially in those sectors where the State is an important client (Dobbin et al., 1987). The State may purchase not only to fulfil its own institutional mission, but also to support private buyers in the decision to purchase (Rothwell, 1991). In this case we refer to "cooperative contracts" whereby public bodies purchase new technology together with private ones. Another type of contract is "catalytic", which occurs when the new technology purchased remains the exclusive property of the private partner (Edquist and Hommen, 1998). In this case the public body has to determine the needs of the private buyer and decide to include alongside the contract procedure other strategic measures such as support in the form of incentives, tax deductions, the diffusion of information and training courses, the use of regulations and the creation of standards or links between producers and consumers. By means of tenders, therefore, the State is able to make the request more sophisticated, and create a cultural environment that is predisposed and receptive towards innovative products (Edler and Georghiou, 2007).

On the other hand, implementing an innovation policy conflicts with the traditional behaviour of public institutions. The structure of incentives in public administration tends to reward contracts that present a lower initial cost and a high degree of reliability for the public service. Innovations, on the other hand, present a greater initial cost with the risk that the service will not be supplied in the best ways or time (Edler and Georghiou, 2007). There are

many other factors that might encourage public functionaries to propose traditional technologies in the contract specifications rather than new ones: a cultural attitude opposed to risk, political pressures favouring short-term results, limited financial resources, and a lack of incentives, motivation and technical competence (Mulgan and Albury, 2003; Tsikriktsis, Lanzolla and Frohlich, 2004).

On the basis of an analysis of the literature carried out thus far, the adoption model for laser technology can now be completed as shown in Figure 2.

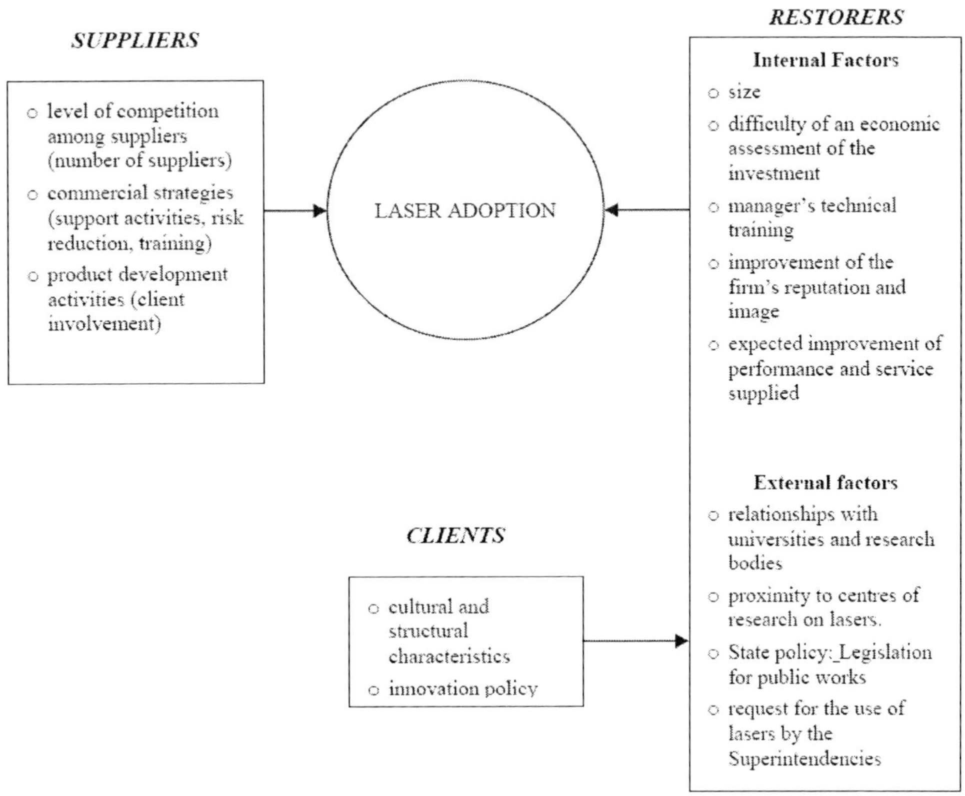

Figure 2. The complete adoption model for laser technology.

5. Objectives and Methodology

The objectives of the present chapter are:

1. to define the client sector within the restoration sector as a major agent in the process of laser adoption and the supplying of lasers;
2. to verify the adoption model of laser technology obtained in the previous paragraph (see Figure 2), with particular reference to the factors introduced in this chapter;
3. to further validate and investigate the internal and external factors that have emerged from the earlier study, both with regard to the suppliers of laser technology and the clients.

The Methodology

The methodology used in the present chapter was developed in two phases. The first phase provided for a direct interview with both Italian suppliers of lasers (in almost all the cases, the interviewee was the technical and/or business manager of the sector dealing with lasers for restoration work), and officials of some Superintendencies (in all the cases the interviewee was the Director of the Superintendency's Scientific Laboratory). The interviews were conducted between 2006 and 2007 with the help of a specific questionnaire prepared in advance for each type of institution/firm interviewed after the first phase of research was concluded.

The suppliers' questionnaire is made up of 38 half-open questions, whereas the second questionnaire for the Superintendencies contains 26 half-open questions. The nature of the questions, grouped in sections, is indicated in Table 4.

According to the literature, the variables correlated to the supply sector that influence firms' adoption of technology were shown to be:

1. the level of competition: number of suppliers, market share and entry barriers;
2. business strategy: innovation differentiation, tax incentives, rental service, client assistance, organization of training courses, sales promotion activities and pressures, if any;
3. product development activities: participation in research projects with research institutes, universities and restoration firms, development of further improvements at clients' request.

The factors correlated to clients, however, were shown to be as follows:

1. the structural and cultural characteristics of the institution: financial trend, organizational structure, resources devoted to investment in innovation, tendency towards innovation, adequate technical competence, participation in research projects with research institutions, universities, restoration firms and suppliers;
2. the innovation policy: communication and information activities, explicit request for adoption in contract specifications, incentives and support activities.

The final part of both questionnaires is dedicated to a discussion of the resistance and driving factors that emerged from the previous study, in order to verify and interpret them further.

Once the data collection phase was completed, the results were elaborated and a subsequent comparison was made between the results obtained and those from the previous study. This purely qualitative method was considered to be the most appropriate on the basis of considerations relating to the number of firms interviewed and the explicit exploratory nature of the research questions the study intended to answer.

Table 4. The questionnaire structure

SUPPLIERS' QUESTIONNAIRE		CLIENTS' QUESTIONNAIRE	
General information about the firm	location, age, type of business, organizational structure, size, share of turnover per product line	General information about the commissioning institute	location, age, operational fields, organizational structure, size, amount and distribution of public funding
Level of competition	number of suppliers, market share of Italian and foreign producers, reasons for the oligopolistic structure, entry barriers	Tendency towards innovation and knowledge of laser technology	technological investments, personnel training knowledge and use of lasers, collaboration with research institutes, universities and suppliers
Business strategies	differentiation of product, laser distribution, sale price, tax incentives, rental service, training and promotional activities, client assistance	Innovation policy instruments towards restoration firms	criteria for selecting restoration firms, explicit requests for laser in contract specifications, support and incentives for the adoption of laser
Product development activities	participation in research projects with institutions, universities and restoration firms, development of further modifications at clients' request	Examination of resistance and driving factors in laser adoption	advantages and disadvantages of lasers, reasons for the delay in its adoption and examination of influencing factors
Examination of resistance and driving factors in laser adoption	advantages and disadvantages of laser, reasons for the delay in its adoption and examination of influencing factors		

The Organizations Interviewed

Given the small number of laser producers and distributors in Italy, the investigation was addressed to all the firms producing (3) and distributing them in Italy[8] (3), and the request for collaboration was accepted by 5 out of 6 of the firms consulted. Of these, the first is a firm of considerable size, while the other four are either small or medium-sized. All five firms are well-established, joint-stock companies operating in north or central Italy (Table 5).

With regard to public commissioners in Italy, 32 Superintendencies are responsible for architecture and the landscape, 25 for artistic, cultural and ethno-anthropological heritage, 23 for archaeology and 21 for archives. The choice of the three Superintendencies in the sample was dictated by the fact that each of them had conducted various restoration projects using lasers and therefore had developed expertise and experience concerning this technology;

[8] No lasers for restoration use are distributed in the Italian market by European or non-European producers.

moreover, they are operating in extremely important Regions in terms of artistic and cultural heritage. To make the sample more complete, in addition to the three public institutions another belonging to the Vatican (institution D) was included, which is particularly important in the restoration sector both for its technical-scientific expertise and the number of orders it allocates (Table 6).

Table 5. Characteristics of suppliers interviewed

Name given	Geographic location	Number of employees	Year founded	Legal status
Firm A	Florence -Tuscany	525	1981	S.p.a.
Firm B	Vicenza – Veneto	12	1996	S.r.l.
Firm C	Varese- Lombardy	61	1985	S.p.a.
Firm D	Milan - Lombardy	12	1988	S.r.l.
Firm E	Vicenza - Veneto	30	1984	S.r.l.

Table 6. Characteristics of the Superintendencies interviewed

Name given	Geographical location	Number of employees in restoration workshop	Year founded
Superintendency A	Florence - Tuscany	25	1966
Superintendency B*	Vicenza - Veneto	/*	1973
Superintendency C	Ravenna - Emilia Romagna	3	1972
Institution D	Rome - Lazio	42	1985

*Superintendency does not have a restoration workshop.

6. Analysis of Results

6.1. The Supply Sector

The Level of Competition

From the analysis conducted, it emerges that the structure of the sector supplying lasers for restoration is essentially oligopolistic. There are three firms in the Italian market, although Firm A holds the majority of Firm C's shares. In particular, the behaviour of Firm C corresponds to the behaviour of Firm A, which has purchased it. The two laser dealers (D and E) distribute the products of Firm A and Firm B respectively. Firm A (larger in terms of employees and financial resources) holds the leadership in the market. The oligopolistic form of the market is motivated by the barriers that firms entering the field have to face. Since there are no restrictions arising from ownership of patents (an absolute barrier) the entry barriers mainly depend on the high costs of research and development, and the high level

technical and scientific expertise necessary for the development of the equipment, offset by a very limited amount of business.

Business Strategies

The third part of the questionnaire is devoted to investigating the business strategies adopted by laser suppliers, such as: innovation differentiation, tax incentives, rental service, client assistance, organization of training programmes, sales promotional activities, pressures, if any.

The firms' business policies are essentially different: Firm A aims for a wide range of lasers developed in their own research and development laboratories, which always offer practical and design improvements, whereas Firm B offers only two models developed from a widely-tested technology. It should be underlined that differentiating laser technology is a very expensive process given that the alteration of any of the fundamental three parameters (wavelength, impulse length and power) involves the construction of new equipment. The prices of lasers offered by both firms are quite similar (€18,000 - €60,000) and there is no discount or reduction policy. With regard to after sales services, Firm A offers assistance and maintenance support, while Firm B offers the possibility of renting the equipment (but at a high cost), assistance in the use and maintenance of the equipment and instalment payments or leasing.

The interviews reveal that the approaches used by all the firms to promote lasers are: meetings with restorers (personal contacts, workshops, seminars), the organization of training courses in laser use, advertising through the distributor, conference participation, magazine publications in the sector and collaboration with Superintendencies and professional bodies. With regard to distribution policy, producers of lasers delegate distribution to firms D and E.

Product Development

The testing of laser equipment is carried out directly by the manufacturers in their laboratories, but it has proven difficult to quantify the average investment in RandD activity on lasers used for restoration. The firms occasionally participate in research projects in collaboration with research institutions, Superintendencies and restoration firms, with the aim of increasing knowledge in the restoration sector and improving laser performance. In any event, none of the manufacturing firms offer lasers specifically developed to suit clients' requirements. Given the high costs of research and development, such a service would be too costly. However, all the firms indicate that in developing technical knowledge about restoration, a primary source of importance has been collaboration with restorers, research institutes, the Superintendencies and to a lesser degree, universities.

Resistance and Driving Factors in Adoption

From a comparison of resistance and driving factors resulting from an empirical analysis of restoration firms (Verbano et al., 2008), what emerges from interviews with suppliers can be summarized as follows:

- a firm's size represents a resistance factor to laser adoption. The initial purchase cost of equipment is a strong deterrent, above all where size is limited.

- the difficulty of making an economic assessment of the investment constitutes a resistance factor. In particular, in addition to the lack of tools and managerial ability there is the firm manager's limited tendency to invest, unless as a response to a series of orders the firm has already obtained. In other words, suppliers are of the opinion that restoration firms take an exclusively short-term view in their assessment because it is linked to public sector contracts;
- the firm manager's lack of technical training does not represent a significant resistance factor. A restorer's technical training is not as important as perhaps the experience he/she has gained in the field or from following specific training courses;
- under current legislation the assignment of public works is based on the criterion of the largest discount, which all the firms surveyed see as one of the principal resistance factors. In the first place the system of tenders favours the large groups and construction firms who, once they have won the public competition, very often subcontract the work to the restoration firms, obliging them to make further cuts. This system leads the firms to adopt the most economical restoration techniques, even if these do not guarantee the same quality of restoration. As a practice 'the largest discount' depresses the sector, compromising the earnings of restoration firms and limiting their innovative force;
- improvement of the firm's reputation and image is considered an important factor; possession of a laser adds a distinctive element to a firm that can be an advantage in the selection process of companies invited to compete in tendering, and in cases where the Superintendencies or private individuals assign work by private contract (especially when it is impossible to use traditional restoration methods and the Superintendencies are familiar with laser techniques ;
- the expected improvement in performance of the service supplied is a strong incentive towards adoption;
- relationships with universities and research institutes is held to be a driving factor in the decision to adopt laser technology, even though there are still only a small number of examples of collaboration between firms and institutes of this kind;
- the request for laser use by public institutions is recognised as the most important driving factor. It constitutes the determining condition for encouraging technological innovation in the sector;
- the geographical proximity of restoration firms to research institutes and suppliers is not a determining factor in laser adoption, also because their clients are spread across Italy and are not concentrated in the supplier's region.

6.2. The Client Sector

Characteristics of Commissioning Bodies

The institutional tasks of public bodies are related to the protection, conservation and restoration of works under their direct authority, namely: the archaeological, historical-artistic and architectural works situated in their Province or Region.

Of the public institutions interviewed, two (A and C) have their own restoration workshop devoted to the restoration of works that are mainly public property, or property

belonging to the institution itself, whereas one (B) has a scientific laboratory that carries out chemical-physical analyses, diagnostics for the study of the state of conservation of artistic artefacts, technical-scientific assistance, research on new methods of diagnostic investigation, conservation and restoration. The other institution (D) has both a scientific laboratory and a restoration workshop; the latter in particular is larger than those of public institutions. Of the four institutions, three have therefore stated they engage in research in the field of diagnostic methods, conservation and restoration.

In terms of economic resources, the public institutions interviewed have declared a sizeable reduction in funding in recent years, with cuts of up to 40% in ministerial contributions. Limited economic resources have led to a reduction in the number of commissions for restoration work (fewer contracts for private firms), but this is also caused by a reduction in spending affecting the provision new jobs (in some cases even highly specialized staff have been dismissed), the participation of officials in training courses and seminars, the reimbursement of travel expenses for officials responsible for checking on restoration work being carried out by the firms under contract, and updating equipment. A further problem to that of funding is the need to revise the organizational structure of these public institutions, which are regulated by a law from 1939, which does not reflect the new roles and responsibilities that have arisen over the years, and which creates excessive administrative bureaucracy (pointless procedures, long delays etc.).

These comments do not apply to institution D, which benefits from greater financing and can therefore invest in specialized staff, new technology, and in controls.

Tendency towards Innovation and Knowledge about Lasers

None of the public institutions has made investments in technology in recent years, and do not foresee doing so in the near future. Only institution D has invested in new technology, among which is the purchase of two lasers, and it plans to make further investments in the field of the cleaning of artwork and work safety.

All four institutions know about lasers and have used it several times in research projects with universities and other institutes or research centres. The interviewees claim that in general the Superintendencies are distrustful towards this technology not only due to their traditional attitude (reluctance towards change), but also due to a lack of experience of its use in the field. In this respect, a European level of standardization of regulations governing the use of lasers is considered important, giving detailed specifications regarding procedures for its use on various materials, and ensuring greater safety in the use of this tool.

The information channels that have proven most important for knowledge on lasers are trade fairs and conventions where an exchange of ideas has been possible between specialists and experts.

Innovative Policy Devices

The Superintendencies state that in their contract specifications they have never stipulated a particular technical approach such as laser use. Two Superintendencies and one private institution declare they have suggested it in some cases, but it should be remembered that the Superintendencies that were selected are not only familiar with this technology but have also taken part in projects on the research and development of laser technology in the field of restoration. It appears, however, that the officials involved in drawing up contracts

have a predominantly humanistic background and therefore have limited technical knowledge about new technologies for restoration.

With regard to the criteria for selecting firms, the major criterion considered is the largest discount offered. Other criteria can be applied, such as the most economically advantageous offer, not only based on costs, but also the firm's qualifications and experience, but the fear of complaints about the reasons for their choice prevent public institutions from adopting this procedure. For institution D, however, assigning a contract or selection based on the firm's résumé prove to be the normal selection procedures.

It is the general opinion that the criterion of the largest discount (that lead to reductions of up to 30% when compared to contract specifications) is the cause of accelerated job completion time, the use of more economical restoration methods and therefore a lowering of the quality of the work. For these reasons some institutions use the criterion of an automatic exclusion for anomalous bids, (although this policy still leads to bids with a 17-20% discount on contract specifications).

Resistance and Driving Factors

Finally, regarding the resistance and driving factors in adopting lasers that emerged from the empirical analysis of the restoration firms, the results of the interviews reveal that:

- the limited size of firms is confirmed as a resistance factor;
- the difficulty of an economic assessment of the investment is considered to be a resistance factor, and is also linked to the first point;
- the firm manager's lack of technical training is not a relevant factor in the adoption of lasers;
- the policy of assigning contracts based on the largest discount is undoubtedly a hindrance to investments in technology; however, the Superintendencies can compensate by using selection criteria (for example, the most economically advantageous bid, even if there is the risk that the Superintendencies choices will be contested);
- the expected improvement in the company image is confirmed as a driving factor, but to a lesser extent compared to other factors;
- the expected improvement in the execution of restoration work is confirmed;
- relationships with research institutes and universities are essentially confirmed, even though in one case it was emphasized that the vendors' sales promotion policy is more important than collaboration with institutes and universities; dealers should organize demonstrations and lower rental prices;
- requests from the Superintendencies to use laser was essentially confirmed by everyone. The problem in this case consists in conducting a diagnostic examination in order to prepare an evaluation, and from this, the specifications, thus confirming the problems involved in the restoration work and the best methods to employ. However, two problems hinder this approach: the lack of funding for diagnostic investigation and the lack of technical skills by those who have to make the assessment (often art historians who have no expertise in art restoration methods);
- the geographical proximity of restoration firms to research institutes and suppliers is not considered an influential factor in the process of adopting lasers, because in

general research institutes and suppliers also collaborate or develop research projects with geographically distant restoration firms.

Conclusion

This chapter has examined the characteristics of the field of laser supply for the restoration of art works, and that of institutes commissioning restoration and conservation, and specifically, the role of these agents in the adoption of laser technology in the restoration sector. The former is a field characterized by an oligopolistic structure, with essentially two agents operating in Italy: the market leader, an international group with an annual turnover of a 94 million euros, and a small firm with 25 employees and an annual turnover of one million euros.

From an analysis of their behaviour it emerges that Firm A produces lasers for use in restoration mainly for reasons linked to the company image rather than for reasons of profit. In fact, the group considers it an asset to advertise their collaboration with a Superintendency in the restoration of an important work of art. Firm B's reasons for working in this sector are different. It was founded to produce lasers for restoration work, and only after some years has it had to enter the more lucrative business of producing lasers for the medical sector.

In short, the elements that characterize the supply sector with regard to the adoption of lasers by firms are:

- the oligopolistic nature of the market, the limited volume of sales, the high costs of research and development of laser technology are responsible for the high price of this technology;
- the firms adopt marketing strategies such as tax incentives, assistance and support, product demonstrations, training courses, media advertising, advertising in scientific journals that might facilitate the adoption of lasers;
- the firms conduct research and experimentation on new laser equipment in collaboration with research institutes, universities and restoration firms, but do not develop equipment to suit the client's specific requirements due to the high research and development costs.

The analysis conducted on the supply sector compared to the one conducted among the restoration firms demonstrates a correlation between a low level of competition among suppliers and the limited "customizing" of the product, and the low rate of laser adoption, thus confirming the relevant literature (David and Olsen, 1992; Harrison and Waite, 2005). With regard to the third variable, it can be observed that although the two firms have adopted marketing strategies, the rate of laser adoption is low. This conclusion may be either due to the fact that the small number of suppliers does not allow them to reach all the restoration firms operating in Italy, and therefore limits them from obtaining the advantages of a diffusion of information among restoration firms, or to the fact that restoration firms apparently attribute little importance to the suppliers' marketing strategies (only 18% of the sample considers the suppliers' marketing strategies as being important in the adoption of lasers, whereas 53% consider them of little importance).

The second objective is the characterization of the field of public sector clients and their propensity towards new technologies. From the analysis of these public institutions a rather problematic situation emerges. The Superintendencies, as non-autonomous, peripheral administrations, depend on the central administration for their running costs and staffing. On the other hand, in recent years there have been severe cutbacks in ministerial contributions, which have led to a reduction in staff, staff training, controls on work carried out by restoration firms, and the amount of restoration work commissioned. Regarding the elements in this field that may influence the adoption of laser, the following are noted:

1. internal cultural and structural factors have been found to be insufficient for promoting innovation in the sector. The Suprintendences do not have the financial resources necessary for investing in technological innovation, nor in training or technological knowledge. If greater economic resources were available it would also be possible to carry out preliminary diagnostic examinations through calls for bids in order to identify restoration problems and the most appropriate methods and techniques to suggest to firms. The Superintendencies show a certain distrust about using new technologies, also because they feel the weight of responsibility for the restoration more than the other entities involved. Even more significant is the problem of the commissioners' lack of technical and scientific expertise in restoration, since they tend to be art history graduates.
2. The Superintendencies do not use public contracts as an instrument for promoting innovation. Most Superintendencies claim they have suggested the use of lasers, (referring here to Superintendencies particularly "enlightened" about laser use), but none has indicated its use in the contract specifications.

The last objective was to confirm the validity of the driving and resistance factors that emerged from the empirical analysis of restoration firms.

The results of this comparison are summarized in the following table (Table 7).

The analysis confirms the relevant factors in the process of adopting laser technology as: limited size, the difficulty of making an economic assessment of the investment, the policy of assigning work based on the largest discount (one of the most severe problems not only for the adoption of new technology, but also for the management of the entire field), the improvement of a firm's reputation following the adoption of laser, the expected improvement in executing restorations, relationships with institutions and universities, and above all the Superintendencies request for the use of lasers, which in the opinion of the suppliers and the Superintendencies themselves is the most important driving factor in laser adoption. The lack of technical training of restoration firm managers, and the geographical proximity of restoration firms to research centres and institutes, prove to be irrelevant in the process of adoption.

In conclusion, a rather complex picture emerges regarding the capacity for innovation demonstrated by the firms in the sector under examination. The elements of complexity can be discerned in the first place in the structural weakness inherent in the extremely small size of these industries, with particular reference to the limited availability of economic-financial resources and managerial knowledge, and in the second place in the client sector, which is

tightly restricted in its role as a promoter of innovation due to public tender regulations, the limitations of available resources, and the lack of a techno-scientific culture. Lastly, further elements of complexity can be discerned in the laser supply sector which occupies a particularly strong position in comparison to the restoration sector, due to both the larger size of the elements that compose it and its oligopolistic structure.

Table 7. Resistance and driving factors according to the earlier research, the suppliers and the Superintendencies

	Resistance factors	Previous research	S*	C**	Driving factors	Previous research	S*	C**
Internal	1. limited size 2. difficulty of economic assessment of investment 3.firm manager's limited technical training	Yes Yes No	Yes Yes No	Yes Yes No	5. improvement of firm's reputation and image 6.expected improvement of performance and service supplied	approx. Yes Yes	Yes Yes	Yes Yes
external	4. policy of assigning contracts based solely on price	Yes	Yes	Yes	7. relationships with universities and research institutions 8. request for laser use by public institutions 9. proximity to laser research centres and to suppliers of laser technology	Yes Yes Weak Yes	Yes Yes No	Yes Yes No

* S = Suppliers, **C = Clients.

In the light of the findings, some possible suggestions identified as a result of this chapter, which may lead to the development of policies that encourage the adoption of laser in this sector are the following:

- for the Superintendencies: stimulate the request for laser use in contract specifications and ensure that the criteria used in selecting bids are more oriented towards technical expertise and the quality of restoration work;
- for the suppliers: offer seminars and free demonstrations to Superintendency officials and intensify the types of collaboration between suppliers and restoration firms both in the product development phase and the marketing phase in order to increase client confidence in suppliers and to promote a greater understanding of this technology.

- for government bodies: promote an awareness of other European (French, English, Spanish) and non-European producers of laser technology in order to increase competition in the sector and in sale prices.

REFERENCES

AVCPLSF (Autorità per la Vigilanza sui Contratti Pubblici di Lavori, Servizi e Forniture), (2007), Relazione al Parlamento, available on line www.autoritalavoripubblici.it/pubblicazioni/Relazione2007.pdf.

Attewell, P. (1992). Technology diffusion and organizational learning: the case of business computing. *Organization Science*, 3(1), 1-19.

Baldwin, J. and Lin, Z. (2002). Impediments to advanced technology adoption for Canadian manufactures. *Research Policy*, 31(1), 1-18.

Baptista, R. (2000). Do innovations diffuse faster within geographical clusters? *International Journal of Industrial Organization*, 18, 515-535.

Bass, F. (1980). The relationship between diffusion rates experience curves and demand elasticises for consumer durables technological innovations. *Journal of Business*, 53, 551-567.

Brandi, C. (1998). *Teoria generale della critica*, Roma, Editori Riuniti, 1998.

Cainarca, G. C., Colombo, M. G. and Mariotti, S. (1989). An Evolutionary Pattern of Innovation Diffusion: The Case of Flexible Automation. *Reserch Policy*, 18, 59-86.

Clark, P.A., Staunton, N. (eds.) (1989). *Innovation in Technology and Organization*. London: Routledge.

Cohen, W. M. (1995). Empirical Studies of Innovative Activity. In P. Stoneman (Eds.), *Handbook of the Economics of Innovation and Technological Change*. Oxford: Blackwell Publishers Ltd.

Cooper, R. B. and Zmud, R. W. (1990). Information technology implementation research: a technological diffusion approach. *Management Science*, 36 (2), 123-139.

Damanpour, F. (1992) "Organizational Size and Innovation", *Organization Studies*, 13(3), pp 375-402.

David, P., Olsen, T. (1992). Technology adoption, learning spillovers and the optimal duration of patent based monopolies. *International Journal of Industrial Organization*, 10, 517-544.

Dewar, R. D. and Dutton, J. E. (1986). The adoption of radical and incremental innovations: an empirical analysis. *Management Science*, 32(11), 1422-1433.

Dholakia, R. R. and Kshetri N. (2004). Factors Impacting the Adoption of the Internet among SMEs. *Small Business Economics* 23(4), 311-322.

DiMaggio, P.J., Powell, W.W. (1983). The iron cage revisited: institutional isomorphism and collective rationality in organizational fields. *American Sociological Review*, 48, 147-160.

Dobbin, F. R., Edelman, L., Meyer, J. W., Scott, R. W., Swidler A. (1987). The Expansion of Due Process in Organizations. In L. G. Zucker (Eds), *Institutional Patterns and Organizations*. Cambridge: Ballinger Publishing Company.

Dos Santos, B. L., Peffers K., (1998). Competitor and vendor influence on the adoption of innovative applications in electronic commerce. *Information and Management*, 34, 175-184.

Edler. J., Georghiou L., (2007). Public procurement and innovation – Resurrecting the demand side. *Research Policy*, 36(10), 949-963.

Edquist, C., Hommen, L., (1998). Government technology procurement and innovation theory. Paper for the project "Innovation System and European Integration" (ISE). Linkoping.

Edquist, C., Hommen, L., Tsipouri, L., (eds.) (2000). *Public Technology Procurement and Innovation*. Dordrecht: Kluwer Academic.

Fink, F. (1998). Guidelines for the successful adoption of information technology in small and medium enterprises. *International Journal of Information Management*, 18(4), 243-253.

Freel, M. S. (2000). External linkages and product innovation in small manufacturing firms. *Entrepreneurship and Regional Development,* 12, 245-266.

Freel, M. S. (2005). Patterns of innovation and skills in small firms. *Technovation,* 25(2), 123-134.

Frambach, R.T., Barkema, H.G., Nooteboom, B., Wedel, M., (1998). Adoption of a service innovation in the business market: an empirical test of supply side variables. *Journal of Business Research*, 41, 161-174.

Gatignon, H., Robertson, T. S. (1989). Technology Diffusion: an empirical test of competitive effects. *Journal of Marketing*, 53, 35-49.

Geroski, P. A. (2000). Models of technology diffusion. *Research Policy*, 29, 603-625.

Harrison T., Waite, K. (2005). Critical factors affecting intermediary web site adoption: understanding how to extend e-participation. *The Journal of Business and Industrial Marketing*, 20, 4/5, 187-199.

Hemmert, M. (2004). The influence of institutional factors on the technology acquisition performance of high-tech firms: survey results from Germany and Japan. *Research Policy,* 33 (6-7), 1019-1039.

Iacovou, C.L., Benbasat, I., Dexter, A.S. (1995). Electronic data interchange and small organizations: adoption and impact technology. *MIS Quarterly*, December, 465-485.

Igbaria, M., Zinatelli, N. and Covaye, A. L. M. (1998). Analysis of information technology success in small firms in New Zealand. *International Journal of Information Management*, 18 (2), 103-119.

Jensen, R.A. (2004) "Multiplant Firms and Innovation Adoption and Diffusion", *Southern Economic*, Vol 70, No 3, pp 661-671.

Kimberly, J. R. and Evanisko, M. J. (1981). Organizational Innovation: The Influence of Individual, Organizational, and Contextual Factors on Hospital Adoption of Technological and Administrative Innovations. *Academy of Management Journal*, 24 (4), 689 – 713.

Kohn, S., Hüsig, S. (2006). Potential benefits, current supply, utilization and barriers to adoption: an exploratory study on German SMEs and innovation software. *Technovation,* 26(8), 988-998.

Kuan, K.K.Y. and Chau, P.Y.K. (2001) "A perception-based model for Edi adoption in small business using a technology-organization-environment framework", *Information and Management*, Vol 38, pp 165-176.

Leonard-Barton, D. and Deschamps, I. (1988). Managerial influence in the implementation of new technology. *Management Science*, 34, 1252-1265.

Lal, K. (1999). Determinants of the adoption of Information Technology: a case study of electrical and electronic goods manufacturing firms in India. *Research Policy,* 28(7), 667-680.

Maxwell, J. R. and Wersterfield D. L. (2002). Technological Entrepreneurism Characteristics Related to the Adoption of Innovative Technology. *SAM Advanced Management Journal,* 67, 9-21.

Merhtens, J., Cragg, P.B. and Mills A.M. (2001). A model of Internet adoption by SMEs. *Information and Management*, 39(3), 165-176.

Ministero dei Beni Culturali (2007). *Riepilogo generale 2007*, (www.beniculturali.it)

Mulgan, G., Albury, D. (2003) (Eds), *Innovation in the public sector*. Strategy Unit, London.

Petroni, G., Turra, F., Verbano C., Venturini K, 2006, "The adoption of laser technology by art restoration firms", in Dan Remenyi (edited by), *Proceedings of the European Conference on Entrepreneurship and Innovation: ECEI 2006*, Academic Conferences Ltd., Reading (England)

Premkumar, G., Roberts, M. (1999). Adoption of new information technologies in rural small business. *OMEGA International Journal of Management Science*, 27(4), 467-484.

Provan K. G., (1980). Board Power and Organizational Effectiveness Among Human Service Agencies. *Academy of Management*, 23, 221-236.

Robertson, T. S. and Gatignon H., (1986). Competitive Effects on Technology Diffusion. *Journal of Marketing*, 50(3), 1-12.

Rogers, E. M. (Eds.) (1995). *Diffusion of innovations*. New York: The Free Press.

Rothwell, R., Dodgson, M. (1991). External linkages and innovation in small and medium-sized enteprises. *RandD Management*, 21 (2).

Rolfstam, M., (2005). Public Technology Procurement as a Demand-side Innovation Policy Instrument: an Overview of Recent Literature and Events. *Danish Research Unit for Industrial Dynamics (DRUID)*. PhD Winter Conference, available on line www.druid.dk/uploads/tx_picturedb/dw2005-1635.pdf.

Sadowski, B. M., Maitland, C. and van Dongen, J. (2002). Strategic use of Internet by small- and medium-sized companies: en explanatory study. *Information Economics and Policy*, 14, 75-93.

Souitaris, V. (2002). Firm-specific competencies determining technological innovation: a survey in Greece. *RandD Management,* 32(1), 61-77.

Tsikriksis, N., Lanzolla, G. and Frohlich, M. (2004). Adoption of e-process by service firms: an empirical study of antecedents. *Production and Operations Management* , 13(3), 216-229.

Romijn, H. and Albaladejo, M. (2002). Determinants of innovation capability in small electronics and software firms in southeast England. *Research Policy,* 31(7), 1053-1067.

Sadowski, B.M., Maitland, C. and van Dongen, J., (2002) "Strategic use of Internet by small- and medium-sized companies: en explanatory study", *Information Economics and Policy*, Vol 14, pp 75-93.

Salimbeni, R., Pini R., Siano S. and Calcagno, G. (2001). Assessment of the state of conservation of stone art works after laser cleaning: comparison with conventional cleaning results on a two-decade follow up. *Journal of Cultural Heritage*, 1, 385-391.

Santarelly, E. and D'Altri, S. (2003). The diffusion of e-commerce among SMEs: theoretical implications and empirical evidence. *Small Business Economics*, 21, 273-283.

Tsikriksis, N., Lanzolla, G. and Frohlich, M. (2004). Adoption of e-process by service firms: an empirical study of antecedents. *Production and Operations Management* , 13(3), 216-229.

Verbano C., Venturini K., Petroni, G., Nosella A., (2008). Characteristics of Italian art restoration firms and factors influencing their adoption of laser technology, *Journal of Cultural Economics*, 32(1), 3-34.

Von Hippel, E., (1986). Lead users: a source of novel product concepts, *Management science*, 32(7), 791-805.

Waarts, E., van Everdingen, Y. M. and van Hillegersberg, J. (2002). The dynamics of factors affecting the adoption of innovations, *The Journal of Product Innovation Management,* 19, 412-423.

Zucker, L.G. (1987). Institutional Theories of Organization, *Annual Review of Sociology*, 13, 443-464.

In: Business and Finance: Performance and Management
Editors: R. Morland and A. Gagglione
ISBN: 978-1-61122-936-3

Chapter 5

CONSOLIDATION AND DETERMINANTS OF BANK EFFICIENCY: EMPIRICAL EVIDENCE FROM MALAYSIA

Fadzlan Sufian*
[a]Khazanah Nasional Berhad, Malaysia
[b]Universiti Putra, Malaysia

ABSTRACT

The present paper examines the impact of mergers and acquisitions on the cost efficiency of the Malaysian banking sector. The analysis consists of three stages. Firstly, by using the non-parametric Data Envelopment Analysis (DEA) approach, we calculate the cost, allocative, and technical efficiency of individual banks during the period 1997-2003. Secondly, we examine changes in the efficiency of the Malaysian banking sector during the pre and post merger periods by using a series of parametric and non-parametric univariate tests. Finally, we employ the multivariate Tobit regression analysis to examine factors that influence the efficiency of the Malaysian banking sector during the pre and post merger periods. The empirical findings suggest that the merger has resulted in a higher mean cost efficiency of the Malaysian banking sector post merger. We find that the acquirers have been relatively more cost efficient in all of the seven merger cases analyzed. The results from the multivariate regression analysis suggest that loans intensity, size, income diversification, and capitalization exhibits positive relationship with bank efficiency. On the other hand, market share and expense preference behaviour are negatively related to bank efficiency levels. The empirical findings suggest that banks in the control group have been relatively more cost efficient than those that were involved in mergers. The results suggest that the variations in Malaysian bank cost efficiency are not significantly related to economic conditions and concentration.

---

* Corresponding author: [a] Khazanah Research and Investment Strategy, Khazanah Nasional Berhad, Malaysia. [b] Department of Economics, Faculty of Economics and Management, Universiti Putra Malaysia. Mailing address: Khazanah Research and Investment Strategy, Khazanah Nasional Berhad, Level 35, Tower 2, Petronas Twin Towers Kuala Lumpur City Centre, 50088 Kuala Lumpur, Malaysia. E-mail: fadzlan.sufian@khazanah.com.my; fsufian@gmail.com. Tel: 603-2034-0197, Fax: 603-2034-0035.

JEL Classification: G21; D24.
Keywords: Mergers and Acquisitions, Data Envelopment Analysis, Multivariate Tobit Regression Analysis, Malaysia.

1. INTRODUCTION

The consolidation of the banking sector in Malaysia started relatively later than the merger and acquisition waves in other developed countries. Although incentives have been introduced by the central bank to promote mergers and acquisitions particularly among the small domestic banking institutions, it was not until after the economic crisis in 1997 that stronger measures to force consolidation between the domestic incorporated banking institutions led to the completion of the merger exercise at the end of 2000.

While there have been numerous studies that examine voluntary bank mergers and acquisitions, virtually nothing has been publish to examine the effect of forced mergers and acquisitions on the efficiency of the acquiring and target banks due to its rarity. Therefore, the case of the Malaysia's merger programme offers an opportunity to assess the extent of the impact of government interventions on the efficiency of the banking sector.

The purpose of the present study is to employ the Data Envelopment Analysis (DEA) method to examine the impact of forced mergers and acquisitions on the cost efficiency of the Malaysian banking sector. We differentiate this paper from previous ones that focus on the Malaysian banking sector and add insights in several respects discussed below.

Firstly, we examine for the first time the impact of mergers and acquisitions on the cost, allocative, and technical efficiency of the Malaysian banking sector. Although a recent by Sufian (2007) has also examine the impact of mergers and acquisitions on the efficiency of the Malaysian banking sector, the study has only examine the impact of mergers and acquisitions on Malaysian banks' technical, pure technical, and scale efficiency. In contrast, the present study examines the cost efficiency of Malaysian banks and its mutually exhaustive components of technical and allocative efficiencies. While technical (in) efficiency is related to managerial factors, allocative (in) efficiency is often associated with regulatory factors (Isik and Hassan, 2002). Within the context of the Malaysian banking sector, it is important to examine this issue as Okuda and Hashimoto (2004) suggests that the management of Malaysian banks were inefficient due to the various forms of government influence and regulations. They suggest that the management of Malaysian banks were unable to pursue managerial efficiency, as they are required by the government to provide loans for specific policy purposes. Thus, it is interesting to examine whether allocative rather than technical efficiency has a greater influence in determining the cost efficiency of the Malaysian banking sector.

Secondly, we run a series of parametric and non-parametric univariate tests to examine the difference in the efficiency of the Malaysian banking sector during the pre and post merger periods. We also run the multivariate Tobit regression analysis to explain the relationship between cost efficiency and bank specific traits such as size, risk, and capitalization while controlling for other macroeconomic and market condition variables. To the best of our knowledge, no study has undertaken such an analysis in respect of the Malaysian banking sector.

In essence, the present paper raises three important fundamental questions: 1) Did the MandAs result in the improvement in Malaysian banking sector's cost efficiency post merger? 2) Did a less efficient bank become the target for acquisition? 3) What are the factors that significantly explain the variations in Malaysian banks' cost efficiency during the pre and post merger periods?

The paper is structured as follows: the next section reviews the main literatures in regard to bank mergers and acquisitions. Section 3 outlines the approaches to the measurement and estimation of efficiency change. Section 4 discusses the results, and finally, section 5 provides some concluding remarks.

2. Related Studies

As surveyed by Berger et al. (1999), a substantial literature investigates the causes and consequences of bank mergers. Bank MandAs may enable banking firms to benefit from new business opportunities created by changes in the regulatory and technological environment. Berger et al. (1999, p. 136) pointed out the consequences of MandAs, which may lead to changes in efficiency, market power, economies of scale and scope, availability of services to small customers and payment system's efficiency. Besides improvements in cost and profit efficiencies, MandAs may entail diverging effects on cost and profit efficiency, as well as on loan and deposit pricing, which may lead banks to earn higher profits. Prager and Hannan (1998) found that bank MandAs have resulted in higher banks' concentration, which in turn leads to significantly lower rates on deposits. Some evidence also suggested that U.S. banks that involved in MandAs improved the quality of their outputs in the 1990s in ways that increased costs, but still improved profit productivity by increasing revenues more than costs (Berger and Mester, 2003, p. 88).

In terms of methodology, the empirical literature analyzing the effects of consolidation on banks' performance follows two main empirical methods. The majority of studies follow event study-type methodology, often based on changes in stock prices around the period of the announcement of the merger. These studies typically try to ascertain whether the announcement of a bank merger creates shareholder value, normally in the form of cumulated abnormal stock market returns for the shareholders of the target, the bidder or the combined entity (see Beitel and Schiereck (2001) for an excellent review).

A second strand of literature measure the impact of financial integration on bank performance via accounting ratios of performance (such as the return on assets, return on equity, etc.) or productive efficiency indicators (such as indicators of cost, profit, or technical efficiency). The potential for scale economies is often one of the main reasons given by practitioners to justify MandAs. However, the majority of U.S. studies find that these potential efficiency gains resulting from size rarely materialize after the merger (Berger et al. 1999). A possible reason could be that some efficiency gains may take longer to accrue such as the benefits derived from cost reductions or scope economies.

With regard to the frontier efficiency techniques, two main approaches are commonly used to assess the impact of MandAs on bank efficiency, namely the parametric and non-parametric approaches. The parametric approach on one hand comprise of three major approaches, namely the Stochastic Frontier Approach (SFA), the Distribution Free Approach (DFA), and the Thick Frontier Approach (TFA), while Data Envelopment Analysis (DEA)

and Free Disposal Hull (FDH) are non-parametric approaches. While both techniques require the specification of a cost or production function or frontier, the former involves the specification and econometric estimation of a statistical or parametric function/frontier, the non-parametric approach provides a piecewise linear frontier by enveloping the observed data points.

The DEA method has been widely applied in the empirical estimation of financial institutions, health care, and education sectors' efficiency worldwide. Notwithstanding, the technique has increasingly been the preferred method to investigate the impact of MandAs on bank efficiency, in particular if the sample size is small. Previous studies undertaken to analyze a small number of MandAs includes among others Avkiran (1999), Liu and Tripe (2002), and Sufian and Majid (2007).

By employing the DEA method to a small sample of 16 to 19 Australian banks during the period of 1986-1995, Avkiran (1999) examined the effects of four mergers on efficiency and the benefits to public. He adopted the intermediation approach and two DEA models. He reported that the acquiring banks were more efficient than the target banks. He also found that the acquiring banks do not always maintain their pre merger efficiency, but that, during the deregulated period, technical efficiency, employees' productivity and return on assets (ROA) improved. There were mixed evidence from the four cases on the extent to which the benefits of efficiency gains from mergers were passed on to the public.

Liu and Tripe (2002) analyzed a small sample of 7 to 14 banks employed accounting ratios and two DEA models to explore the efficiency of 6 bank mergers in New Zealand between 1989 and 1998. They found that the acquiring banks to be generally larger than their targets, although they were not consistently more efficient. They found that five of the six merged banks had efficiency gains based on the financial ratios, while another only achieved a slight improvement in operating expenses to average total income. Based on the DEA analysis, they found that only some banks were more efficient than the target banks pre merger. The results suggest that four banks had obvious efficiency gains post merger. However, they could not decisively conclude on possible benefits of the mergers on public benefits.

Using a small sample size of 6 banks, Sufian and Majid (2007) employed Data Envelopment Analysis (DEA) to examine the effects of MandAs on the Singapore domestic banking groups' efficiency. They applied a variant of the intermediation approach to two models to detect for any efficiency gains (loss) resulting from the MandAs. The results from both models suggest that the merger has resulted in higher mean overall efficiency of Singapore banking groups post merger. They do not find evidence of more efficient acquirers compared to the targets, as the findings from both models suggest that both the targets are more efficient relative to the acquirers. The empirical results further support the hypothesis that the acquiring banks' mean overall efficiency improved post merger resulting from the merger with a more efficient bank.

3. METHODOLOGY AND THE CHOICE OF VARIABLES

3.1. Data Envelopment Analysis

The non-parametric Data Envelopment Analysis (DEA) method is employed with variable returns to scale (VRS) assumption, to measure input oriented cost efficiency of Malaysian banks. DEA involves constructing a non-parametric production frontier based on the actual input-output observations in the sample relative to which efficiency of each bank in the sample is measured (Coelli, 1996). To discuss DEA in more technical terms, let us assume that there is data on K inputs and M outputs for each N bank. For the ith bank, these are represented by the vectors x_i and y_i respectively. According to Charnes et al. (1978) the input oriented measure of a particular bank is calculated as:

$$\begin{aligned}&\min_{\theta,\lambda} \theta,\\ &y_i + Y\lambda \geq 0\\ &\theta x_i - X\lambda \geq 0\\ &\lambda \geq 0\end{aligned} \tag{1}$$

where θ is a scalar representing the value of the efficiency score for the ith bank which will range between 0 and 1. λ is a vector of N x 1 constants. The linear programming has to be solved N times, once for each bank in the sample. In order to calculate efficiency under the assumption of VRS, the convexity constraint ($N1'\lambda = 1$) will be added. The convexity constraint determines how closely the production frontier envelops the observed input-output combinations and is not imposed in the constant returns to scale (CRS) case.

Next, in order to estimate cost efficiency, the objective function of the program is altered to capture total bank costs (Fare et al. 1985). The linear program is specified as

$$\min_{x_i, \lambda_i} w'_i x_i$$

subject to $\quad y_i, \leq Y\lambda_i$

$$x_i \leq X\lambda_i$$

and $\quad \lambda_i \geq 0 \qquad (2)$

Letting x^*_i be the cost minimizing vector of input for bank i, cost efficiency (CE) is given by $CE_i = w'_i x^*_i \,/\, w'_i x_i$. Given estimates of CE and technical efficiency (TE), allocative efficiency (AE) is estimated by the ratio $AE_i = CE_i/TE_i$. The solution of the cost efficiency program provides the cost minimizing input vector conditional on the observed technology in the sample. If the ratio $x_{ik} = x^*_{ik} < 1$, the bank is under utilizing input k; and if $x_{ik} = x^*_{ik} > 1$, the bank is over utilizing input k.

Allocative efficiency represents how optimally input factors are mixed to minimize total input costs given output quantity and input prices. Firms achieve cost efficiency by adopting the best practice technology (becoming technically efficient) and choosing the optimal mix of input (becoming allocatively efficient), conditional on output and input prices. Technical efficiency for a given bank is defined as the ratio of the input usage of a fully efficient bank producing the same output vector to the input usage of the bank under consideration (Fare et al. 1985).

3.2. Multivariate Tobit Regression Analysis

As defined in equations 1 and 2, the DEA score falls between the interval 0 and 1 ($0 < h^* \leq 1$) making the dependent variable a limited dependent variable. A commonly held view in previous studies is that the use of the Tobit model can handle the characteristics of the distribution of (in) efficiency measures and thus yielding results that can provide important policy guidelines to improve performance (Coelli et al. 1998). The standard Tobit model can be defined as follows for observation (bank) i:

$$y_i^* = \beta' x_i + \varepsilon_i$$
$$y_i = y_i^* \text{ if } y_i^* \geq 0$$
$$\text{and } y_i = 0\text{, otherwise} \qquad (3)$$

where x_i is a vector of explanatory variables and β is the set of parameters to be estimated. $\varepsilon_i \sim N(0, \sigma^2)$ denotes the error term. y_i^* is a latent variable and y_i is the efficiency score obtained from the DEA model[9].

By using the efficiency scores as the dependent variables, we estimate the following model:

$$\gamma_{jt} = \beta_0 + \beta_1 \Sigma Characteristics + \zeta_2 \Sigma Econ + \varepsilon_{jt} \qquad (4)$$

where, γ_{jt} is the cost efficiency of the jth bank in period t obtained from the DEA model, *Characteristics* is a set of bank specific traits variables and *Econ* is a vector of economic and market conditions.

---

[9] The likelihood function (L) is maximized to solve β and σ based on 193 observations (banks) of y_i and x_i is $L = \prod_{y_i=0}(1-F)\prod_{y_i>0}\frac{1}{(2\Pi\sigma^2)^{1/2}} \times e^{-[1/(2\sigma^2)](y^i-\beta x_i)^2}$ where, $F_i = \int_{\infty}^{\beta x_i/\sigma} \frac{1}{(2\Pi)^{1/2}} e^{-t^2/2} dt$ The first product is over the observations for which the banks are 100 percent efficient (y = 0) and the second product is over the observations for which banks are inefficient (y >0). F_i is the distribution function of the standard normal evaluated at $\beta' x_i / \sigma$.

3.3. Data and Construction of Variables

We use annual bank level data of all Malaysian commercial banks covering the period 1997-2003. The variables are collected from published balance sheet information in annual reports of each individual bank, while the macroeconomic variable is sourced from various issues of Bank Negara Malaysia's annual reports. The total number of commercial banks operating in Malaysia varied from 33 banks in 1997 to 22 banks in 2003 due to entry and exit of banks during the past decade. This gives us a total of 193 bank year observations. The sample represents the whole gamut of the industry's total assets.

As in most recent studies, (e.g. Isik and Hassan, 2002; Pasiouras, 2007), we adopt the intermediation approach. Accordingly, three inputs and three output variables are chosen. The input vectors used are (X1) Total Deposits, (X2) Capital, and (X3) Labour, while, (Y1) Total Loans, (Y2) Investments, and (Y3) Non-Interest Income are the output vectors. To measure cost and allocative efficiencies the input prices are (P1) Price of Deposits, (P2) Price of Labour, and (P3) Price of Capital. The summary of data used to construct the efficiency frontiers are presented in Table 1.

The bank specific variables included in the second stage multivariate regression models are, LNDEPO (log of total deposits), LOANS/TA (total loans divided by total assets), LNTA (log of total assets), LLP/TL (loans loss provisions divided by total loans), NII/TA (non-interest income divided by total assets), NIE/TA (total overhead expenses divided by total assets), and EQASS (book value of stockholders' equity as a fraction of total assets). To examine the relationship between cost efficiency and the acquiring banks, a binary dummy variable DUMACQ is included in regression model 2. A binary variable CON_GRP is included in regression model 3 to examine the relationship between cost efficiency and banks that are not involved in any merger during the years under study. To measure the relationship between economic and market specific factors and bank efficiency, LNGDP, PRE_MER, POST_MER, and CR_3 are used. The independent variables and their hypothesized relationship with efficiency are detailed in Table 2.

Our data cover the registered MandAs that took place in the Malaysian banking sector during the year 2000. To be included in the sample, both the target and the acquiring banks must not have been involved in any other merger in the three years prior to the merger. In addition to the banks that were involved in MandAs during the study period, we have also included 19 other domestic and foreign banks that have not been involved in any MandAs during the years as a control group in the analysis. In the spirit of maintaining homogeneity, only commercial banks that make commercial loans and accept deposits from the public are included in the analysis. Therefore, Investment Banks, Finance Companies, and Islamic banks are excluded from the sample. In the study population, there were seven major MandAs that fit into our sample which were analyzed:

Case 1: Affin Bank Berhad acquisition of BSN Commercial Bank Berhad.

Case 2: Alliance Bank Berhad acquisition of Sabah Bank Berhad.

Case 3: EON Bank Berhad acquisition of Oriental Bank Berhad.

Case 4: Hong Leong Bank Berhad acquisition of Wah Tat Bank Berhad.

Table 1. Descriptive Statistics for Inputs, Outputs, and Input Prices (in million of RM)

	Y1	Y2	Y3	X1	X2	X3	P1	P2	P3
Min	53,411.00	205.00	14.00	131,352.00	1,248.00	1,898.00	0.005	0.002	0.009
Mean	12,335.73	3,767,524.55	180,873.30	888,037.68	184,255.20	152,612.30	0.056	0.008	0.252
Max	109,070.50	36,423.40	1,800,718.00	137,864.10	1,417,961.00	1,419,973.00	1.461	0.019	7.340
S.D	5,790.82	2,346,414.05	80,638.77	6,551.73	61,636.41	78,243.08	0.084	0.001	0.411

Notes: Y1: Loans (includes loans to customers and other banks), Y2: Investments (includes dealing and investment securities), Y3: Non-Interest Income (defined as fee income and other non-interest income, which among others consist of commission, service charges and fees, guarantee fees, and foreign exchange profits), X1: Total Deposits (includes deposits from customers and other banks), X2: Capital (measured by the book value of property, plant, and equipment), X3: Personnel Expenses (inclusive of total expenditures on employees such as salaries, employee benefits and reserve for retirement pay)[10], P1: Price of Deposits (interest expense divided by total deposits), P2: Price of Labour (personnel expenses divided by total assets), P3: Price of Capital (capital cost and depreciation divided by fixed assets).

Source: Banks annual reports and authors own calculations.

[10] As data on the number of employees are not readily made available, personnel expenses have been used as a proxy measure.

Case 5: Maybank Berhad acquisition of The Pacific Bank Berhad.

Case 6: Public Bank Berhad acquisition of Hock Hua Bank Berhad.

Case 7: Southern Bank Berhad acquisition of Bank Hin Lee Bank Berhad.

Table 2. Descriptive of the Variables Used in the Regression Models

Variable	Description	Hypothesized Relationship with Efficiency
	Bank Characteristics	
LNDEPO	Natural logarithm of total deposits	+/-
LOANS/TA	Total loans over total assets	+/-
LNTA	Natural logarithm of total assets	+/-
LLP/TL	Loan loss provisions over total loans	-
NII/TA	Non-interest income over total assets	+
NIE/TA	Non-interest expense over total assets	-
EQASS	Total book value of shareholders equity over total assets	+/-
DUMACQ	Binary variable that takes a value of 1, if a bank is an acquiring bank, 0 otherwise.	+/
CON_GRP	Binary variable that takes a value of 1, if a bank does not involve in any merger during the years, 0 otherwise.	+/
	Economic/ Market Conditions	
LNGDP	Natural logarithm of gross domestic products	+/-
CR_3	Proxy for the concentration in terms of assets of the three largest banks.	+/-
PRE-MER	Binary variable that takes a value of 1 for the pre merger years, 0 otherwise.	+/
POST_MER	Binary variable that takes a value of 1 for the post merger years, 0 otherwise.	+/

4. EMPIRICAL RESULTS

In the spirit of Rhoades (1998), we develop a [-3, 3] event window, to investigate the effect of MandAs on Malaysian bank efficiency. The choice of the event window is motivated by Rhoades (1998, p. 278), who pointed out that there has been unanimous agreement among the experts that about half of any efficiency gains should be apparent after one year and all gains should be realized within three years after the merger. The whole period (i.e. 1997-2003) is divided into three sub-periods: 1997-1999 refers to the pre merger period, 2000 is considered as the merger year, and 2001-2003 represents the post merger period, when the MandAs are expected to have some impact on Malaysian bank efficiency. We expect to be able to capture the effects of MandAs on the efficiency of Malaysian banks during this period. During all periods the targets and acquirers' mean cost efficiency along with its decomposition of allocative and technical efficiency scores are compared. This could help shed some light on the sources of inefficiency of the Malaysian banking system in general, as well as to differentiate between the targets' and acquirers' efficiency scores. To allow inefficiency to vary over time, the efficiency frontiers are constructed for each year by solving the linear programming (LP) problems rather than constructing a single multi-year frontier.

4.1. Did the Merger Result in a Higher Bank Efficiency Levels?

Table 3 illustrates the CE estimates, along with its decomposition into AE and TE. It is apparent that during the pre merger period Malaysian banks have exhibited a mean CE of 83.5%. Overall, the results suggest that the Malaysian banking system has performed relatively well in its basic function – transforming deposits to loans, with relatively minimal input waste of 16.5%. Thus, the results imply that during the pre merger period Malaysian banks could have produced the same amount of outputs with only 83.5% of the amount of inputs used. In other word, Malaysian banks could have reduced their inputs by 16.5% and still could have produced the same amount of outputs. The decomposition of CE into its AE and TE estimates suggest that during the pre merger period, the inefficiency of the Malaysian banking sector was largely due to TE (42.6%) rather than AE (4.9%). While technical (in) efficiency is related to managerial factors, allocative (in) efficiency is often associated with regulatory factors (Isik and Hassan, 2002). Thus, the results imply that during the pre merger period the cost inefficiency in the Malaysian banking sector was largely due to managerial practices rather than regulatory forbearance.

During the post merger period, the findings suggest that the merger has resulted in the improvement of Malaysian banking sector's CE. It is apparent from Table 3 that the Malaysian banks have exhibited mean CE of 86.9% during the post merger period, higher than the 83.5% recorded during the pre merger period. A closer look at the decomposition of CE into its AE and TE components reveals that the improvement in CE during the post merger period was mainly attributed to the improvement in TE. It is also interesting to note that despite earlier evidence implying that the lack of competition may result in lower TE (see Sathye, 2001), it is apparent from Table 3 that all Malaysian banks have reported higher mean TE score during the post merger period.

To examine the difference in the efficiency of the acquiring banks between the two periods i.e. before and after the mergers, we perform a series of parametric (*t*-test) and non-parametric (Mann-Whitney [Wilcoxon] and Kruskal-Wallis) tests. The results are presented in Table 4. The results from the parametric *t*-test support the findings that the Malaysian banking sector has exhibited a higher mean CE post merger (0.83328 < 0.86530), but is not statistically significant at any conventional levels. The decomposition of the CE into its AE and TE components suggest that the improvement in the Malaysian banking sector's CE post merger was mainly attributed to a higher TE (0.57555 < 0.89896) and is statistically significant at the 1% level.

Table 3. Summary of Mean Efficiency Levels of Malaysian Banks

Bank	ABB	Pre Merger*			During Merger**			Post Merger***		
		CE	AE	TE	CE	AE	TE	CE	AE	TE
Affin Bank	AFF	0.883	0.972	0.533	0.764	0.920	0.836	0.792	0.927	0.853
Alliance Bank	ALB	0.914	0.988	0.539				0.869	0.978	0.888
Arab Malaysian Bank	AMB	0.916	0.916	0.855	0.971	0.971	1.000	0.846	0.971	0.871
Ban Hin Lee Bank	BHL	0.759	0.959	0.413						
Bumiputra-Commerce Bank	BCB	0.975	0.975	0.741	0.801	0.965	0.831	0.850	0.973	0.873
Bank Utama	BUB	0.884	0.961	0.411	0.912	0.988	0.923	0.966	0.966	1.000
BSN Commercial Bank	BSN	0.683	0.780	0.591						
EON Bank	EON	0.903	0.966	0.517	0.850	0.973	0.874	0.925	0.895	0.842
Hock Hua Bank (Sabah)	HHS	0.398	0.916	0.281						
Hock Hua Bank	HHB	0.733	0.987	0.355						
Hong Leong Bank	HLB	0.895	0.981	0.462	0.915	0.915	0.754	0.721	0.920	0.786
Maybank	MBB	0.998	0.998	0.519	0.823	0.948	0.870	0.879	0.969	0.907
Oriental Bank	OBB	0.840	0.988	0.450						
Phileo Allied Bank	PAB	0.796	0.950	0.609						
Public Bank	PBB	0.959	0.990	0.428	0.700	0.932	0.755	0.785	0.955	0.822
RHB Bank	RHB	0.995	0.995	0.617	0.890	0.947	0.944	0.895	0.961	0.930
Sabah Bank	SBH	0.599	0.986	0.378						
Southern Bank	SBB	0.916	0.964	0.492	0.835	0.950	0.880	0.871	0.926	0.942
Pacific Bank	PAC	0.758	0.984	0.423						
Wah Tat Bank	WTB	0.523	0.969	0.309						
ABN-Amro Bank	ABN	0.587	0.843	0.580	0.693	0.945	0.791	0.843	0.896	0.942
Bangkok Bank	BBB	0.738	0.849	0.453	0.568	0.972	0.586	0.958	0.988	0.969
Bank of America	BOA	0.544	0.794	0.536	0.352	0.522	0.957	0.788	0.954	0.826
Bank of Nova Scotia	BNS	1.000	1.000	1.000	0.875	0.875	1.000	0.751	0.911	0.831
Bank of Tokyo	BOT	0.944	0.944	0.903	0.951	0.951	1.000	0.947	0.947	1.000
Citibank	CIT	0.891	0.988	0.628	0.922	0.971	0.949	0.985	0.985	1.000
Deutsche Bank	DEU	0.784	0.784	0.877	0.816	0.816	1.000	0.963	0.992	0.971
Hongkong Bank	HBB	0.952	0.994	0.475	0.627	0.948	0.665	1.000	1.000	1.000
JP Morgan Chase	JPM	1.000	1.000	1.000	1.000	1.000	1.000	0.816	0.968	0.843
OCBC Bank	OCB	0.989	0.995	0.593	0.861	0.945	0.914	0.759	0.941	0.805
OUB Bank	OUB	0.959	0.998	0.825	1.000	1.000	1.000	0.892	0.972	0.916
Standard Chartered Bank	SCB	0.996	0.996	0.549	0.909	0.952	0.955	0.887	0.975	0.909
UOB Bank	UOB	0.860	0.962	0.609	0.799	0.923	0.870	0.858	0.940	0.916
Mean		0.835	0.951	0.574	0.819	0.927	0.885	0.869	0.955	0.870

* 1997-1999; ** 2000; *** 2001-2003.

CE – Cost Efficiency; AE –Allocative Efficiency; TE – Technical Efficiency.

The results from the parametric *t*-test are further confirmed by the non-parametric Mann-Whitney [Wilcoxon] and Kruskal-Wallis tests. On the other hand, it is clear that the Malaysian banking sector has also exhibited a higher AE during the post merger period (0.95000 < 0.95376), but is not statistically significant at any conventional levels. However, both the non-parametric Mann-Whitney [Wilcoxon] and Kruskal-Wallis tests suggest that the difference is statistically significant at the 5% level (z and $\chi^2 = 0.038$). Thus, we conclude that the Malaysian banking sector has exhibited a higher CE during the post merger period mainly attributed to the improvement in TE.

Table 4. Summary of Parametric and Non-Parametric Tests

	Test Groups					
	Parametric Test		Non-Parametric Test			
Individual Tests	*t*-test		Mann-Whitney [Wilcoxon Rank-Sum] test		Kruskall-Wallis Equality of Populations test	
Hypotheses			$Median_{Acquirer}=Median_{Target}$			
Test Statistics	t (Prb > t)		z (Prb > z)		χ^2 (Prb > χ^2)	
	Mean	t	Mean Rank	z	Mean Rank	χ^2
Cost Efficiency (CE)						
Pre Merger	0.83328	-1.237	83.80	-0.064	83.80	0.004
Post Merger	0.86530		84.28		84.28	
Allocative Efficiency (AE)						
Pre Merger	0.95000	-0.284	90.55	-2.075**	90.55	4.306**
Post Merger	0.95376		74.93		74.93	
Technical Efficiency (TE)						
Pre Merger	0.57555	-11.261***	58.64	-8.013***	58.64	64.203***
Post Merger	0.89896		119.14		119.14	

Note: Test methodology follows among others, Aly et al. (1990), Elyasiani and Mehdian (1992), and Isik and Hassan (2002).

***, **, * indicates significant at the 0.01%, 0.05%, and 0.10% levels respectively.

4.2. Are the Acquirers the More Efficient Banks?

We now turn to the assessment of how the mergers and consolidation process affects the CE of the involved banks. First, we analyze the pre merger performance of the banks concerned. Theoretically, the more efficient banks should acquire the less efficient ones. A more efficient bank is assumed to be well organized, and has a more capable management. The idea is that since there is room for improvement concerning the performance of the less efficient bank, a takeover by a more efficient bank will lead to a transfer of the better management quality to the inefficient bank. This will in turn lead to a more efficient and better performing merged unit. In order to see whether indeed it is the case that banks that are more efficient acquire the inefficient ones, we calculate the difference in the technical

efficiency between the acquiring and the acquired banks. This efficiency difference is measured as the mean CE of the acquiring banks, minus the mean CE of the acquired banks for the last observation period before consolidation.

It is clear from Table 5 that during the pre merger period, in all of the seven merger cases analyzed the acquirers were relatively more cost efficient compared to the targets. In the next step, we again perform a series of parametric (*t*-test) and non-parametric (Mann-Whitney [Wilcoxon] and Kruskal-Wallis) tests to verify whether the difference between the acquirers' and targets' efficiencies. The results are presented in Table 6.

Table 5. Summary of Mean Efficiency Levels of Targets and Acquirers Banks

Bank	Target/Acquirer	Acquirer More Efficient Than Target	Pre Merger		
			CE	AE	TE
			AFF + BSN		
Affin Bank	ACQUIRER	YES	0.883	0.972	0.533
BSN Commercial Bank	TARGET		0.683	0.780	0.591
			ALB + SBH		
Alliance Bank	ACQUIRER	YES	0.914	0.988	0.539
Sabah Bank	TARGET		0.599	0.986	0.378
			EON + OBB		
EON Bank	ACQUIRER	YES	0.903	0.966	0.517
Oriental Bank	TARGET		0.840	0.988	0.450
			HLB + WTB		
Hong Leong Bank	ACQUIRER	YES	0.895	0.981	0.462
Wah Tat Bank	TARGET		0.523	0.969	0.309
			MBB + PAC		
Maybank	ACQUIRER	YES	0.998	0.998	0.519
Pacific Bank	TARGET		0.758	0.984	0.423
			PBB + HHB		
Public Bank	ACQUIRER	YES	0.959	0.990	0.428
Hock Hua Bank	TARGET		0.733	0.987	0.355
			SBB + BHL		
Southern Bank	ACQUIRER	YES	0.916	0.964	0.492
Bank Hin Lee Bank	TARGET		0.759	0.959	0.413

CE – Cost Efficiency; AE –Allocative Efficiency; TE – Technical Efficiency.
The font in bold indicate banking group that is relatively more efficient.

The results seem to suggest that the acquirer were relatively more cost efficient (0.92395 > 0.69910) and is statistically significant at the 1% level (*p*-value = 0.000), mainly attributed to a higher TE (0.49852 > 0.41695) and is statistically significant at the 5% level (*p*-value = 0.015). The target banks were also found to be relatively less allocatively efficient compared

to the acquiring banks (0.97981 > 0.95029) although is not statistically significant at any conventional levels.

The *t*-test results are further confirmed by the results derived from the Mann-Whitney [Wilcoxon] and Kruskal-Wallis tests. We therefore can conclude that the acquiring banks were relatively more cost efficient compared to the target banks mainly attributed to a higher technical efficiency.

4.3. The Determinants of Bank Efficiency

Regression results focusing on the relationship between bank efficiency and the explanatory variables are presented in Table 7. The equations are based on 193 bank year observations during the period 1997-2003. As pointed out by Saxonhouse (1976), heteroscedasticity can emerge when estimated parameters are used as dependent variables in the second stage analysis. Thus, following Hauner (2005) and Pasiouras (2007) among others, QML (Huber/White) standard errors and covariates are calculated. Several general comments regarding the test results are warranted. The model performs reasonably well in at least two respects. For one, results for most variables remain stable across the various regressions tested. Secondly, the findings suggest that all explanatory variables have the expected signs and in most cases are statistically different from zero.

Table 6. Summary of Parametric and Non-Parametric Tests

	Test Groups					
	Parametric Test		Non-Parametric Test			
Individual Tests	*t*-test		Mann-Whitney [Wilcoxon Rank-Sum] test		Kruskall-Wallis Equality of Populations test	
Hypotheses			$Median_{Acquirer}$=$Median_{Target}$			
Test Statistics	t (Prb > t)		z (Prb > z)		χ^2 (Prb > χ^2)	
	Mean	t	Mean Rank	z	Mean Rank	χ^2
Cost Efficiency (CE)						
Acquiring Banks	0.92395		30.74		30.74	
Target Banks	0.69910	-6.137***	12.26	-4.897***	12.26	23.980***
Allocative Efficiency (AE)						
Acquiring Banks	0.97981		24.02		24.02	
Target Banks	0.95029	-1.348	18.98	-1.338	18.98	1.790
Technical Efficiency (TE)						
Acquiring Banks	0.49852	-2.546**	25.93	-2.340**	25.93	5.474**
Target Banks	0.41695		17.07		17.07	

Note: Test methodology follows among others, Aly et al. (1990), Elyasiani and Mehdian (1992), and Isik and Hassan (2002).

***, **, * indicates significant at the 0.01%, 0.05%, and 0.10% levels respectively.

Table 7. Multivariate Tobit Regression Analysis

$$\gamma_{jt} = \alpha + \beta_1 \text{LNDEPO} + \beta_2 \text{LOANS/TA} + \beta_3 \text{LNTA} + \beta_4 \text{LLP/TL} + \beta_5 \text{NII/TA} + \beta_6 \text{NIE/TA} + \beta_7 \text{EQASS} + \beta_8 \text{DUMACQ} + \beta_9 \text{CON\_GRP} + \zeta_{10} \text{LNGDP} + \zeta_{11} \text{CR\_3} + \zeta_{12} \text{PRE\_MER} + \zeta_{13} \text{POST\_MER} + \varepsilon_j$$

The dependent variable is bank's cost efficiency scores derived from the DEA. LNDEPO is a measure of bank's market share calculated as a natural logarithm of total deposits. LOANS/TA is a measure of loans intensity calculated as the ratio of total loans to total bank assets. LNTA is a proxy measure of bank size measured as the natural logarithm of total bank assets. LLP/TL is a proxy measure of risk calculated as the ratio of total loan loss provisions divided by total loans. NIE/TA is a measure of bank management quality calculated as total non-interest expenses divided by total assets. NII/TA is a measure of bank's diversification towards non-interest income, calculated as total non-interest income divided by total assets. EQASS is a measure of capitalization measured by banks' total shareholders equity divided by total assets. LNGDP is natural logarithm of gross domestic product. DUMACQ is a binary variable that takes a value of 1 if a bank is an acquiring bank, 0 otherwise. CON_GRP is a binary variable that takes a value of 1 if a bank does not involve in any merger during the years, 0 otherwise. CR_3 is the 3 bank concentration ratio. PRE_MER is a binary variable that takes a value of 1 for the pre merger years, 0 otherwise. POST_MER is binary variable that takes a value of 1 for the post merger years, 0 otherwise.
Values in parentheses are z-statistics
***, **, and * indicate significance at 1, 5, and 10% levels.

	Model 1	Model 2	Model 3
CONSTANT	0.033503	0.555323	2.851602
	(0.024409)	(0.296216)	(1.398936)
Bank Characteristics			
LNDEPO	-0.132731***	-0.133582***	-0.142583***
	(-3.170883)	(-3.191900)	(-3.796337)
LOANS/TA	0.384778***	0.384370***	0.382405***
	(3.643812)	(3.641999)	(3.751492)
LNTA	0.187428***	0.189415***	0.198570***
	(4.122873)	(4.188661)	(4.854654)
LLP/TL	0.576919***	0.566038**	0.562391**
	(2.100929)	(2.074357)	(2.130303)
NII/TA	9.804759***	9.699273***	8.573176***
	(6.839889)	(6.819815)	(6.454208)
NIE/TA	-10.30275***	-10.26364***	-9.171609***
	(-5.572294)	(-5.543964)	(-5.203553)
EQASS	0.523860***	0.520757***	0.445261***
	(3.467039)	(3.479499)	(2.993309)
DUMACQ		-0.010251	
		(-0.568562)	
CON_GRP			0.054468***
			(3.198932)
Economic/ Market Conditions			
LNGDP	-0.054484	-0.097765	-0.339190
	(-0.356242)	(-0.538183)	(-1.545575)
CR_3	0.005531	0.004198	0.010315
	(0.601277)	(0.419263)	(1.006072)
PRE_MER		-0.012026	
		(-0.384468)	
POST_MER			0.045627*
			(1.724996)
Log likelihood	136.1750	136.3407	142.3594
R^2	0.458806	0.459735	0.492401
Adj. R^2	0.429070	0.423717	0.458562
No. of Observations	193	193	193

In models 2 and 3 regressions when we add the other group of variables to the baseline specification that include the bank specific attribute variables, the coefficients of the baseline variables stay mostly the same: they keep the same sign, the same order of magnitude, they remain significant as they were so in model 1 regressions (albeit sometimes at different levels), and with few exceptions, do not become significant if they were not in model 1 regressions. Therefore, for models 2 and 3 regressions, we will only discuss the results of the new variables added to the baseline specification.

The proxy for market power, LNDEPO reveals a negative relationship and is statistically significant at the 1% level, suggesting that the more cost efficient banks are associated with banks with a lower market share. On the other hand, LOANS/TA reveals a positive relationship and is statistically significant at the 1% level. The findings imply that banks with higher loans-to-asset ratios tend to have higher cost efficiency scores.

Thus, bank loans seem to be more highly valued than alternative bank outputs i.e. investments and securities. Likewise, LNTA shows positive coefficients suggesting that the larger the bank, the more efficient the bank will be, purely because of the economies of scale arguments. Hauner (2005) offers two potential explanations for which size could have a positive impact on bank efficiency. First, if it relates to market power, large banks should pay less for their inputs. Second, there may be increasing returns to scale through the allocation of fixed costs (e.g. research or risk management) over a higher volume of services or from efficiency gains from a specialized workforce. Thus, assuming that the average cost curve for Malaysian banks is U-shaped, the recent growth policies of the small and medium Malaysian banks seem to be consistent with cost minimization.

The coefficient of LLP/TL entered all regression models with a positive sign, which is in consonance with Berger and DeYoung's (1997) *skimping* hypothesis. To recap, Berger and DeYoung (1997) suggests that under the *skimping* hypothesis, a bank maximizing long run profits may rationally choose to have lower costs in the short run by skimping on the resources devoted to underwriting and monitoring loans, but bear the consequences of greater loan performance problems. Similarly, the empirical findings seem to suggest that NII/TA has consistently exhibit strong positive and significant relationship with CE. The elasticity and CE with respect to NII/TA is quite high and is statistically significant at the 1% level. The results imply that banks tend to become more efficient as they increase their income from non-interest sources.

The results seem to suggest that NIE/TA has consistently exhibit negative relationship with bank efficiency and is statistically significant at the 1% level. The finding is in consonance with the *bad management* hypotheses of Berger and DeYoung (1997). Low measure of cost efficiency is a signal of poor senior management practices, which apply to input-usage and day-to-day operations. Clearly, efficient cost management is a prerequisite for the improved efficiency of the Malaysian banking system i.e. the high elasticity of cost efficiency to this variable denotes that banks have much to gain if they improve their managerial practices.

EQASS exhibits positive relationship with bank cost efficiency in all regression models. The empirical findings seem to suggest that the more cost efficient banks, *ceteris paribus*, use less leverage (more equity) compared to their less efficient peers. The findings may also imply that the more efficient banks are involved in riskier operations and in the process tend to hold more equity, voluntarily or involuntarily, i.e. the reason may be due to deliberate efforts by banks to increase the safety cushions.

Interestingly, after controlling for other bank specific traits and macroeconomic variables, we do not find a significant relationship between the acquiring banks (DUMACQ) and cost efficiency. It can be observed from Table 7 that the control group banks are relatively more efficient compared to the banks that have been involved in mergers and acquisitions during the period under study. A plausible reason is that more than 80% of the banks in the control group are foreign banks. Thus, this should come as no surprise because of the ability of the foreign owned banks to capitalize on their access to better risk management and operational techniques, which is usually made available through their parent banks abroad.

During the period under study, the empirical findings seem to suggest that macroeconomic conditions (LNGDP) and the three bank concentration ratio (CR_3) do not significantly explain the variations in Malaysian banks' cost efficiency. Similarly, the binary variable PRE_MER do not enter the regression model significantly. On the other hand, the variable POST_MER entered the regression model with a positive sign suggesting that the Malaysian banking sector has been relatively more cost efficient during the post merger period compared to the pre merger period. However, the results should be interpreted with caution as the coefficient of the variable is weak and is only statistically significant at the 10% level.

Conclusions and Directions for Future Research

Applying a non-parametric frontier Data Envelopment Analysis (DEA) approach, the paper investigates the effects of mergers and acquisitions on the cost efficiency of the Malaysian banking sector. The sample period is divided into three sub-periods, i.e. pre merger, during merger, and post merger to compare the differences in the Malaysian banking sector's mean cost, allocative, and technical efficiency levels during all periods. A multivariate Tobit model is employed to examine the relationship between cost efficiency and size, capitalization, and risk.

The results from the DEA suggest that Malaysian banks have exhibited mean cost efficiency of 83.5% during the pre merger period, suggesting mean input waste of 16.5%. We find that during the merger year, Malaysian banks' cost efficiency level deteriorated slightly to 81.9%, which was mainly due to technical rather allocative inefficiency. Despite that, during the post merger period, Malaysian banks have exhibited higher mean cost efficiency levels compared to the pre merger period. The empirical findings seem to suggest that the improvement in cost efficiency during the post merger period was largely attributed to the improvement in technical rather than allocative efficiency. We find that the acquirers have been relatively more cost efficient in all of the seven merger cases analyzed.

The results from the multivariate regression analysis suggest that LNDEPO has a negative relationship with cost efficiency, implying that the more cost efficient banks are associated with banks with a lower market share. On the other hand, LOANS/TA reveals a positive relationship implying that banks with higher loans-to-asset ratios tend to have higher cost efficiency scores. LNTA shows positive coefficients suggesting that the larger the bank, the more efficient the bank will be, purely because of the economies of scale arguments. The coefficient of LLP/TL entered all regression models with a positive sign, which is in consonance with Berger and DeYoung's (1997) *skimping* hypothesis. Similarly, the empirical findings seem to suggest that NII/TA has consistently exhibits strong positive and significant

relationship with CE. The results imply that banks tend to become more efficient as they increase their income from non-interest sources.

The findings seem to suggest that NIE/TA consistently exhibit negative relationship with bank efficiency levels. The finding is in consonance with Berger and DeYoung's (1997) *bad management* hypothesis. Clearly, efficient cost management is a prerequisite for the improved efficiency of the Malaysian banking system. EQASS exhibits positive relationship with bank cost efficiency suggesting that the more cost efficient banks, *ceteris paribus*, use less leverage (more equity). The findings may also imply that the more cost efficient banks are involved in riskier operations and in the process tend to hold more equity, voluntarily or involuntarily.

We do not find a significant relationship between the acquiring banks (DUMACQ) and cost efficiency. On the other hand, the findings suggest that the control group banks are relatively more efficient compared to the banks that have been involved in mergers and acquisitions. A plausible reason is that more than 80% of the banks in the control group are foreign banks. Thus, the empirical findings seem to suggest that the foreign banks have succeeded in capitalizing on their advantages and exhibit a higher level of cost efficiency compared to their domestic bank peers.

The results seem to suggest that Malaysian banks have been relatively more efficient during the post merger compared to the pre merger period. However, the coefficient of the variable is weak and is only statistically significant at the 10% level. On the other hand, the empirical findings seem to suggest that macroeconomic conditions, the three bank concentration ratio, and the pre merger period do not significantly explain the variations in Malaysian banks' cost efficiency.

Due to its limitations the paper could be extended in a variety of ways. Firstly, future research into the efficiency of Malaysian banks could consider the production function along with the intermediation function used in this study. Secondly, the non-parametric frontier analysis used in this paper could also be combined with the stochastic frontier analysis method of estimating the frontier. This should testify to the robustness of the results against alternative estimation methods. Finally, investigation of changes in productivity over time as a result of technical change or technological progress or regress by employing the Malmquist Total Factor Productivity Index could yet be another extension to the current paper.

REFERENCES

Aly, H.Y., Grabowski, R., Pasurka, C. and Rangan, N. (1990), Technical, Scale and Allocative Efficiencies in U.S. Banking: An Empirical Investigation, *Review of Economics and Statistics* 72, 211-218.

Avkiran, N.K. (1999), The Evidence on Efficiency Gains: The Role of Mergers and the Benefits to the Public, *Journal of Banking and Finance* 23, 991-1013.

Beitel, P. and Schiereck, D. (2001), Value Creation at the Ongoing Consolidation of the European Banking Market, Working Paper, University of Witten/Herdecke.

Berger, A.N. and DeYoung (1997), Problem Loans and Cost Efficiency in Commercial Banks, *Journal of Banking and Finance* 21, 849-870.

Berger, A.N. and Mester, L.J. (2003), Explaining the Dramatic Changes in Performance of U.S. Banks: Technological Change, Deregulation and Dynamic Changes in Competition, *Journal of Financial Intermediation* 12, 57-95.

Berger, A.N., Demsetz, R. and Strahan, P. (1999), The Consolidation of the Financial Services Industry: Causes, Consequences and Implications for the Future, *Journal of Banking and Finance* 23, 135-194.

Charnes, A., Cooper, W.W. and Rhodes, E. (1978), Measuring the Efficiency of Decision Making Units, *European Journal of Operational Research* 2, 429-444.

Coelli, T., Prasada-Rao, D.S. and Battese, G.E. (1998). *An Introduction to Efficiency and Productivity Analysis.* Boston: Kluwer Academic Publishers.

Coelli, T. (1996), A Guide to DEAP Version 2.1: A Data Envelopment Analysis (Computer Program), Working Paper, CEPA, University of New England, Armidale.

Elyasiani, E. and Mehdian, S. (1992), Productive Efficiency Performance of Minority and Non-Minority Owned Banks: A Non-Parametric Approach, *Journal of Banking and Finance* 16, 933-948.

Fare, R., Grosskopf, S. and Lovell, C.A.K. (1985), *The Measurement of Efficiency of Production.* Boston: Kluwer-Nijhoff Publishers.

Hauner, D. (2005), Explaining Efficiency Differences Among Large German and Austrian Banks, *Applied Economics* 37, 969-980.

Isik, I. and Hassan, M.K. (2002), Technical, Scale and Allocative Efficiencies of Turkish Banking Industry, *Journal of Banking and Finance* 26, 719-766.

Liu, B. and Tripe, D. (2002), New Zealand Bank Mergers and Efficiency Gains, *Journal of Asia Pacific Business* 4, 61-81.

Okuda, H. and Hashimoto, H. (2004), Estimating Cost Functions of Malaysian Commercial Banks: The Differential Effects of Size, Location and Ownership, *Asian Economic Journal* 18, 233-259.

Pasiouras, F. (2007), Estimating the Technical and Scale Efficiency of Greek Commercial Banks: The Impact of Credit Risk, Off-Balance Sheet Activities, and International Operations, forthcoming in *Research in International Business and Finance.*

Prager, R.A. and Hannan, T.H. (1998), Do Substantial Horizontal Mergers Generate Significant Price Effects? Evidence from the Banking Industry, *Journal of Industrial Economics* 46, 433-454.

Rhoades, S.A. (1998), The Efficiency Effects of Bank Mergers: An Overview of Case Studies of Nine Mergers, *Journal of Banking and Finance* 22, 273-291.

Sathye, M. (2001), X-Efficiency in Australian Banking: An Empirical Investigation, *Journal of Banking and Finance* 25, 613-630.

Saxonhouse, G.R. (1976), Estimated Parameters as Dependent Variables, *American Economic Review* 66, 178-183.

Sufian, F. and Majid, M.Z.A. (2007), Deregulation, Consolidation and Banks Efficiency in Singapore: Evidence from Event Study Window Approach and Tobit Analysis, *International Review of Economics* 54 (2), 261-283.

Sufian, F. (2007), Mergers and Acquisitons in the Malaysian Banking Industry: Techncial and Scale Efficiency Effects, *International Journal of Financial Services Management* 2 (4), 304-326.

Reviewed by:
(1) Professor Dr. Muzafar Shah Habibullah, Department of Economics,
Faculty of Economics and Management, Universiti Putra Malaysia
(2) Dr. Law Siong Hook, Department of Economics,
Faculty of Economics and Management, Universiti Putra Malaysia

In: Business and Finance: Performance and Management ISBN: 978-1-61122-936-3
Editors: R. Morland and A. Gagglione

Chapter 6

THE CHANGING FACE OF INTERNATIONAL HRM AND BUSINESS: CASE STUDIES OF JAPANESE AND TAIWANESE COMPANIES OPERATING IN CHINA

***Ying Zhu*[*], *Imogen Chen*[**] *and Takamichi Mito*[***]**

[*]Department of Management and Marketing,
The University of Melbourne, VIC 3010, Australia
[**]School of Communication, Culture and Languages,
Victoria University, VIC. 8001, Australia
[***]Department of Japanese Studies,
The Chinese University of Hong Kong,
Shatin, N.T., Hong Kong

ABSTRACT

Under the influence of globalization, different international business strategies require the support of unique international human resource management (HRM) policies and practices in order to make the business successful. A critical challenge is how to integrate international business strategies and international HRM. The increasing debate on this topic highlights the problems in balancing the policies of HQ control, global integration and localization. However, the difficulty is how to achieve a balanced approach between these policies in reality.

This chapter looks at the integration between international business strategies and international HRM by carrying out case studies of Japanese and Taiwanese companies operating in China. There are several reasons for carrying out this research: 1. China is one of the most dynamic economies in East Asia. It has both huge amounts of FDI and many multinational enterprises (MNEs) operating within its borders. This research will have general implications of MNEs operating in one of the largest emerging economies in East Asia. 2. Japanese and Taiwanese MNEs have been the leaders in terms of offshore investment and production in East Asia. In fact, both Japanese and Taiwanese MNEs are the leading groups of foreign investors in China and other parts of Asia. By investigating these two types of MNEs,

[*] Tel: 61-3-83449771; Fax: 61-3-93494293; Email: y.zhu@unimelb.edu.au

we will have a better understanding of their strategic considerations regarding offshore investment and business operations as well as their approach towards the integration of international business strategies and international HRM. The feedback from of this project will benefit Japanese and Taiwanese MNEs as well as other MNEs for future successful operation in China.

Following the central theme of this research project, we are most interested in the following perspectives of these cases: 1. their international business strategies, vision and goals; 2. their different international staffing strategies, such as using parent country nationals (PCN), third country nationals (TCN) and host country nationals (HCN); 3. the roles of headquarters (HQ) vs. subsidiary in terms of business strategy formulation, control and evaluation; 4. the detailed policies and practices of global integration and localization; 5. the future direction for improvement.

In order to have a comprehensive understanding of the relevant issues, we have set out this chapter as follows: Section 2 reviews the relevant literature that is related to a balanced approach of global integration and localization. Section 3 details the case studies and the investigation of the detailed policies and practices in relation to the five perspectives identified above. Section 4 discusses our findings and Section 5 concludes the chapter by highlighting our major findings and implications for both theoretical understanding as well as for empirical practice. Section 5 concludes the chapter by identifying the unique research outcomes of this project, the limitation as well as future research direction.

1. INTRODUCTION

Different international business strategies require the support of unique international HRM policies and practices in order to make the business successful. A critical challenge is how to integrate international business strategies and international HRM. The increasing debate on this topic concerns the choice between the policies of HQ control, global integration and local responsiveness (Evans et al., 2002). However, the difficulty arises in how to achieve a balanced approach between these policies in reality. Traditional practice among MNEs emphases HQ control, but this becomes increasingly problematic due to a lack of flexibility and business integration within local markets. Recently, some MNEs have emerged with global experience and have redirected their focus towards global integration with certain efforts of localization policies in order to correct the weakness brought by the of HQ control Model.

This research project aims to analyze the balanced approach strategy of integration between international business strategies and international HRM through case studies of Japanese and Taiwanese companies operating in China. There are several reasons for developing this project: 1.) China is one of the most dynamic economies in East Asia with huge FDI and many MNEs operating in China. The outcome of this research will have have general implications for MNEs operating in one of the largest emerging economies in East Asia. 2.) Japanese and Taiwanese MNEs have been the leaders in terms of offshore investment and production in East Asia. They are also the major source of foreign investment in China (and other parts of Asia). By investigating these two types of MNEs, this paper aims to provide a better understanding about the strategies used in making offshore investments, general business operations, and the basic integration between international business strategies and international HRM. The feedback from this project will benefit Japanese and Taiwanese MNEs as well as other MNEs with an eye for future successful business operations in China.

We are particularly interested in the following perspectives of these cases studied: 1.) their international business strategies, vision and goals; 2.) their different international staffing strategies, such as using parent country nationals (PCNs), third country nationals (TCNs) and home country nationals (HCNs); 3.) the role of HQ vs. subsidiaries in terms of business strategy formulation, control and evaluation; 4.) the detailed policies and practices of global integration and localization; and 5.) future areas for improvement.

In order to have a comprehensive understanding of the relevant issues, we have set out this chapter as follows: Section 2 reviews the relevant literature that is related to a balanced approach of global integration and localization. Section 3 details the case studies and the investigation of the detailed policies and practices in relation to the five perspectives identified above. Section 4 discusses our findings and Section 5 concludes the chapter by highlighting our major findings and implications for both theoretical understanding as well as for empirical practice.

2. Global Integration and Localization

The key element crucial to this topic is about the challenge of international HRM: how to operate an international business in an interconnected world where people are the source of sustainable competitive advantage (Evans et al., 2002). The field of international HRM has extended from an initial focus on managing expatriation to more complicated issues, such as localization of management, international coordination, global leadership development, cultural due diligence and integration (ibid). It is difficult to handle global integration and localization and it seems that a balance between the two is the key. Another challenge is that the complexities of international business are no longer restricted to large MNEs but are also of concern for small to medium-sized enterprises (SMEs) (Brewster and Scullion, 1997). Size influences or determines the behavior and performance of companies in their business strategies and related HR policies and practices (Ding et al., 2000).

The evolution of international HRM literature has led to an increasing consideration of integrating international business with international HRM policies and practices (Bartlett and Ghoshal, 1989; Porter, 1986; Prahalad and Doz, 1987). The importance of MNEs of adopting an international orientation in both business operations and people-management is critical for international business success. Recent research into international HRM has acknowledged the importance of linking HR policies and practices to organizational strategy, resulting in a literature on strategic international HRM (Schuler et al., 1993; De Cieri and Dowling, 1999; Brewster et al., 2005). New areas of investigation on strategic international HRM include the link between strategy-structure configuration in MNEs and demands for global integration, as opposed to the need for local responsiveness (Whitley, 1992; Rosenzweig and Nohria, 1994; Sparrow and Hiltrop, 1994). Those favoring a global integration perspective view it as highly important to maximize global integration and coordination, and to ensure that subsidiaries are globally integrated with other parts of the company or/and strategically coordinated by the parent company. In contrast, those holding a local responsiveness perspective consider it mandatory to be highly responsive to the local situation,, and allow subsidiaries to enjoy as much autonomy as possible. There is less need for integration in this instance (Brewster et al., 2005). However, the current literature on these two perspectives is dealt in a contradictory manner. However, in reality, integrating both perspectives in a balanced way is a more

realistic approach. Therefore, our design of this research project is to seek to identify some key features of such a balanced approach.

So far, the published research on Japanese and Taiwanese companies' international business and IHRM in China have focused on areas such as business strategies and performance (Zhu, 2006), international and local staffing strategies (Delios and Bjorkman, 2000; Zhu, 2006), control and coordination between HQ and subsidiary (Legewie, 2002; Zhu, 2006), strategies of localization (Zhu, 2006), and general illustration of key factors influencing HRM practices of overseas subsidiaries in China (Farley et al., 2004). Generally speaking, Zhu (2006) explores and summarizes the general trends of business strategies and performance found in Japanese and Taiwanese companies operating in China. According to Zhu, the key driving factor for Japanese companies operating in China is to occupy a substantial market with two strategic goals, namely, to implement strategies of localization and to strengthen their uniqueness or difference (ibid). As for their Taiwanese counterparts, their major goal is to relocate their production to China in order to reduce the cost of production (mainly labor costs). In the end, HQ is responsible for most decision making in securing a long-term strategic future, identifying success factors for local effectiveness and global integration, receiving orders and directing RandD, while the subsidiaries focus on manufacturing and sales in the local market (ibid).

On international and local staffing strategies, Delios and Bjorkman (2000) claim that Japanese expatriates are performing two primary functions, that is to say, the control function and knowledge transference function. Both functions are responsibilities largely assumed by expatriates in their operations in China. However, due to a lack of experience in China, Japanese MNEs tend to encourage subsidiaries to employ more competent local mangers; however, a problem arises in that there is a short supply of capable local managers (ibid). In contrast, Taiwanese companies are more familiar with the social customs and culture in China; they are thus more willing to let go of local control and regional autonomy to their subsidiaries (Zhu, 2006). In terms of staffing, an increasing number of HCNs have been promoted into higher ranking management positions and IHRM in Taiwanese companies can be identified as being a regiocentric nature (Zhu, 2006). In addition, PCNs from Taiwan tend to live permanently in China and localize themselves by way of marrying local people or relocating the whole family from Taiwan to mainland China. By comparison, Japanese PCNs still follow a rotation arrangement of about 4-year expatriate duration, which makes it hardly possible for the PCNs to develop an in-depth understanding of the Chinese local culture, social customs, mentality, business practices or the characteristics of the local market. All these are potentially useful and helpful to their business operations in China (ibid).

The issues of HQ control and coordination and strategies of localization have become increasingly important. Legewie's (2002) research analyzes the international management control system that Japanese MNEs employ to coordinate the activities of their subsidiaries in China. The findings indicate that Japanese expatriate-focused models continue to be characterized by an insider-outsider mentality, which prevents a real internationalization of overseas operations in the 'transnational' sense. The existing system creates problems such as unpopularity of Japanese companies as employers among Chinese employees when compared with their US and European competitors (Ma, 1998), and a lack of flexibility in market response (Legewie, 2002). As for Taiwanese companies, the different role and responsibility between HQ and the subsidiary are clearly designated (Zhu, 2006). HQ retains complete control in decision-making and in directing the business, while the subsidiaries focus on

controlling production and recruiting and managing HCNs (ibid). In addition, many Taiwanese companies have gradually expanded their subsidiaries in the mainland with a scale larger than their HQs in Taiwan. There is also an increasing trend of relocating most business operations to mainland China and just retaining a small proportion of business, such as RandD and marketing, in Taiwan. This business trend requires further localization strategies (ibid). By conducting a survey of 286 foreign subsidiaries from the US, Japan and Germany operating in China, Farley et al. (2004) identified significant differences in financial control from HQ, organizational form, and time length since entry. In fact, the push factors from the parent-firm economic considerations and venture structure and the pull factors such as local conditions and the norm of local HRM practices both play significant roles in influencing the HRM practices of their subsidiaries in China.

Based on these key aspects of existing research areas, we have designed this research project to explore the relevant issues by addressing the following research questions: 1.) What are the major international business strategic goals and what impact will the chosen strategic goals likely have on the international staffing strategies? 2.) What are the roles of HQ vs. subsidiary in terms of business strategy formulation, control and evaluation? 3.) How do MNEs handle the challenge in balancing HQ control and localization?

3. Case Studies

In order to tackle the three key questions mentioned above, fieldwork was conducted involving a visit and a 2-hour interview with MNEs in China. These MNEs included 10 Japanese-owned companies operating in Hong Kong and Guangdong Province, 8 Taiwanese-owned companies operating in Guangdong Province (i.e. Dongguan and Zhongshan), Jiangsu Province (ie. Suzhou and Jiaxing),and Shanghai. Interviewees were either senior managers or HR managers of the company. Of the 18 companies interviewed, 16 were wholly-owned foreign companies (10 Japanese and 6 Taiwanese) and 2 joint ventures (both with Taiwanese capital). The ownership structure of these companies supports the argument made by Walsh and Zhu (2007) in that foreign investment in China shows a tendency of moving away from joint-ventures towards wholly-owned companies for better control and development in recent years. The case studies covered a cross-section of size (i.e. large-sized companies vs. small- and medium-sized companies), ownership (i.e. wholly-owned vs. joint-venture) and type of business (i.e. manufacturing, trade and services) (see Table 1). To keep these companies anonymous, each company was allocated a code between J1 and J10 for the Japanese-owned companies and T1 and T8 for the Taiwanese-owned companies.

International Business Strategies, Vision and Goals

Among our sample cases, there was a wide range of international business strategies, visions and goals. The key information on all these aspects is summarized in Table 2. The company visions, missions and goals, as identified by our sample companies, included: expanding international business, market competition and global network (7 cases),

Table 1. Company profiles (2007)

Company	Ownership	Age (years)	Location HQ/subsidiary	Employment Size	Business	Turnover (US$ mil)	Market	Position of Market Competition
J1	Wholly-owned	30	Tokyo/Hong Kong	800	Banking	>200	100% domestic	High
J2	Wholly-owned	12	Shizuoka/Hong Kong-Guangdong	27	Sales & services	>200	100% domestic	Medium
J3	Wholly-owned	36	Tokyo/Hong Kong	330	Import/export, sales & services	>44	96% domestic 4% overseas	High/medium
J4	Wholly-owned	45	Tokyo/Hong Kong	680	Sales	N/A	90% domestic 10% overseas	High
J5	Wholly-owned	16	Tokyo/Hong Kong	110	Manufacturing, sales & product procurement	>180	10% domestic 90% overseas	Medium
J6	Wholly-owned	30	Osaka/Hong Kong	38	Sales (of parent company's products)	>250	100% domestic	High
J7	Wholly-owned	19	Tokyo/Beijing-Hong Kong	170	Manufacturing logistics support and sales	>800	5% domestic 95% overseas	Medium
J8	Wholly-owned	4	Osaka/Hong Kong	4	Texture trading	>4	40% domestic 60% overseas	High
J9	Wholly-owned	5	Tokyo/Hong Kong	30	Manufacture & sale of electric machinery	>48	100% domestic	High
J10	Wholly-owned	28	Tokyo/Hong Kong	496	Manufacturing and sales Manufacture and trade of	>300	83% domestic 17% overseas	High

Company	Ownership	Age (years)	Location HQ/subsidiary	Employment Size	Business	Turnover (US$ mil)	Market	Position of Market Competition
T1	Wholly-owned	18	Tainan/Dongguan, Guilin, Jiaxing, Shanghai	20,000	textiles & footwear	>20,000	50% domestic 50% overseas	High
T2	Joint-venture	5	Taipei-Norway-Singapore/Beijing, Shanghai, Suzhou	1,000	Therapeutic services	>800	100% domestic	High
T3	Wholly-owned	9	Taipei/Zhongshan	700	Manufacture of electronic components	>30	2% domestic 98% overseas	Medium
T4	Joint-venture	17	Taipei/Shanghai	6	Trade of textiles machinery	N/A	100% domestic	Medium
T5	Wholly-owned	5	Tainan/Guangdong	20	Manufacture of metal products	>12	33% domestic 67% overseas	Medium
T6	Wholly-owned	7	Tainan/Dongguan	200	Manufacture & sale of medical instruments	N/A	100% overseas	Medium
T7	Wholly-owned	4	Tainan/Dongguan	200	Manufacture & sale of electronics	>20	100% overseas	High
T8	Wholly-owned	10	Tainan/Shanghai	10,000	Manufacture & sale of textiles	>25,000	70% domestic 30% overseas	High

Table 2. Contextual information of the cases

Company	Strategy/vision/ goals	Reason for investment	Any changesince establishment: 1. Capital 2. Employee	Ratio of management team: 1. PC N 2. TC N 3. HC N	Business strategy formulation: HQ vs. Subsidiary (S)	Business control & evaluation: HQ vs. Subsidiary (S)	Satisfaction with business performance
J1	Provide good service Building trust & global network	Market	1: No 2: Small no. of retrenchment & new recruitment of university graduates	1: 6 top & 64 mid-management 2: 0 3: 20 mid-management	HQ: global planning S: in put through discussion with HQ; 6-m, 1-y & 3-y plans: Profit target, assets, no. of new client and quality of service	HQ: use balance score card to evaluate performance of branch, group and individual S: report to HQ every month	Very satisfactory
J2	Increasing market sharein South China with good after-sale service	Goodlocation & market	1: No 2. Shift workforce to Southern China	1: 5 (3 in 1998) 2: 13 (2 in 1998) 3: 9 (8 in 1998)	S: making proposals, 6-m, 1-y & 3- y plans in consultation with HQ	HQ: evaluate performance against budget and target S: execute plans to meet corporategoals	Neither satisfactory nor dissatisfactory
J3	Innovation Creativity Advanced technology	Goodlocation Quality of labour Market	1: No 2: Expanding	1: 3 2: 0 3: 25	HQ: set up guidelines and approvethe plan submitted from S S: follow the guideline and make proposals	HQ: provide guidelines and advice S: evaluate monthly business & individual performance	Neither satisfactory nor dissatisfactory
J4	Good corporate citizen & reputation	Legal & regulatory systems Quality of labour Infrastructure	1: No 2: No	1: 19 (27 in 2003) 2: 2 (0 in 2003) 3: 120 (120 in 2003)	S: localized decision-making	HQ: Budgetcontrol S: Manage monthly targetof perfomance	Very satisfactory

		Goodlocation					
J5	Best services to customers	Goodlocation Infrastructure Legal & regulatory systems	1: No 2: Fluctuate regarding the business needs (decline in recent years)	1: 20 (74 in 1996) 2: 30 (50 in 1996) 3: 56 (186 in 1996)	S: take initial strategy in consultation with HQ	HQ: communication & evaluation of business performance S: execute and manage targets	Neither satisfactory nor dissatisfactory
J6	Excellent reputation & trust of customers	Market	1: No 2: Increase	1: 1 (4 in 2003) 2: 0 3: 11 (11 in 2003)	S: in charge of decision	HQ: evaluate the budget target S: monthly performance evaluation and report	Satisfactory
J7	Corporate social role and citizenship	Support production in China	1: 4-folded increase 2: Shift workforce to Southern China	1: 6 2: 0 3: 15	HQ: plan & policy formulation S: implementation & formulation of local business plan	HQ: control of corporate budget S: manage the realization of goals and performance	Satisfactory
J8	Conscience and wisdom	Goodlocation Quality of labour	1: No 2: Increase	1: 2 (1 in 2004) 2: 0 3: 2 (I in 2004)	S: in charge of decision	HQ: evaluate budget and performance S: evaluation of performance	Very satisfactory
J9	Environment, human health and safety and new energy	Infrastructure and market	1: No 2: Restructuring	1: 3 (2 in 2003) 2: 3 (0 in 2003) 3: 24 (2 in 2003)	HQ: initiate the principle S: formulate businessstrategy	HQ: set up standard and evaluate performance S: evaluate performance of PCN, TCN & HCN	Satisfied with sales Not satisfied with profit
J10	Living & working togethe for the common good	Market and goodlocation	1. Increase 2. Increase	1. 3 (17 in 2002) 2. 0 3. 64 (42 in 2002)	HQ: discussion and endorsement of subsidiary plan S: initiate annual	HQ: monitoring budget, plans and performance annually	Very satisfactory

Table 2. (Continued)

					and 3-year plans	S: developing and implementing local plans and budget	
T1	High quality & internationalization of business	Cost of doing business	1: Increase 2: Increase locals	1: 200 (replace the 2nd best team with the 1st bests team) 2: 0 3: 800	HQ: control over budget & HR S: operating production & sale	HQ: budget control & performance management S: implementation	Satisfactory
T2	Creating value and improve human health	Market	1: Increase 2: Increase	1: 2 2: 5 3: 0	HQ: determine business plan S: consultation with HQ on key decisions	HQ: set up goals and policies, monitoring performance S: operation and evaluation of performance	Very satisfactory
T3	Internationalization of business and reduction of cost	Cost of doing business Good location	1: No 2: Increase	1: 4 2: 0 3: 40	HQ: set up major policy S: implementation and decision-making autonomies	HQ: control budget, resources and allocation S: decision on local operation	Neither satisfactory nor dissatisfactory
T4	Extendng new market & opportunity	Market	1: Increase 2: Increase	1: 1 2: 1 3: 1	HQ: interference on key decisions, including HR S: some autonomies	HQ: total control S: responsible for sales & creating market	Neither satisfactory nor dissatisfactory
T5	Competition, network, speed, excellent services	Market and cheap labour with good quality	1: Increase 2: Increase	1: 2 (3 in 2002) 2: 0 3: 3 (0 in 2002)	HQ: in charge of business strategy S: implementation	HQ: total control through intranet S: managing daily production and business operation	Satisfactory
T6	R & D, creating new brand name	Cost of doing business	1: No 2: No	1: 5 (3 in 2000) 2: 0	HQ: in charge of business strategy	HQ: get business order & allocate	Neither satisfactory nor

		Goodlocation		3: 10 (8 in 2000)	S: manage production, quality and performance	resources S: manage daly operation and HRM /HRD	dissatisfactory
T7	Excellent customer services and new products	Market	1: Increase 2: Increase	1: 3 2: 0 3: 10	HQ: in charge of businessstrategy S: implementation & production	HQ: total control throughintranet and Tele-conference S: manage daly production and businessoperation	Neither satisfactory nor dissatisfactory
T8	Expanding market andimprove competitivenes	Market Cost of doing business	1: Increase 2: Increase	1: 100 (800 in 1990) 2: 0 3: 400 (100 in 1990)	HQ: set up the major policy and direction S: implementation	HQ: total control throughintranet, teleconference, frequentsite visit S: manage daly production and businesswith some autonomies	Satisfactory

developing good services and trust (6 cases), corporate reputation, social role (including environment, health and safety) and corporate citizenship (6 cases), innovation, quality and RandD (3 cases).

Some also mentioned conscience and wisdom, environment, health and safety, and reduction of costs. Although there was some overlap between the cases studied, it is clear there is a growing awareness of the importance of social responsibility and good corporate citizenship, in addition to the ability to compete in the rapidly expanding global market.

As for major reasons for investment (see Table 2), the majority identified market and location as their key reasons (16 cases). Other reasons mentioned were cost considerations for local businesses (5 cases), good quality of workers (3 cases), and good legal and regulatory systems (both cases were located in Hong Kong, where legal environment is different from the remainder of China). It was very clear that companies invest in China, particularly in Southern China, mainly because of the market potential and good location (e.g. closer to a port or developed economic areas). This is consistent with the information listed in Table 1 under market orientation, where most companies' registered their interest in the local market as a major reason for investments. This demonstrated that foreign companies came to China not only for exporting to overseas markets, but also for a growing interest in China's domestic market. The market economy has brought forth substantive increases in personal income and has resulted in stronger consumerism among domestic consumers.

In terms of business changes since their establishment (see Table 2), the majority of companies did not have much change in capital, but most had substantial changes in the areas of staffing.

International Staffing

International staffing strategies refer to a strategic use of PCNs, TCNs and HCNs (Evans et al., 2002). As indicated earlier in the literature review, there are different reasons and rationales, such as HQ control, HQ-subsidiary balanced relationship and local responsiveness, for choosing different types of employees. In general, our samples suggest a more localized HR employment. As a result of meeting market and management demands of more established subsidiaries (e.g. J4, J5, J6, J10, T1, T5, and T8), Table 2 demonstrates that the majority of companies have experienced an increase in the number of HCNs employed in managerial positions (15 cases), thus showing a reduction in the employment of PCNs. Moreover, as a result of business expansion at the subsidiary level, some companies have increased the number of managerial positions. These positions have been made available not only to PCNs but also to HCNs (eg. J2, J8, J9, and T6). Some companies have indicated that, after some speedy development of their business, the initial team of PCNs could not cope with the new challenges. A "more capable" new team of PCNs have thus been sent by their parent companies to replace the initial team. In the case of T1, the company originally relied on the second tier PCN team to set up and operate its subsidiaries in various regions, but the entire team has been replaced by the first tier PCN team in recent years in order to increase a chance for further globalization of its business. However, the use of TCNs is not common, particularly with Taiwanese-owned companies. Our interview data has shown that only a limited number of TCNs were employed, including 13 employed by J2, 2 by J4, 30 by J5, 3 by J9, 5 by T2, and 1 by T4. Most of these TCNs were expected to possess special skills in

either management or technology and have been recruited for special tasks that both PCNs and HCNs may not be able to provide within those organizations. A more detailed discussion on the major obstacles for the promotion of HCNs to senior management positions will follow.

HQ vs. Subsidiary: Strategy Formulation, Control and Evaluation

The roles of HQ vs. subsidiary in terms of business strategy formulation, control and evaluation are significant issues, as they determine the outcome of MNEs' international business approach as to whether HQ control or local responsiveness is favored. In our interviews, we asked two questions related to this issue. 1.) Who is in charge of business strategy formulation, HQ or subsidiary? 2.) How is the business being controlled and evaluated? As summarized in Table 2, despite the fact that there are overlaps in certain aspects across the models, three distinct models have been identified: Model 1 (M1): HQ dominant management, Model 2 (M2): HQ-subsidiary collaborative management, and Model 3 (M3): Localized management. Generally speaking, companies under M1 can be characterized as emphasizing a high level of HQ control through formation of business plans and policy, and controlling subsidiaries over budget, HR and performance management. Their subsidiaries are required to carry out frequent reporting, fully implementing HQ's plans and policies, along with managing daily production and business with limited autonomy. The HQ control is normally achieved by the use of an intranet and teleconferencing. Among our samples, J7, T1, T4, T5, T7 and T8 can be categorized as being M1.

As for M2, key characteristics are consultation on business strategy, planning and policy between HQ and subsidiary, HQ's control over budget only and having the subsidiary manage routine targets and performance, together with HR policy and practices with approval of HQ. Under M2, subsidiaries have more input into the formulation of business strategy and designing business plans (i.e. 6 months, 1 year and 3 years), in addition to managing business or production with a certain degree of autonomy, and managing subsidiary's HR performance. In order to achieve control and coordination, HQ can use a balance score-card for performance evaluation and demand regular reporting from subsidiaries. Among our samples, J1, J2, J3, J9, T2, T3, and T6 can be categorized under M2.

The characteristics of M3 can be identified as localized business decision-making, policy initiation by subsidiaries which are in charge of business execution and performance management, including HR, with the HQ being the ultimate evaluator. Among the samples, J4, J5, J6, J8 and J10 can be categorized under M3.

From the division of these three models, we can see that there is a trend moving away from a traditional HQ control model of M1 and towards a balanced approach between HQ-subsidiary management collaboration (M2). However, localized management, namely M3, is still the minority.

The companies overall evaluation of their own business performance is mixed among the sample companies (see Table 2). Generally speaking, a majority of the companies (11 cases) indicated that their performance in China has been between satisfactory and very satisfactory, while the other 7 cases indicate that it has been neither satisfactory nor dissatisfactory. No company in the sample was dissatisfied. This result can be seen as a positive sign of foreign business operation in China. This positive result is very different from many previous studies,

many of which have pointed out negative aspects of doing business in China. (Please cite leading literature here).

Policies and Practices of Global Integration and Localization

The issues related to policies and practices of global integration and localization are fundamental for an understanding of MNEs' global business operations. In the following section, we explore these issues through nine important perspectives (see Table 3).

1) HQ's Key Cultures and Policies to Follow

For the M1 group, the key areas that HQs want subsidiaries to follow are execution of HQ's policy and principles, and complete loyalty to the leadership of HQ. Additionally, compliances with HQ's culture, production standards, budget and strategic control are also among important requirements for subsidiaries to achieve. As for the M2 group, subsidiaries are required to comply with HQs in terms of HQ's operation principles, cost and quality control, and production standardization.

Apart from these, they are also given strong encouragement to follow the local culture, customs and rules in order to be a good corporate citizen locally. As for the M3 group, the HQ's influence is more associated with principle, philosophy, vision, and moral standards rather than hard-core policies and actions. HQs maintain a more general approach in their relationship with subsidiaries and allow their subsidiaries more autonomy to manage routine day-to-day business activities.

2) Key Local Cultures and Norms to Deal with

The local operations that concern the M1 group are mostly related to a high turnover rate of local employees, and inconsistency in regional regulations (i.e. regulations may change from region to region). They thus direct most of their attention to meeting the local demands in the differing local political, cultural and regulatory systems, and the need of building good local relationship (*guanxi*) for business. In contrast, the M2 group has more detailed approaches taking into consideration the local way of doing business, such as following the local way of managing HR, engaging fully with local cultures and norms, conforming to local regulations, understanding and meeting the local demands and customers' needs, together with the use of local staff for better incorporation of local ways of business operations and building local *guanxi*. As for the M3 group, they also share characteristics with the other two groups in areas such as following the local culture, laws and norms. Furthermore, they also explicitly acknowledge the importance of following the local customs and norms, due to the fact that localization can never be achieved unless local customs and norms are incorporated into the company and made to play a role in it.

3) How to Integrate the Two Forces: HQ Control vs. Localization?

As for a balanced approach for integrating the two forces of HQ total control and local responsiveness, the different groups have opted for different orientations.

Table 3. Policies and practices of global integration and localization

Key aspects	M1: J7, T1, T4, T5, T7, & T8	M2: J1, J 2, J3, J9, T2, T3, & T6	M3: J4, J5, J6, J8 & J10
1. Key parent company's cultures and policies to follow.	Vertical relationship with HQ and following HQ's policy, PCNs' personnel management hold at HQ (J7); HQ's 5 principles (loyalty, innovation, reputation, responsibility & realism) (T1); Complete loyalty & leadership of HQ (T4); HQ's management culture (T5); Quality standards and control of budget and accounting systems (T7); HQ's control of strategies (T8).	HQ's traditional practices, eg. annual examination, monthly report (J1); HQ strongly insists that the S should follow local customs and rules so that the latter can be a good corporate citizen (J2 & J3); HQ's philosophy, policy and general affairs, including HRM (J9); HQ's direction and standardization (T2); Cost control, consistent quality, provision of procedures and guide book, R&D (T3); HQ holds principles for the S to follow and operation strategies and quality control must be consistent (T6).	Following HQ's principle and achieving globalisation of management (J4); Following HQ's business philosophy (J5); Implementing HQ's culture which emphasizes on following and expanding the core business, but not engaging speculation, being honest (J6), Following HQ's vision of operation with moral and wisdom (J8); HQ encourages company to follow the local law and customs and subsidiary is seen as local company (J10).
2. Key local cultures and norms to deal with.	High turnover rate of HCNs (J7); Inconsistent local regulations (T1); Local supply and taxation regulations (T4); Local policies on labour, environment and trade (T5); Political and cultural differences and difficulty of building local relations (T7); Local regulations (T8).	Following the local way of managing HR, eg. performance-based pay & less seniority-orientation (J1); Fully engaging with local cultures and norms (J2); High turnover rate of HCNs (J3); Following local regulations and norms and understand the local demand and customers' needs (J9); Try to use local staff for understanding local way of doing business (T2); Following local regulations and building local *guanxi* are important (T3 & T6).	Following all the local customs and norms because localization would not be realized unless we do so (J4); Following local laws, norms and cultures and we think it is natural thing to do (J5); Following local norm and regulations (J6); Individuality is strong locally (J8); To be a good local corporate citizen (J10).
3. How to integrate the two forces?	Relying on local senior management to	Using general and specific training	Since HQ has developed a global

Table 3. (Continued)

	consider both foces when executing policies (J7); Encouraging PCN s to be more localized, eg. through marriage with locals (T1); Encouraging PCNs to stay permanently andusing HC Ns as consultant (T 4); The most importantconsideration is to reduce transaction cost, then following local regulations may reducecost (T5 & T7); Consistence between HQ and S and hiring more HCNs as local managers (T8).	programs for both PCNs and HCNs managersfor cross-cultural understanding (J1); IntegratingHQ's p olicies and local businesscultures (J2); Try to understand and observe through the help of long-term HC Ns (J3); Promoting transformational role of PC N andHC N managersto link HQ and subsidiary together (J9); Emphasising on educaton and communication and building consciences (T2); All production procedures and audting systemset by HQ and PCNs andHC Ns design the details of the flow charts and implementplus monthly report (T 3); Balance between following HQ's operation strategies and quality control and local business culture(T 6).	standard, we do notneed to put much effort on integration work (J4); By fo llowing local law, cultures and norms in order to prevent any conflicts, and adopting local HRsystems by local HR manager(J5); Accounting systems are different between home country and host country, so we need to train people to be able to manage both (J6) Nil (J 10).
4. The processes and mecharisms being used to help PCNs and TC Ns to be familiar with localized policies and practices.	Nothing particular excepttransfer of information (J7); Encouraging PCN s to study local policy and decision-makingprocess(T1); Preparation, information collection & frequent local visits (T 4); Via inform al channels such as chats with those how had years of work experience in China (T 5); Using local consultant for local information (T7); More experiencedexpatriates will provide useful information (T 8).	Pre-departure training for PC Ns and local support, eg. accommodaton, shopping, school for children and medical services (J1); Transfer of information and know-how from the predecessors and pre-departure training for PC Ns (J2); Nil (J3); Enforcing communication and share of information among the staff and corresponding to the need of PC Ns & TCNs (J 9); Informal assistance (T2); Seek information and assistance from expatriates who havealready workedin	Pre-departure training on inter-cultural communication and language etc. and accepting PCNs with overseaswork experience (J4); Adopting local way of business operation and HR practices through the assistance ofexperienced HC Ns (J 5); Occasional training held atHQ and subsidiary levels (J6); Nil (J8); Brief briefing due to small no. of PC Ns (J10).

		PRC (T3); Pre-departure information sessions for PCNs (T 6).	
5. The processes and mechanisms being used to help local employees to be familiar with HQ's cultures and policies.	Communication with HCNs regarding development of principles and policies (J7); Using a strict mechanism to control for HCNs to follow (T1); On-line communication with HCNs and HQ's visits for HCNs (T4); HQ provides flow charts and training guidebook to control local HCNs (T5); HQ has made clear regulations for HCNs to follow (T7); Through the instruction of PCNs to influence HCNs (T 8).	Training for key HCNs at HQ, eg. finance, accounting and other customer's services. On the job training for new HCNs for 1 year (J1); On the job training at both HQ and subsidiary levels (J2); Sharing the HQ's guidelines with HCNs (J3); Regular training for outstanding HCNs at HQ (J 9); Setting up clear regulation and punishing wrong doing by reducing performance points (T2); Training for new HCNs (T 3); On-line training and communications (T6).	Orientation and guidance training for newcomers, and regular recreation program, on job rotation based on horizontal task force(J4); Adopting localization practice and no needs for HCNs to be familiar with HQ's system (J5); Occasional training (J6); Occasional training at HQ (J 8); Through internal newsletter and CEO's speech (J10).
6. Languages for communications	Japanese with HQ and English with local (J7); Taiwanese with HQ and Mandarin with local (T 1, T4, T5, T7, & T 8).	Japanese with HQ and English with local (J 1, J2, & J3); Japanese with HQ and local (J9); Mandarin and English with HQ and Mandarin with local (T2); Mandarin with HQ and local (T3 & T6).	English with both HQ and local (J4); Japanese and English with HQ and among management team, and English with local (J5 & J10); Japanese and English with HQ, and English among management team and with local (J6); Japanese with HQ and among management team, and Japanese & English with local (J8);
7. The major obstacles for the promotion of local staff into senior management position.	Language & understanding (J7); Lack of trust and ethics (T 1); Lack of motivation (T4); Problem with communication and	Language, cultural barriers and trust issues (J1); Difficulty in communications (J2 & T3);	No, we have a succession plan (J4); Intrinsic understanding of the business of HQ (J5); No, we have local senior managers(J6);

Table 3. (Continued)

	loyalty (T5 & T7); Lack of experience (T8).	Lack of good candidates for senior management (J3); The difficulty to adjust cultural differences (J9); HCNs do not meet the standards for senior management (T2); Lack of leadership quality among HCNs and company is still providing training to the HCNs (T6)	No, both PCNs and HCNs have the same opportunity to get promotion (J8); No, all management team can be local at any time (J10).
8. The company salary and benefit systems for PCNs, TCNs and HCNs.	PCNs: home country pay (no less & no gain) (J7 & T 4); home country pay plus overseas allowance (T1, T5, T7 & T8); TCNs: N/A; HCNs: managerial staff with local pay structure & manager allowance; employee with average local pay level and benefit (J7, T1, T4, & T7).	PCNs: home country pay (J3, J9, T2 & T6); home country pay plus overseas allowance (J1, J2 & T3). TCNs: Same as PCN's home country pay (T2); TCN's home country pay plus allowance (J9); HCNs: managerial staff with local pay, performance-based bonus and lower interest rate home loan (J1); Managerial staff with local pay structure & manager allowance (J2, J3, J9, T2, T3 & T6); Employee with local basic salary plus performance-based bonus (J1 & T6); Employee with local basic salary plus housing allowance (J2); Employee with average local pay level and benefit (J3, J9, T2 & T3).	PCNs: home country pay (J4, J5, J6 & J10); home country pay plus overseas allowance (J8); TCNs: TCNs' home country pay plus allowance (J4); host country average standard and benefit (J5); HCNs: managerial staff with local pay & manager allowance (J4, J5, J6 & J10); Managerial staff with performance-based pay and overseas training (J8); Employee with local basic salary and benefit (J4, J5, J6 & J10); Employee with performance-based pay (J8).
9. The processes of evaluating effective management systems to maintain the balance between global integration and local responsiveness in the future.	HQ evaluates subsidiaries and provides feedback based on their global standards (J7); Developing product diversity and global business system to gain market competition (T1); Problems with HRM and need relying on HQ control but not subsidiary (T4); Adopting more international standardization and training (T5 & T8); Adopting diversity management in terms of location and multi-business (T7).	Further localization policy, eg. promoting HCNs to senior position (J1); Relying on HQ's overseas business divisions' effort to remain the balance (J2); Corresponding appropriately in order to fit in the global market, and HQ should not intervene specific activities of subsidiary (J3); Listening to the advices from subsidiary before making decision at HQ (J9); Making globalisation as the goal for every business unit (T2); Nil (T3); More localized HR policy and international standardisation (T6).	The local practices should reflect the global standards (J4); Adopting a management system which is able to give priority to local issues (J5); Integrating two systems: sending HCNs to HQ to learn new practices and at the same time to meet local requirement and changes in particular labour market competition (J6). Nothing special was done (J8); Internal communication, regional-based information sharing, regular meeting between HQ's managers and subsidiary managers & employees (J10).

For example, the approach that the M1 group adopted tended to emphasize more on HR control to balance the tendency to have more localized staffing. Several procedures have been adopted, including an increasingly heavy reliance on local senior management when executing policies. In addition, they encouraged PCNs to become more localized by living like the locals.

Some Taiwanese PCNs have achieved localization through marriage with a local, a prolonged stay at the subsidiary, employing HCNs as consultants or promoting HCNs into management positions. Some companies have attempted to reduce costs incurred by localization (e.g. T5 and T7). As for the M2 group, conducting training is one of the key mechanisms for improving the awareness of both PCNs and HCNs in mutual understanding and conscience building. Long-term assignments for PCNs and long-employment of HCNs are another way to ensure stable cross-cultural management. More detailed activities include the promotion of transformational roles of PCNs and HCNs in linking HQ and the subsidiary together. As for the M3 group, they do not have to spend time and energy on the detailed procedures mentioned above, since their HQs already have a clear global strategy and production standards with a focus on localization. However, formal and informal training remains the most effective way to familiarize employees with different local business practices such as accounting systems and other regulatory systems.

4) The Assistance Provided for PCNs and TCNs to Be Localized

The companies within the M1 group have done nothing in particular to facilitate the localization of PCNs and TCNs except for transferring and collecting some local information via formal channels (e.g. the services of accounting and legal firms) as well as informal channels (e.g. hearsay from experienced expatriates), and encouraging PCNs to study the local policy as it relates to the company and its decision-making process. In contrast, companies within the M2 group developed substantial policies and mechanisms to enable PCNs and TCNs to become familiar with local policies and practices. Activities undertaken have included formal pre-departure training for PCNs, transfer of information and know-how from predecessors, and assistance in day-to-day local support (e.g. accommodation, shopping, schooling for children and medical services). The M3 group has also emphasized the need for pre-departure training, particularly in the areas of intercultural communication and language learning. The selected PCNs normally have prior overseas work experience. Through the assistance of experienced HCNs, the companies found that it is much easier for new PCNs to meet local requirements and demands than before.

5) The Assistance Provided for HCNs to Get Familiar with HQ

Again, different model groups have adopted different approaches in assisting their HCNs to learn the corporate culture and operation principles valued most by the HQ. Among the M1 group, companies have emphasized clear and constant communications with HCNs regarding HQ's principles and policies, arrangement of visits by HCNs to HQ, and informing HCNs of HQ culture through the instruction of PCNs or through clear instruction of regulations.

As for the M2 group, more activities have been arranged, such as training for the key HCNs at HQ in the area of finance, accounting and other customer services; on-job-training for HCNs at both HQ and subsidiary levels; and communicating and sharing HQ's guidelines with HCNs. Because more attention is given to localization, the M3 group has not paid as much attention towards facilitating HCNs to be familiar with HQ. Instead, activities such as

occasional training for key HCNs at HQ, induction training for new HCNs, internal newsletters and CEO's speeches have been arranged from time to time. By doing so, it is believed that HQ and the subsidiary are able to secure a better level of consistency in business operations.

6) Languages for Communications

An examination of the dominating language(s) used for communication within companies may reveal significant information on the cultural norms and opportunity for promotion of HCNs (see next point). Among the M1 group, the Japanese cohort has adopted Japanese as the only linguistic code for communication with HQ and English for communication with locals, while the Taiwanese cohort used the Taiwanese dialect (Southern Min) with HQ and Mandarin with locals. As for the M2 group, three Japanese MNEs have a policy similar to that of the M1 group, but one company (i.e. J9) uses Japanese only for communication with both HQ and locals. As for the Taiwanese, one company (i.e. T2) has indicated that Mandarin and English are used when communicating with HQ and Mandarin is used with locals. The two other Taiwanese companies (i.e. T3 and T6) use Mandarin for communication with both HQ and locals. Among the M3 group, one Japanese company (i.e. J4) uses English for communication with both HQ and locals, two Japanese companies (i.e. J5 and J10) use Japanese and English for communication with HQ and with the management team at the subsidiary, and English with locals. One Japanese company (i.e. J6) uses Japanese and English for communication with HQ and English with the management team and with locals at the subsidiary. Another Japanese company (i.e. J8) uses Japanese for communication with HQ and with the management team at the subsidiary, but both Japanese and English for communication with locals.

From these diversified patterns of language use between HQ and the subsidiary as well as among other people at the subsidiary, some key characteristics can be ascertained.

First, the majority of companies have adopted the parent company's language for communication between HQ and subsidiary, which suggest a strong influence from HQ in the choice of language for communication. It is a phenomenon shared by all companies, no matter what model group the company belongs. Some companies have adopted both the parent company's language and English for communication between HQ and subsidiary, and this indicates a certain degree of globalization in terms of their approach to business operations as well as business needs (i.e. market requirements).

Second, the language for communication within the management team at the subsidiary level can have three options: the parent company's language, English or the local language. Among our sample, there are different orientations. In the case of Taiwanese-owned companies, it is possible for Taiwanese companies to use Mandarin for communication at all levels since Mandarin is the official language in both China and Taiwan. However, one thing worth noting here is that, over the past few decades, the Taiwanese dialect (Southern Min), spoken by over 70% of the total population in Taiwan has emerged as the major business language widely used in privately-owned enterprises particularly in the southern part of Taiwan. Since 4 out of the 8 Taiwanese-owned companies had a HQ in the south (i.e. T1, T5, T6 and T7), it is also natural for the PNCs of these companies to use the Taiwanese dialect for communication with HQ and among themselves. In such cases, the use of the Taiwanese dialect represents an in-group language and increases solidarity. As for the two companies, one with English-speaking shareholders (T2) and the other with Japanese shareholders (T4), it

is natural for PNCs to use their common language, English or Japanese, to communicate with HQ or among PCNs.

Language use in the Japanese companies portrays a different picture and reveals several interesting patterns: a.) companies which used only Japanese indicate a strong PCNs' control and lack of foreign language capacity by PCNs; b.) companies which used both Japanese and English have indicated a sense of global integration of both company and individuals (PCNs and HCNs), and PCNs and HCNs are able to use language other than their mother tongues; c.) and there is no example of using the local language for communication among the management team at the Japanese companies. This shows that most Japanese PCNs do not have good language training before placement. This reflects a certain degree of ethnocentric management practice.

Third, the languages for communication between PCNs and local employees at the subsidiary level are relatively straightforward; that is, using Mandarin among the Taiwanese companies or English among the Japanese companies. Once again, the Taiwanese companies have certain advantages compared with other foreign owned companies. In addition, the lack of local language competency by PCNs is one of the disadvantages of Japanese companies and it reinforces the perception of ethnocentric management practices.

7) The Obstacles to the Promotion of HCNs

Following the point made in the previous section, it is clear that language competency can be one of the major obstacles preventing HCNs from being promoted to a senior position, particularly in a Japanese company, due to the fact that Japanese is used as the only means of communicating with HQ and among the management team at the subsidiary level. HCNs' lack of language ability and cultural understanding can lead to cultural barriers and lack of trust. Other obstacles to HCNs' promotion in both Japanese and Taiwanese companies include a lack of work ethic, management experience, leadership skills and strong motivation on the part of HCNs, and difficulty in communicating with the HQs of the M1 and M2 groups. As for the M3 group, there is a certain degree of promotion for HCNs in some of the companies. For example, J6 has local senior managers, J8 treats both PCNs and HCNs as equal as regards to promotion, and J10 has a localized management team.

8) Salary and Benefits for PCNs, TCNs and HCNs

There are many different compensation systems identified among our sample companies. Generally speaking, there are two systems of compensation for PCNs: one is based on the home country pay structure (10 companies) and the other is based on the home country pay plus overseas allowance (8 companies). For HCNs, there is a division between managers and employees. The majority of the companies pay managerial staff, following a local pay structure together with managers' allowance (10 companies). Others add management performance-based bonus, low interest rate home loans or overseas training as extra benefits. As for HCN employees, the majority are paid at an average local pay level plus benefits. Some subsidiaries add performance-based bonuses and housing allowances. TCNs are paid differently. Some (i.e. T2) are paid the same as PCN's home country pay and others are paid as TCN's home country pay plus allowance (J9 and J4), or host country average pay standard plus other benefits (J15).

9) Future Improvement for Maintaining the Balanced Approach

The final perspective concerns the adoption of certain processes to evaluate effectiveness in management systems in order to maintain a balance between global integration and local responsiveness in the future. Our sample companies again vary in their approaches. For the M1 group, a reliance on global standards is crucial for maintaining consistency between HQ and subsidiary. Other elements include diversifying production and globalizing the business system in order to maximize market competition, improving international HRM by relying on international standardization, and diversity management to address the complexity of multi-location and multi-business. Within the M1 group, a certain degree of HQ orientation indicate that these companies still emphasize the top-down approach in decision making, whether towards managing international business in general or IHRM in particular.

In contrast, among the M2 group, further localization policies have been devised and regarded as the most important element for future development. Such policies include promoting HCNs to senior positions, non-intervention from HQ in specific activities of the subsidiary, consultation with the subsidiary before making decisions at HQ level, making globalization as the goal for every business unit, and availability of more localized HR policy and international standardization. It is obvious that in comparison with the M1 group, the M2 group has a more balanced approach towards future action. On the one hand, a continuation of the localization policy is identified as the foremost priority for future development. On the other hand, their international standardization and global-oriented goal will guide them to further develop their international business strategy as well as IHRM. Among the M3 group, a balanced approach was also significant in statements reflecting this direction, such as 'the local practices should reflect the global standards' (i.e. J4), and 'adopting a management system which is able to give priority to local issues' (ire. J5). Some companies have tried to integrate the two systems through sending HCNs to HQ to learn new practices in order to meet local requirements and changes in the labor market competition (i.e. J6), or through improving information sharing by way of encouraging better internal communication, regionally-based information sharing, and regular meetings between HQ's managers and subsidiary managers and employees (i.e. J10). It is quite clear that the companies within the M3 group have attempted, to a certain degree, to prioritize localization as their future direction, meanwhile recognizing the importance of global standards and HQ's effort in integrating international business strategy and IHRM policies.

4. Discussion

At the beginning of the chapter, we identified three key research questions and now we explored the issues related to these three questions. The first research question was on the correlation between having an international business strategic goal and its impact on staffing policies and strategies. Generally speaking, the majority of the companies identified occupying or increasing the share of the Chinese market as the most important goal for their business investment in China. This has signaled a shift in the goal of MNEs' investment in China, changing from using China as an enclave for export in the early years to targeting China as a market destination in more times. Evidence shows that the majority of our sample companies have made China their markets. This has consequently exerted significant influence on their international staffing policy. In addition, most companies have experienced

a many-fold increase in staff numbers following the expansion of their business (cf. Table 2), the speedy development of the Chinese economy and the maturity of the Chinese market. As Table 2 shows, most companies are satisfied with their business in China and no company expressed dissatisfaction. As the local market is becoming increasingly important for their business, a change in the general trend in staffing has been identified in our samples. That is to say, international staffing strategy has shifted towards localization with a growing proportion of HCNs (as managerial staff members and ordinary employees). We have also witnessed decreases in the number of PCNs and TCNs. In particular, the number of TCNs has become fairly small. In addition, since the business has become more competitive and complicated, some initial PCNs teams have been replaced by a more capable PCNs team. Furthermore, as explained in the previous sections, a limited number of TCNs are employed for the special management or technology skills required by those companies. Judging from all these, we can conclude that with international business strategic goals shifting from an export orientation to Chinese domestic market penetration, MNEs in China also tend to adopt a more localized international staffing strategy by increasing the recruitment of HCNs into managerial positions.

The second research question concerned the role of HQs vs. subsidiaries and their impacts on business strategy formulation, control and evaluation. Based on the evidence drawn from our samples, three models can be identified, namely M1: HQ-dominant management system, M2: HQ-subsidiary collaborative system and M3: localized management system. These three models are as follows:

(1) M1 emphasizes a high level of HQ control through formation of business plans and policies, and control subsidiary over budget, HR and performance management, while subsidiaries have to carry out frequent reporting, fully implement HQ's plan and policy, along with managing routine business activities with some autonomies.
(2) M2 has adopted a more balanced approach by consultation on business strategy, plan and policy between HQ and subsidiary. HQ control mainly deals with budgetary matters but subsidiaries manage routine targets and performance as well as HR policy and practices with approval from HQ. Within the M2 group, subsidiaries will have more input than the M1 group in decision-making, business management and HR policy practices.
(3) M3 has shifted towards more localized orientation, such as localized business decision-making and policy initiation made by the subsidiaries. Within the M3 group, some subsidiaries are given mandate for autonomous execution and performance management (including HR), but HQ's role is to evaluate long-term overall business performance.

Among our sample companies, there was a trend, generally shifting from the traditional top-down control model of M1 towards the balanced approach of M2. The M3 Model, totally-localized management is still in the minority.

The third research question concerned about how MNEs respond to the challenge of balancing HQ control and localization. Through interview data in relation to the nine perspectives, we can identify some patterns among the sample companies, in relation to the three models M1, M2 and M3. The first three perspectives explored include: 1.) key HQ's cultures and policies to follow; 2.) key local cultures and norms to deal with; and 3.)

integration of globalization and localization. When the three perspectives are analyzed in conjunction with the three models, there is a clear division of the models among the companies. Generally speaking, the M1 group has a more detailed description regarding Perspective 1 but is less concerned with Perspective 2. In contrast, M2 and M3 groups have a more general approach towards Perspective 1, in particular related to HQ principles, philosophy and vision. A much more explicit recognition of Perspective 2 is found in M3 but less so with M2. As for Perspective 3, the M1 group adopted the strategy of relying on local senior management to manage the balance between HQ control and localization. At the same time this group encourages PCNs to become more localized (e.g. via a longer residency in the country or marriage with locals) and promotes HCNs into senior position. As for the M2 and M3 groups, training is the key for getting familiar with different business systems as well as maintaining a balanced approach between HQ control and localization.

The second area relates to organizational assistance available for PCNs and TCNs to be localized, as well as for HCNs to be familiar with HQ, identified as perspectives 4 and 5. As for PCNs and TCNs' localization process, the M1 group only collects and transfers local information and encourages staff to study the local policy and decision-making process. However, the M1 group tends to emphasize more the need of HCNs to be familiar with HQ through HQ's visit and training regarding HQ's principles and policies. PCNs also provide detailed instruction to HCNs at the subsidiary level. As for the M2 group, the emphasis is on the importance of both perspectives through the arrangement of pre-departure training, transferring information and know-how from their predecessors, and providing local support. As for the assistance for HCNs, the M2 group also provides more activities such as training for key HCNs at HQ and on-the-job training for all HCNs at the subsidiary. Due to the fact that the M3 group pays substantial attention to localization, such companies concentrate their efforts mainly on facilitating PCNs and TCNs to become localized, rather than HCNs to be familiar with HQ. As required, the M3 group emphasizes pre-departure training in the areas of inter-cultural communication and language and uses experienced HCNs for assistance.

The third area is related to languages for communication and obstacles for HCNs' promotion. Most companies have adopted the parent country language for HQ-subsidiary communication. Taiwanese-owned companies have a unique advantage of a shared language, due to Mandarin being the official language in both mainland China and Taiwan. Taiwanese is also used between some HQs and their PCNs, particularly the HQs located in south Taiwan. However, among the Japanese-owned companies, there are different patterns of language use between PCNs and HCNs, such as using Japanese between PCNs and HCN managers and English between PCNs and HCN employees; or English between PCNs and all HCNs. But hardly any Japanese-owned companies use Chinese for communication between PCNs and HCNs. This reflects different degrees of internationalization of communication among Japanese-owned companies, with a dominant use of parent country language for communication. This potentially imposes obstacles for the HCNs to be promoted, due mainly to a lack of the required Japanese language proficiency. Other factors influencing HCNs' promotion in both Japanese and Taiwanese companies include lack of management experience, ethical standards, leadership skills, strong motivation, and difficulty in cross-cultural communications.

The fourth area concerns international compensation. The difference among PCNs or TCNs' benefits mainly between people paid with home country pay or home country pay plus overseas allowance. Most companies have adopted the so-called 'Going Rate Approach' as

the prevailing market rate in order to make the compensation arrangement consistent with the parent company pay systems, with adjustment of regional difference. As for the HCNs' benefits, most companies have linked the pay system with the average local level, together with some consideration of performance incentives such as performance-based bonuses or other welfare consideration like housing allowances.

The final area concerns about future improvement for maintaining a balanced approach. There are also apparent divisions among the three model groups. As for M1 group, relying on the global standard for production manufacturing is crucial in maintaining consistency between HQ and the subsidiary. In the IHRM area, international HR standardization and diversity management are regarded as effective ways of managing multiple locations and multiple businesses. As for the M2 group, increased localization is given as the most important element for future development, and targeted mainly at promoting HCNs to senior positions, no intervention from HQ on specific activities of the subsidiary, and more localized HR policies. As for the M3 group, a balanced approach is clearly reflected in their future development such as integrating global standards and giving priority to local issues. In addition, promoting effective internal communications between HQ and the subsidiary and among PCNs and HCNs via regionally-based information sharing and regular meetings are highlighted in their future integration agenda.

These findings, summarized above, also shed some light on the implications for theory and practice. In our literature section, we focused on work done on the difficulty of achieving a balanced approach between the policies of HQ control, global integration and localization (i.e. Evans et al., 2002). Above all, it is suggested that there is a general trend of movement among MNEs, shifting along the line from an initial emphasis of HQ control towards global integration with certain amount of localization policies. Unfortunately, this approach seems vague and requires substantial explanation. In this particular area, our research findings, in fact, provide a complementary contribution to fill this gap through the identification of three models among these sample MNEs: M1 for those with a HQ dominant management system, M2 with a HQ-subsidiary collaborative management, and M3 with a localized management system. As indicated in our discussion, there is a clear shift among our sample companies, moving gradually from M1 towards the balanced approach of M2, while M3 remains in the minority. In addition, the host country China is no longer a production center with abundant cheap labor. It has now emerged as a growing market for the sale of their products and services. It should be noted, however, that we have found no clear correlation between the company model and its history (age), size, sector and market orientation. That is to say, each model group has companies with characteristics of being old or young, large or small, and offering different business services and market orientation. Therefore, those variables are not important factors in determining the model.

However, the location of the subsidiary has some influence on developing the likely characteristics corresponding to the various models. For example, companies located in Hong Kong and Guangdong areas tend to have a more de-centralized and balanced approach, and some with a more localized management approach. This suggests a relatively high level of trust in the relationship between HQ and subsidiaries as well as its HCNs in these areas. In contrast, subsidiaries located in the northern inland areas inclined to rely on a more centralized HQ-control orientation. These phenomena can be related to the relatively lower labor quality of HCNs and business environment in these areas. This, in turn, encourages HQ

to take more control and tighter supervision of the local staff and everyday business operations.

Compared with what is found in the literature on Japanese- and Taiwanese-owned companies operating in China, our findings show some similarities with and differences from the previous findings (Zhu, 2006). Japanese companies operating in China occupy a substantial market with two strategic goals, namely to implement strategies of localization and at the same time to strengthen their uniqueness or difference. Among the sample companies, most Japanese-owned companies' responses confirmed that occupying a substantial market was their strategic goal. A large number of Japanese companies have adopted a more balanced approach or even a more localized approach in international business management and IHRM. But certain uniqueness such as directing RandD, maintaining quality control and using Japanese language for communication are still significant in their routine business operations. As for the Taiwanese-owned companies, the strategic goal is to reduce the cost of production. Due to several factors, our Taiwanese samples have a more HQ-control orientation in their international business operations as well as IHRM practices. Nevertheless, Taiwanese PCNs have a much easier channel of communication compared with Japanese PCNs due mainly to having a common language and cultural elements shared between Taiwanese and mainland Chinese. Therefore, PCNs from Taiwan seem to adapt easier to living in China and localizing themselves. These are consistent with the previous research (i.e. Zhu, 2006). In contrast, the Japanese PCNs still follow the rotation arrangement of overseas expatriation and tend to fall short of fully understanding the local culture and their way of doing business, when compared with Taiwanese PCNs. In addition, the opportunities for HCNs to be promoted to senior positions are still limited with many obstacles facing them. Lack of language competency (the Japanese language in particular) and cultural understanding are identified as the major barriers for the promotion of HCNs in Japanese-owned companies. In addition, lack of work ethics, management experience, leadership skills and strong motivation to do more than what is just required are the key obstacles for HCNs to be promoted.

CONCLUSION

Given the increasing importance of MNEs operating in China, one of the largest emerging economies in the world, a better understanding of the rationale and activities of these MNEs in relation to their international business strategies and IHRM would benefit the business community, regulatory governing bodies and individuals working in this area. By building on this understanding, government policymakers and business organizations as well as academics can work for future improvement. This example of qualitative research has given a relatively in-depth look at the key factors that influence the behavior of MNEs operating in China in general, and Japanese and Taiwanese MNEs in particular. Three complementary models have been developed, with a hope that they can contribute further to the current but rather vague approaches to global integration vs. localization. We are aware of the limitation of the current research in terms of sample size and the methodology with mainly qualitative analysis. It is therefore identified that in our future research, we should enlarge the size of the sample companies, adding some more variables such as ownership, source of capital and location, as well as adopting both qualitative and quantitative methods

in order to better predict the outcome in terms of the inter-relationships among those variables.

REFERENCES

Bartlett, C. A. and Ghoshal, S. (1989) *Managing across Boundaries: The Transnational Solution.* Boston, MA: Harvard Business School Press.

Brewster, C. and Scullion, H. (1997) 'A Review and an Agenda for Expatriate HRM', *Human Resource Management Journal,* 7(3): 32-41.

Brewster, C., Sparrow, P. and Harris, H. (2005) 'Towards a New Model of Globalizing HRM', *International Journal of Human Resource Management*, 16(6): 949-70.

De Cieri, H. and Dowling, P. (1999) 'Strategic Human Resource Management in Multinational Enterprises: Theoretical and Empirical Developments'. In P.M. Wright, L.D. Dyer, J.W. Boudreau and G. T. Milkovich (eds.) *Strategic Human Resource Management in the Twenty First Century*. Greenwich, CT: JAI Press, pp. 305-27.

Delios, A. and Bjorkman, I. (2000) 'Expatriate Staffing in Foreign Subsidiaries of Japanese Multinational Corporations in the PRC and the United States', *International Journal of Human Resource Management*, 11(2): 278-93.

Ding, D. Z., Goodall, K., and Warner, M. (2000) 'The end of the "Iron Rice-Bowl": Whither Chinese Human Resource Management?' *International Journal of Human Resource Management,* 11(2): 217-236.

Evans, P., Pucik, V. and Barwoux, J.L. (2002) *The Global Challenge: Frameworks for International Human Resource Management.* Boston: McGraw-Hill Irwin.

Farley, J.U., Hoenig, S. and Yang, J.Z. (2004) 'Key Factors Influencing HRM Practices of Overseas Subsidiaries in China's Transition Economy', *International Journal of Human Resource Management,* 15(4): 688-704.

Legewie, J. (2002) 'Control and Coordination of Japanese Subsidiaries in China: Problems of an Expatriate-Based Management System', *International Journal of Human Resource Management,* 13(6): 901-919.

Ma, C. (1998) 'Foreign-Funded Enterprises in China: The Difficult Task of Talent-Keeping and Its Impact on the Wage Structure', *JETRO China Newsletter,* 132:2-9.

Porter, M.E. (1986) 'Changing Patterns of International Competition', *California Management Review*, 28(2): 29-40.

Prahalad, C.K. and Doz, Y. (1987) *The Multinational Mission: Balancing Local Demands and Global Vision.* New York: The Free Press.

Rosenzweig, P. and Nohria, N. (1994) 'Influences of Human Resource Management Practices in Multinational Firms', *Journal of International Business Studies*, 20(2): 229-52.

Schuler, R., Dowling, P. and De Cieri, H. (1993) 'An Integrative Framework of Strategic International Human Resource Management', *Journal of Management,* 19(2): 419-59.

Sparrow, P.R. and Hiltrop, J.M. (1994) *European Human Resource Management in Transition.* London: Prentice Hall.

Walsh, J. and Zhu, Y. (2007) 'Local Complexities and Global Uncertainties: A Study of Foreign Ownership and Human Resource Management in China', *International Journal of Human Resource Management,* 18(2). 249-67.

Whitley, R.D. (ed.) (1992) *European Business Systems: Firms and Markets in Their National Contexts*. London: Sage.

Zhu, Y. (2006) *Taiwanese Businessmen in China: An Observation Report (2000-2004)*. Taipei: Caixun.

In: Business and Finance: Performance and Management ISBN: 978-1-61122-936-3
Editors: R. Morland and A. Gagglione

Chapter 7

THE MICROCLUSTER VALUE CHAIN ANALYSIS*

Josep Capó-Vicedo, Manuel Expósito-Langa and José-Vicente Tomás-Miquel**
AERT Research Group. Universitat Politècnica de València

ABSTRACT

This paper tries to study the particular workings of clusters, proposing a tool that helps with the empowerment and development of inter-organisational networks that might exist in them. It is a new tool for territorial strategic analysis focused in clustering policy based on the innovation; the microcluster value chain analysis.

Territorial competitiveness should be looked for by starting from the generation of external economies, from strategic decisions taken by those responsible for the interrelated networks, and from the identification and the empowerment of the key relationships among the agent leaders. These are the objectives that the tool proposed will try to resolve.

To achieve this, the most important thing will be to know how to locate and to diffuse the necessary knowledge to be able to identify the opportunities or key success factors that can motivate the creation of concrete inter-organisational networks in the heart of a microcluster.

Keywords: SMEs, clusters, interorganizational networks, value chain.

INTRODUCTION

In recent years, the balance between knowledge and resources has changed so dramatically in the developed economies that the former has become the most decisive factor in relation to standard of living. Knowledge has become even more important than traditional resources such as land, machinery and work.

---

* This work has been developed within the project "The transformation of industrial districts: heterogeneity, outsourcing and relocation", funded by the Program for Support R & D 2008" of the Polytechnic University of Valencia

** E-mail address: pepcapo@doe.upv.es. Phone: +34966528466 Fax: +34966528585. Corresponding author: Business Management Department, Universitat Politècnica de València. Plaza Ferrándiz y Carbonell, 3 – 03801 – Alcoy (Alicante) – Spain.

Cooperation with others of their similar size, a larger size or a smaller size is a strategic alternative that allows enterprises to take advantage of the competitive advantages of the companies with which they have decided to associate themselves, whether these agreements are of a horizontal or vertical kind. If these agreements are carried out among a large number of companies, they can knit a lattice of relationships that create compact networks through the links established. These inter-organisational networks are usually developed in a concrete geographical environment, forming clusters.

On this subject, the new theories of growth establish a clear dependence between economic growth and the rate of accumulation of physical and human assets, this being defined as levels of knowledge, abilities and competences (OECD, 2001). The abilities and competences required nowadays are no longer only technical, but give more importance to social and organisational skills, which allow personnel to work in more fluid and interactive environments.

However, the existence of economic systems based on Small and Medium Enterprises (SMES) represents an important barrier for transition to take place from traditional economies to those based on knowledge. The European Observatory for the SMES (OES, 2003) states that, in order to develop a competitive base for these companies, on one hand it is necessary to develop human resources, and on the other, to obtain competences from outside by cooperating with external organisations, especially from those geographically close to the company.

The fact that these small and medium companies are located in a certain territory can favour greater product specialization, greater flexibility and a considerable increase in competitiveness. The grouping in function of a group of abilities, knowledge, technologies or markets, can be a catalyst that impels the innovative process in companies. In this case, the existing implicit knowledge in a territory plays a vital role, by means of the establishment of mechanisms of collaboration and participation, formal or informal, of the different public and private agents of the territory.

This paper tries to study the particular workings of these territorial clusters, proposing a new tool for territorial strategic analysis focused in clustering policy based on the innovation; **the microcluster value chain analysis**.

Territorial competitiveness should be looked for by starting from the generation of external economies, from strategic decisions taken by those responsible for the interrelated networks.

To achieve this, the most important thing will be to know how to locate and to diffuse the necessary knowledge to be able to identify the opportunities or key success factors that can motivate the creation of concrete inter-organisational networks in the heart of a microcluster.

Evolution of Industrial Districts and Specialised Territorial Clusters

Another important question to be kept in mind in the analysis of technological evolution processes is the fact that most of them – practically all of them in the case of manufacturing industry – are associated with a certain territory. These processes have had an influence on and, in their turn, are the results of, the historical evolutions that have occurred in these territories.

That is to say, as many authors have studied, from Marshall to Porter, Sabel, Pyke and Sengenberger, etc., when industrial processes are analysed, from the beginning of the Industrial Revolution in the 18th century up to the present day, there appear a series of phenomena of the concentration of specialised production in certain regions of advanced countries. These phenomena are the consequence of the external economies generated in the territories due to being situated close to the specific resources for a determined production chain, as Marshall correctly defined them in his study of 1919 "Industry and Trade", in which he was the first to describe the concept of industrial districts as the phenomena of the concentration of specialised production units.

When, about the year 1987, Giacomo Becattini revived Marshall's theory of industrial districts, others began to study again the phenomena of the concentration of processes of strategic change, many of them in the form of groups of local small and medium sized companies. The Italian school of the Marshall Industrial District – (Sebastiano Brusco, Roberto Cagmani, Fabio Sforzi, etc.) – have made a social and economic paradigm of industrial districts, resorting to an analysis of their evolution in their different stages of development and to the interpretation of the hierarchy of processes and production units in their network of agents, in order to justify and try to diagnose their evolutionary process.

The model, in territorial groupings, of industrial elements specialising in a determined sector of production created by Porter and known by the name of "clusters", has permitted a big advance in the understanding of the reasons why these phenomena present a high degree of geographical concentration in certain parts of advanced countries. Porter showed that the reasons for international competitive success are related to two causes: a) the geographical concentration of specialised industrial elements, and b) the presence of the appropriate determining factors of territorial competitiveness. According to this author, these are the reasons why the companies in these specialised clusters are highly successful in selling their products in international markets.

Porter's writings, referring first of all to the concept of industrial clusters (Porter 1980) and later to regional clusters (Porter, 1998 a, b) have had great influence, since they showed the importance of the close relationship existing between the economic elements that compose a cluster and the competitiveness of the companies operating within it.

The concept of a regional cluster, referring to a geographical concentration of interdependent companies (OECD, 2001; Rosenfeld, 2002), is closely related to other academic concepts utilised, such as Marshallian Industrial Districts, specialised production areas and local production systems.

The success of the networks of specialised companies in a large number of advanced countries, situated in specific territorial concentrations, has increased the interest in the study of these phenomena of geographical industrial concentration in the last two decades, both in the academic world and in organisations responsible for the creation of industrial policies and territorial development (Regional Clusters in Europe. EU, 2002). It has also increased interest both in manufactured goods (e.g. the "Terza Italia") and in the development of high-technology products (e.g. Silicon Valley). In the last decade, clusters have been recognised as areas in which conditions are very favourable either for stimulating productivity and innovation in the integrating companies or for the formation of HRs and the creation of new businesses.

The policy of clustering is giving excellent results in the most dynamic regions of the world, especially when applied to groups of small to mid-sized companies operating in a co-

ordinated network (networking); e.g the Emilia Romana in Italy, Scotland in the UK, Arizona in the USA, Silicon Valley in California, Highway 128 in Boston USA, Valencia, Catalonia and in the Basque Country in Spain, etc.

The success of the most dynamic clusters is closely related to the way in which the leading companies and organizations in its economy manage their knowledge; that is to say, the process of creation, storing, structuring and diffusion of information and knowledge by means of pro-active policies of business and institutional co-operation. In this aspect, the development of Information and Communication Technologies (ICT) and the range of the Information Society in the territory are the determining factors.

In this sense it is important to mention that not all firms aggregate into territorial or geographical clusters. Some firms deliberately locate outside the cluster that encompasses the majority of the firms in their industry because they feel that employee retention will be higher (i.e., competitors will not be as likely to steal their employees) and their trade secrets will be easier to keep. These firms use to form "virtual" clusters, based in the use of ICT.

However, in all these processes it is obvious that there should exist a synergetic Structural Network of Relations (SNR) among the industrial entities, generating valuable external economies for most of them.

Collaboration in a Geographical Region: Clusters and Networks

The world we live in has become a global economy in which the use of ICT and advanced logistics enables relations to be established between businesses in any part of the world. Nevertheless, in order to establish successful inter-organisational relations or alliances it is important to be able to count on the so-called **business ecosystems** (Camarinha-Matos, 2002), i.e. on environments favourable to networks of businesses that use similar strategies and practices, where there exists mutual trust among the companies involved, as well as an atmosphere of community and stability.

The fact that businesses can be concentrated geographically in the form of clusters is a key factor for the SMES in their evolution towards the knowledge-based economy. Some companies are finding out that they can get more benefit from their organisational knowledge, even increasing their competences, within an interactive cluster that possesses informal inter-business links favourable to the creation and transfer of knowledge.

Nowadays, firms tend to stay close to one another, in search of a reserve of trained workers and specific local infrastructures. The firms that compose the cluster can obtain economies of proximity, for example, and even obtain economies of scale through the specialisation of the individual companies, joint purchase of raw materials, etc. On this aspect, as regards the range of knowledge, the proximity of institutes, universities, etc., these are proving to be more important factors than the mere fact of being in a geographical cluster.

Another important factor in clusters is the fact that, although it may sound paradoxical, the grouping of businesses is of great importance, in spite of the advances in the ICT, since the correct assimilation of tacit knowledge and innovation needs an environment of cooperation and mutual trust among people, who are more easily reachable in such circumstances. Regarding this aspect, the ICT have not yet been able to achieve better results in the exchange of knowledge (not information) than interpersonal relations.

Clusters facilitate other kinds of cooperation and association among businesses, since the continual contact and the fact of being close to one another help to establish good relations. Cooperation in networks is the norm when businesses are situated close to one another, although there are some networks of businesses separated by considerable distances. Networks can be formed among firms in a supply chain or between associated businesses.

The network organisational model involves the maximum fragmentation of the company, since it is based fundamentally on a union of companies in which each one specialises in a certain activity. This structure does not happen at random, but is an attempt to incorporate the efficiency of the functional structure, the effectiveness of divisional autonomy and the capacity to transfer skills within the group, but with no one firm exercising a strict control on the elements required to produce goods or services.

The dominant company in the value creation process of the entire system is that which will assume the responsibility of integrating the network, facilitating good relations among all the members. It must therefore reinforce its professional staff and directors in order to efficiently manage the new structure.

It should be pointed out that the fact that the different networks have the objective of providing businesses with the necessary flexibility to respond to the changing and heterogeneous demands of the market does not mean that they are intrinsically unstable or that they will not last longer than the short term and have to function merely as tactical connections. Networks may also create stable links among companies with strategic objectives, such as the so-called strategic networks. Depending on the kind of relationship, these networks may tend to be either stable or dynamic.

Necessity for a Greater Degree of Detail: Clusters and Micro-Clusters

But we understand that the aforementioned models, both the Marshallian industrial districts and Porter's cluster, although valuable and taken as a starting point, are insufficient to define pro-active clustering policies and must be added to. In the particular case of "Porter's diamond", one of the reasons for this insufficiency is that the field of analysis proposed by this author, in terms of a cluster related to a territorial technical specialisation, is too wide and it is therefore necessary to study in greater detail the specialisation of the product.

Porter's definition of a territorial cluster *("A geographically proximate group of interconnected firms and associate institutions in a particular field, linked by commonalties and complementarities"* (Porter, 1998)) does not give sufficient detail to understand how the directors of the specialised companies in a territory can take specific strategic decisions for change. Porter's conception of a cluster and his model of analysis of the diamond – based essentially on the analysis of advanced and specialised determinants of competitiveness – although it can allow the specific identification of the real concrete factors that caused development in the immediate past, is insufficient to identify the specific factors for basing future processes of strategic change, since its analytic process is essentially centred on the structural analysis of the industrial sector.

To say that one must "boost the critical specialised factors" does not tell very much to the director of a company, or even to a political administrator of a territory. The direction of the strategy must be indicated so that plans can be made for specific business strategy, competitive strategy, technological strategy, what technological research to conduct and

promote, the markets to be aimed for, the emerging market sectors, the requirements of new products and processes, etc. When these are decided, the specific requirements in resources – knowledge, training, technology, machinery, infrastructure, etc. – which must be acquired, improved or developed to achieve the objectives can be decided, both in the individual company and on a territorial scale.

To achieve this degree of analytical detail, it is necessary to go beyond a SWOT analysis or the classic structural analysis of an industrial sector. One must go down to the level of in which business competition takes place: companies compete with each other with products in markets. And this brings us to the concept of the Territorial Micro-cluster; a group of specialised companies established in the same region and related to each other, not only by the technology used (industrial sector) and their geographical proximity (Marshallian Industrial District) but by the binomial (product + market), since:

- Firms that do not manufacture the same product do not compete with each other (unless they make substitutable products).
- Firms that do not sell in the same markets do not compete with each other.

It is important to remark that in the two above cases firms not compete for the same customers, but they compete on many other levels. They may compete for employees, investor dollars, community tax abatements or other forms of support, etc.

In fact, the following diversity of types of relationship could be detected among the members of a microcluster:

- **Indifference:** the members take no account whatsoever of the existence of the other member in the decision-making process. The repercussions of any action on the other member are not considered, nor is consideration given to the possible consequences to the company of the actions of the other member.
- **Competition:** two members compete with each other to obtain something that both want: markets, clients, any type of resources (human, financial, technological, physical, etc.), using different types of strategies to achieve their ends. According to the type of strategy and their attitudes to each other, the result of the competition for the microcluster may be:
    - **Negative**: The “I win-you lose” type relationship destroys value.
    - **Positive:** The “win-win” relationship creates value for the microcluster.
- **Collaboration:** The two members adopt formal or informal attitudes that help each other to achieve their objectives while each is intent on achieving his own.

The two latter attitudes, competition and cooperation, are not mutually exclusive in a relationship between two members, unlike the first (indifference), which certainly excludes any other possibility. In the particular case of the relations between two competitors, the adoption of strong reciprocal competition in the market and positive cooperation in the rest of the activities, productive or not (contact with the administration, support for universities and research centres) is beneficial for the territorial system. This is called “co-opetition”, for the concepts of competition and cooperation, and is considered the relationship most likely to generate value for the microcluster.

Adopting this approach of structuring the territorial clusters in micro-clusters – composed of firms inter-related by the value chain of the production of final goods and services, or by intermediaries that perform the same function or sell in the same market – the degree of analysis can be widened and can pass from general considerations and strategies to identifying specific strategies and objectives that allow the companies in the microcluster to maintain their competitive edge in international markets, as it is remarked in table 1.

Table 1. Strategic differences between the traditional cluster analysis and the proposed microcluster analysis

Traditional Cluster Analysis	Proposed Microcluster Analysis
General value and/or cost reductions To invest in R+D+I To invest in research infrastructures	To develop and control a certain Internet-based distribution channel To train a certain number of technicians in a specific technology To start up a rapid prototype production centre To make a project for holding a new specialised international commercial fair for a new type of emerging product

It is thus proposed, in this type of studies, to take the evolutive analysis down to the level of the territorial Micro-clusters, defined in terms of the binomial (product <> market), which is the real battleground in which business-firms compete. The reasons are evident: a key factor for the competitiveness of manufacturers in a micro-cluster may not be such, or may even be negative, for companies outside it.

The Geographic Concentration of Innovation: Territorial Innovation Systems

To continue with the subject matter of the foregoing sections, recent theories of endogenous growth emphasise the fact that accumulation of knowledge and the consequent technological development are the real powers behind localised strategic changes. As certain authors have pointed out (Feldman, 1994; Sharp, 1998), the phenomena of technological cooperation directed towards strategic change – innovation in products and/or processes – are increased by geographic concentration. The flow of information and knowledge directed towards innovation is faster the smaller the physical distance between the persons responsible for taking business decisions in these fields. Innovative activity therefore presents a high degree of geographic concentration, which is even greater than that of economic activity as a whole.

This gives importance to Regional Innovation Systems (RIS) in territorial clusters (universities, technological institutes, research centres, etc.). Following Cooke et al. (2000), we understand that an RIS, in its turn, consists of two subsystems:

- The subsystem of the exploitation and application of knowledge, basically composed of the companies that form the vertical networks of supply in the value chain; and
- The subsystem of the generation and diffusion of knowledge, consisting principally of public organisations and institutions.

In this sense it is important to analyze the specific processes that have taken place in successful clusters, and therefore concentrates on the identification of the key factors in territorial competitiveness that in the past have provided powerful means to generate value and giving competitive advantages to local firms obtained from the capacities and abilities present in the elements of the local economy.

The problem, in terms of industrial and economic policies, is how to generate, distribute, manage, apply and utilise this knowledge, in order to maintain and increase the competitiveness of businesses at present in operation. The past may be unrepeatable, but it is important to achieve analogies and conclusions that permit us to control future conditions.

A Critical Analisis of the Model of the Value Chain

If the existing architecture of the relationships among the elements of a microcluster is studied, the means by which value is generated internally can be studied from the network of relationships *(netchain)* existing among the firms and organisations and the influence of the quantity and quality of these relationships in the value chain of the system of production.

Lazzarini et al. (2001) correctly distinguished the difference between the concepts of "Supply Chain Analysis" (SCA) and "Network Analysis" (NA) with the aim of differentiating the sequential vertical hierarchical "customer–supplier" relationships of the supply chain (SCA) compared to the existing systemic relationships among the various typologies of the firms and organisations involved in a microcluster (NA), in which the connections or interdependencies refer to situations in which each actor makes a discrete independent contribution, formal or informal, to a given task, or in which reciprocal relationships exist where such contributions are mutually dependent.

Porter's Value Chain Model

Porter (1980, 1990) has also made an important contribution to understanding production processes by introducing the term "Value Chain". The value chain of *a firm* is a system of internal interrelated processes in which each of them – each link in the chain – adds value to the final product or service.

In Porter's proposal, the total value of the product or service created by the firm is measured by the total sum that buyers are prepared to pay to acquire this product or service. In this model, the value activities of a firm are structured in nine generic categories, divided into two groups:

a) Primary activities, which are those involved in the physical, chemical or physical-chemical transformation, marketing and distribution of the product; as well as those involved in product support and after-sales service.
b) Auxiliary activities, or those that deal with production factors and provide the infrastructure that allows the primary activities to take place (Porter and Miller, 1985).

Need for a Deeper Analysis

Based on the considerations of the preceding points, we can state that Porter's generic Model of the Value Chain, which divides the activities carried out in the production of goods and services into principal and secondary, or auxiliary, activities, is insufficient to apply a strategic analysis to a Microcluster.

Here we have another objection similar to that in the preceding section, relative to the determining factors in territorial competitiveness: it is no use talking to a business manager of principal and secondary activities, or even of essential activities - *core competences* in the line of Hamel and Prahalad (1990) – since he will not be able to use them to make strategic decisions if he cannot identify them.

More detail is needed in the analysis in order to diagnose what are the key factors for success that specifically must make him take certain decisions in his business and/or in relation to the other firms or organisations with which he is associated; customers, suppliers, related companies, public and private institutions, etc.

Also, we must not forget that Porter's model of the Value Chain was created for a specific company, and this is an additional disadvantage in its application to an analytical study of clusters and microclusters of business companies.

It is precisely the interrelations among the production phases in an industrial sector, performed by *different companies,* but geographically close to each other, that allow us to consider the concept of a Value Chain *extended* to the entire production process in a certain territory, on the basis of their relationship in terms of (product – market). This gives rise to a new concept that we consider can facilitate the strategic analysis process that we are aiming for: the *Framework of the Value Chain of a Microcluster.*

THE DESIGN OF THE FRAMEWORK OF THE VALUE CHAIN OF A MICROCLUSTER

For a Microcluster defined in terms of product and market it is possible to identify each and every one of the specific production phases involved in the transformation of the initial inputs in useful goods and services for the final consumer of the chosen objective markets. At the same time, by concentrating on a production phase, the specific technologies used or that can be used to perform this phase in the most efficient and efficacious way possible can be identified with precision.

In this way the generic concept of the production Value Chain (Porter, 1985) may be amplified towards the specific design of the Framework of the Value Chain in the Microcluster, in the form of a graphic block diagram in which each of the "boxes" of the framework corresponds to a certain phase or link in the production chain. Each of these links is identified with a certain stage whose start and finish are perfectly defined. Such a high degree of detail even allows us to know the value generated in each phase, such as the economic cost of the resources consumed in production, and this facilitates the identification of the stage or stages in which the evolutive process is centred.

In the initial design of this framework, considering the activities defined in this way, the companies that carry out the work are not taken into account, or if they are or are not situated

in the territory in question. It is a case of drawing the traditional or habitual process in which goods or services have been produced up to the present time in the territory, without considering the specific companies involved in their production.

The knowledge and the historic processes associated with a territory give a territorial microcluster its singularity and uniqueness; otherwise the Framework would be confused with another generic technological process.

Thus, by production phase (*a link* in the Value Chain) we understand the group of operations in a certain phase of the specific production process of a product, from the initial inputs of raw materials until the finished product comes into the hands of the final consumer. A phase, stage or link in the chain of value that can be unmistakeably identified from these two characteristics;

- It has perfectly defined initial and final events (markers).
- It generates value – even if at times this may be low or non-existent, in terms of the appreciation of the final consumer, as has been defined in the preceding section – and it has certain costs related to the activities carried out, which correspond to the economic cost of the resources consumed in production (materials, labour, power, information, management, etc).

From the foregoing information we can therefore design the specific Framework of the Value Chain of a Microcluster, creating a graph in the form of a flow diagram with blocks or boxes representing the links. In this diagram, each square or box must correspond to a perfectly defined phase belonging to a value-generating activity with its associated costs in proportion to the resources consumed in its performance. This degree of detail permits a critical analysis of each specific activity carried out (each box), showing the precise relationship of the value generated in the activity for the market with its associated specific costs.

Also, it must be remembered that each of the phases may be performed by internal companies or by companies from outside the territory in question, showing the opportunities for introducing value internally, in those cases in which the value/cost relationship is important and the activity is carried out outside the territory, i.e. by firms outside the Microcluster.

Identification of Opportunities for Innovation in Microclusters from the Determination of Key Factors of Success

The creation of value by innovation can be achieved by means of Innovation in Products and/or by Innovation in Processes.

In the preceding section we defined the differences between the basic concepts of Cost, Price and Value as the starting point to explain the importance of Innovation for businesses, since their profits depend on it.

We said that the best situation occurs with Price located between the company's Cost and the buyer's subjective Value of the product, so that, when an agreement is reached for the

exchange of the product at the stipulated Price, both sides consider that they have taken an advantage from the exchange. In this way – and only in this way – wealth is created in our society. If Price is below Cost, wealth is destroyed in the form of a loss for the selling company, and if Price is above the buyer's subjective Value, wealth is destroyed when he uses his savings in exchange for nothing or for goods that will not give him the satisfaction or the service that he wanted.

So, Innovation is the basis of the creation of wealth for society and of profits for businesses. This is why it is enormously important. The difficult part is to find the right lines to follow that allow companies, by means of increasing value and/or reducing costs, to remain competitive in international markets; the determination of what we call *the key factors in competitive success.*

This is perhaps the most difficult objective to achieve in the endless search for success in business, both for individual companies and for specialised territorial clusters.

With this in mind, we propose to analyse the value chain of a microcluster, i.e. using the Framework of the Value Chain defined in the preceding section. This would mean extending Grant's analysis (1995) by amplifying it to the specialised production links of a microcluster, putting together the blocks of the different stages of production, even if they are each carried out by different firms. Grant uses the value chain of a business company for the possibilities it offers both in the formulation of strategies based on cost reduction and in differentiation.

Individual Analysis of the Links in the Chain

The detailed analysis of the production process and of the technology used in each link, relating them to the percentage of the final value estimated to be generated in this stage and to the associated costs, allows diverse alternatives to be diagnosed:

- For the phases that generate no value, from the point of view of the final consumer: they are simply eliminated.
- For the phases with high costs in relation to final value: a continual search for a greater level of efficiency through the use of new technologies, outsourcing, and if necessary contracting out the work involved in the phase, even using firms outside the geographical region if costs such as salaries, taxes, etc. are lower there.

These are the normal criteria used in the analysis of the principal links in the value chain.

Analysis of the Position of a Specific Phase in the Sequence of Links and Possibilities for Change and/or Change in Relationship with Other Links

One of the greatest successes in industrial sectors, especially in the "mature" sectors (textiles, shoe-making, etc.) has come from a reconstruction of the chain of value, designing completely new production methods, normally based on a "revolutionary" concept (Hamel y Prahalad, 1994) of the Framework of the Value Chain and achieved by a total or almost total restructuring of the technological relationships of the various links.

In the case of the mature sectors, since the products are the traditional ones (clothing, shoes, etc.), the "revolution" has taken place by the intensive use of new technologies (ICT) in the auxiliary activities of the old production chain.

At other times, when the "revolution" cannot be so radical, great innovative advances are achieved by combining antagonistic variables (dipoles), already related to the features or attributes of the product, thus alternating or changing production processes.

Key Factors of Success

The generation of value by obtaining advantages over competitors is attained by companies by utilising the differentiating characteristics (singular characteristics and strategic assets) and applying them in markets where they can be exploited to commercial advantage (Kay, 1993).

The strategic resources to obtain these advantages, as Gary Hammel describes (2000), are to be found in the area of key competences (what the company knows), strategic assets (what the company possesses) and key processes (what the company does).

A key factor in success is therefore the combination of resources and knowledge that a company must have to be used in value-generating or cost-reducing activities to give it an advantage over its competitors.

At this point the necessary question should be; How do we identify a key factor in success? How do we get together and organise the necessary resources and knowledge to beat the competition? And we must not forget that this identification must be done at the start! That is to say, before it actually gives market success.

There is only one answer, and that is by intuition. That is to say, a creative process with information sufficient both in quantity and quality, and with experienced managers responsible for making business decisions, will generate different future strategic alternatives from which the managers from experience and intuition will be able to choose the one or ones with most potential.

In their studies on creativity, Edward de Bono, 1994, and Malcolm Westcott (1968) recognise the importance of the intuitive process in creating and choosing new business ideas. However, for intuition to work well – as a mental function – it is absolutely necessary for it to be based on a long process of work and experience in which knowledge management is a fundamental process, preparing minds for the intuitive phase. This matter has little to do with luck or coincidence and a lot to do with generating relevant information and knowledge by profound analysis in order to generate viable alternatives. And it is intuition, based on the generated knowledge, that in the end impels the minds of the decision takers to choose which one or ones of the alternatives has the most potential to generate value.

The information and knowledge generated both in the analytical process of the structure of microclusters in terms of (product – market) and in the process of the critical analysis of the Framework of the Value Chain must provide sufficient strategic alternatives for the managers of the companies and other bodies involved in the microcluster to be able to intuitively choose the key success factors to be included in the process of strategic change.

However, within a microcluster the alternatives generated have to be shared among the principal organisations involved. What actions must be taken to accomplish this? There are two possible ways, which are not mutually exclusive:

- By means of holding strategic *Benchmarking* sessions in which the principal managers and institutional directors of the Microcluster take part. In these sessions the results of the analysis are explained and a list is given of the most important future alternatives in the sector, discussing and approving those which appear to be the most promising.
- By correspondence, by means of a Delphi type survey, in which proposals for the best alternatives are given and other suggestions are invited, which will be discussed in a second or third round by the managers of the Microcluster.

In both cases the relevant supporting documented information ought to be available to the managers so that they have complete and up to date information on the territory.

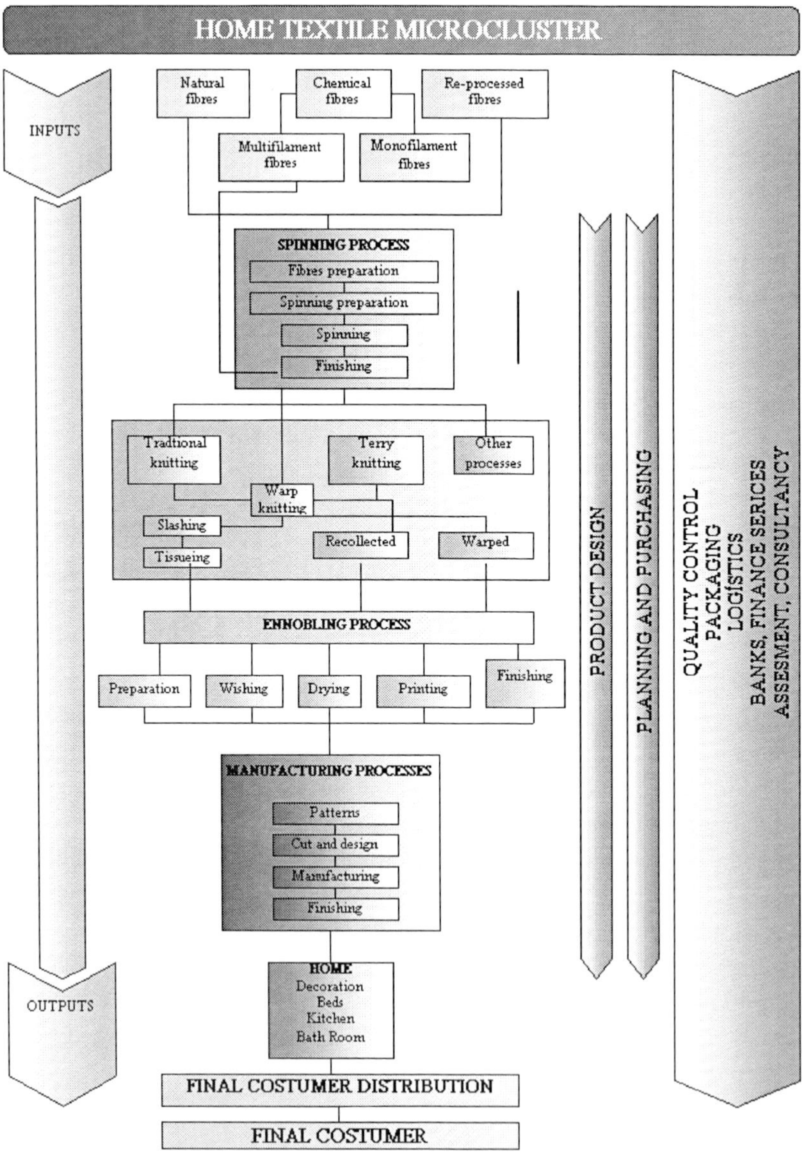

Figure 1. Framework of the Value Chain of the Valencia Home Textile Microcluster.

To illustrate what we have explained, we give in the following figure a simplified map of the value Chain of the Valencia Household Textiles Microcluster. In it some of the key success factors are shown, derived from the analysis of the Microcluster.

CONCLUSIONS

From the information and knowledge gained in the analysis of the microcluster in terms of (product – market), and from the critical analysis of its Framework of the Value Chain, specific strategic alternatives are generated from which the managers involved in the microcluster can use their intuition to isolate the key success factors to be used for strategic changes, as well as the most appropriate technological and industrial policies – in a clustering approach.

In all cases, any strategic decision taken by the leaders of the microcluster must include improved cooperation among its members, making full use of the market potential for the development of new products and services to satisfy clients' new needs and propitiating the development and/or diffusion of new technologies to meet these new needs.

Therefore, it must be remembered that within the concept of the value chain, the information and knowledge that flow through it must also be taken into consideration. According to Rayport and Sviokla (1995), parallel to the physical value chain, along which the goods or services progress, a virtual value chain is generated, along which the information flows that continuously feeds the various members, including the clients, which implies a continuous process of improvement by all the members involved.

This is especially important if we consider the proposed concept of the microcluster value chain. The companies that form this microcluster value chain will have to concentrate on what they really know how to do better than their competitors, and also learn to cooperate with other companies to generate value in an atmosphere of mutual trust. For this microcluster value chain to be basically oriented towards the client, responding to his needs, desires and demands, a new organizational system becomes necessary that is capable of adapting to, and even of anticipating, changes, and of seizing whatever business opportunities are presented.

This form of organization would be that which corresponds to the process of the given value chain necessary to respond to each key factor detected, composed of the members that have the knowledge, competences and skills necessary to carry out the integrated activities through ICT, cooperating with mutual trust, in a context of minimum of hierarchical levels, continually adapting and forming an open, flexible system.

The members of this new organization should agree on a form of management in order to create a common environment of understanding, substituting the concept of obedience for that of shared decisions and negotiation. This is especially important because among the members of the organization, or virtual netchain, there are no traditional hierarchical relationships, since they are independent organizations in a situation of temporary cooperation to deal with a specific market opportunity, so that the establishing of objectives must always be by common agreement among them.

References

Becattini, G. (1989). *Sectors and/or districts: some remarks on the conceptual foundations of industrial economics*. Ed. Goodman et alt.

Becattini, G. (1992). "*El distrito industrial marshaliano como concepto socioeconómico"*. Cap. 4 de Los distritos industriales y las pequeñas empresas. Min. de Trabajo y Seg. Soc. España.

Becattini, G. (1994). *El distrito marshalliano: una noción socioeconómica*. Cap. 2 de Las regiones que ganan. Benko, G. et alt. (eds).

Becattini, G. (1996). *Sistemas productivos locales y mercados globales*. Rev. Investigación Comercial, nº 754

Benko, G. and Lipietz, A. (1994). *Las regiones que ganan*. Ed. Alfons el Magnànim. Valencia.

De Bono, Edward (1994). *El pensamiento creativo*. Ed. Paidós. Barcelona.

Feldman, M. (1994). *The Geography of Innovation*. Dordrecht.

Grant, Robert M. (1995). *Contemporary strategy analysis: concepts, techniques, applications. Blackwell Publishers*. Cambridge, Massachusetts.

Hamel, G. and Prahalad, C.K. (1994). *Competing for the future*. Harvard Business School Press.

Hammel, Gary (2000). *Leading the Revolution*. Harvard Business School Press.

Kay, John (1993). *Foundations of Corporate Success*. Oxford University Press.

Lazzarini, S. G., Chaddad, F. R. and Cook, M. L. (2001). Integrating supply chain and network analyses: the study of netchains. *Journal on Chain and Network Science*, 1 (1), 7-22.

OCDE Territorial Development Policy Committee (1999). Regional Review The Valencian Central Districts. OCDE, París, 3 de diciembre.

Porter, M. E. (1980). *Competitive Strategy: Techniques for analysing industries and competitors*. New York: The Free press.

Porter, M. E. and V. E. Millar (1985). How information gives you competitive advantage. *Harvard Business Review*, Vol. 63, July-Aug., 149-160.

Porter, M. E. (1998 a). *"Clusters and Competition" y "Competing Across Locations" en "On Competition"*. Harvard Business School Press.

Porter, M. E. (1998 b). Clusters and the new economics competition. *Rev. Harvard Business Review,* nov – dec.

Prahalad, C. K. and Hamel, G. (1990). The core competence of the corporation. *Harvard Business Review,* Vol. 68, May-June, 79-91.

Pyke, F. and Sengenberger, W. (1992). *Industrial districts and Local Economic Regeneration*. International Institute for Labour Studies, Geneve.

Rosenfeld, Stuart A. (2002). Just Clusters. Economic development strategies that reach more people and places. A Synthesis of Experiences. Supported by a grant from the Ford Foundation. *Regional Technology Strategies*, Inc. Carrboro, North Carolina. www.rtsinc.org

Sabel, Ch. (1992). Studies Trust: Building New Forms of Cooperation in a Volatile Economy. In Industrial Districts and Local Economic Regeneration. *Frank Pyke and Werner*

Sengenberger, comp. International Institute for Labour Studies, International Labour Office. Geneve.

Scott, B. R. (1989). Competitiveness: Self Help for a Worsening Problem. *Harvard Business Reviews*, 67 (4). 115 - 121.

Sforzi, F. (1989): *"Sistemi locali e sviluppo economico: alcune reflessioni".* Rev. Impresa & Stato, nº 4.

Sweeney, G. (1991). Technical culture and the local dimension of entrepreneurial vitality. *Entrepreneurship and Regional Development,* vol. 3.

Westcott, Malcolm (1968). *Toward a Contemporary Psychology of Intuition.* Holt, Rinehard & Winston. New York.

In: Business and Finance: Performance and Management ISBN: 978-1-61122-936-3
Editors: R. Morland and A. Gagglione

Chapter 8

SEEING THROUGH THE EYES OF CLIENTS: THE LINK BETWEEN MICROFINANCE AND WELL-BEING IN RURAL GHANAIAN HOUSEHOLDS

Cynthia Arku[1,*], Helen Hambly Odame[2,**] and Frank S. Arku[3,]***

[1] Northern Alberta Development Council, Lac La Biche, Alberta, Canada
[2]School of Environmental Design and Rural Development
University of Guelph, Guelph Ontario, Canada
[3]Department of Rural and Community Development, Presbyterian University College, Akuapem Campus, Akropong, Eastern Region, Ghana

ABSTRACT

Income-generating work for women is one of many attempts of the international community and national governments of developing countries to improve well-being of rural households, and empower women. While people draw their interpretation and indicators of well-being from their subjective cultural contexts, many development interventions lack reference to the perceptions of beneficiaries on what advances their well-being. This article presents an investigation of how rural women and men in the Bogoso area of Ghana perceived well-being and the impact of women's microfinance work on their perceived well-being indicators. Findings show that living within a peaceful household environment is the most important well-being indicator to the people, and that microfinance contributed significantly to reducing household conflicts, as household's and children's needs were frequently met. Thus, this article recommends attention to interventions that enhance the ability of rural households to be more engaged in economic activities to promote peace within their households. It also encourages efforts to conscientize and build capacities of household members to be affected by women's work in mitigating potential conflict triggers.

Keywords: Rural households, well-being, culture, gender, conflict, microfinance.

---

[*] E-mail address: cbanner2005@yahoo.ca
[**] E-mail address: hhambly@uoguelph.ca
[***] E-mail address: fsarku@gmail.com

1. INTRODUCTION

Income-generating work for women has gained relevance in the world today. Its potential in reducing poverty[1] in developing countries, particularly rural households, cannot be overemphasized (Gross and Schafer, 2001; Guérin, 2006). Gender and feminist advocates indicate that the roles of men and women affect their development, thereby calling for development interventions that focus on both genders to reduce poverty (Moser, 1989). More emphasis is suggested to be put on women since gender relations tend to marginalize them; unlike their male counterparts, women largely engage in reproductive work, which often does not yield incomes, and consequently limits their access to productive resources (Porter and Sweetman, 2005). According to Kerr (1998) women engaging in reproductive roles, coupled with their lack of access to resources, is related to child poverty.

It is against this background that poverty reduction programs such as microfinance, that target women have gained popularity, especially in developing countries where poverty is widespread. Microfinance, which is described as "the provision of financial services dealing with very small deposits and loans" (Bastelaer, 1999 p. 6), aims to enable women to engage in income-generating work, given that increased income for women promotes better health, nutrition and education for children (Mayoux, 2001; 2005). A lack of such basic needs as food, education and health, in the absolutists view, depict clearly that there is absolute poverty; a situation that do not require comparison with other standards of living to know that poverty exist (Sen, 1983). Also, it is well-documented that women engaging in productive work and earning independent incomes can potentially meet their strategic gender needs as they become empowered, have greater bargaining power and are less at risk of domestic violence (Hashemi *et al.* 1996).

Development objectives that ultimately seek to enable women to achieve independence within cultures where marriage is primarily an imperative to womanhood, may run the risk of overlooking critical dimensions that may shape development interventions to support women's well-being. Kabeer (1994) discussing the purpose of marriage maintains that, it is an interdependent union held together by cooperation, adding that although the gender division of labour within a household can act to sustain society, priorities of some members may be better served than others. Kabeer (1994) citing Evenson's (1976) analysis of the workings of the household noted the reality of negotiations which often occur before one can have access to household resources. The negotiation process, according to Becker (1965, 1976, 1985), evades conflicts when viewed within the New Household Economics theory – which emphasizes the intrinsic capacity of households to maximize joint utility. In this theory, pure altruism that seeks to achieve common household goals, along with the presence of a household head making decisions in the interest of all household members, are said to eliminate potential household conflicts. Critiques indicate that household heads may not know much about the needs of women and children, and their interests may lie elsewhere or within a wider economic and political sphere - not necessarily within their immediate household (Whitehead, 1981; Harris, 1981). Moser also (1993) suggests that cultural and economic factors cause equal and unequal resource allocation within the household, contributing to either support or inhibit the well-being of its members.

[1] Poverty reduction and well-being promoter are used interchangeably in this article

The concept of well-being has been perceived in two ways. First, it consists of material (economic) needs such as food, housing, productive resources and other assets for human survival. Second, it encompasses non-material elements, including psychological and spiritual dimensions such as the absence of physical or verbal violence and happiness in a marriage. Both the material and non-material dimensions of well-being are not only interconnected, but are equally important because each of them contributes to happiness and peace of mind (Afshar, 2005; Narayan *et al.* 2000; Copestake, 2008). Nevertheless well-being is influenced by many factors of which culture is paramount.

People's socio-cultural[2] contexts which entail values, belief systems and customs give rise to perceptions of well-being, which Diener and Suh (2000) referred to as subjective well-being. And due to the differences in what constitutes culture from one society to another or the subjectiveness of well-being (Shek *et al.* 2005; Veenhoven, 2005, 2008; Arku *et al.* 2008), attempting to measure and compare well-being among varied cultural contexts is a complex task (Afshar, 2005; Diener and Suh, 2000; Shah, 1998).

According to Townsend (1985: 662) ".... people have needs which can only be defined by virtue of obligations, associations and customs of such memberships". Although what constitutes well-being, in other words well-being indicators, that measure if people's well-being is met is partly informed by a variety of cultural aspects, culture has not been well integrated into designing, implementing, monitoring and evaluating development interventions. For example, Ver Beek's (2000) review of the policies of three northern development organizations revealed that in addition to a lack of policy in addressing matters of spirituality as an element of culture, there is a conscious avoidance of the topic of culture.

Also, what is often missed in development planning is how people perceive an intervention can contribute to meeting their subjective well-being. Goetz's (1992: 12) study cited the frequent portrayal of Bangladesh women "as silent and passive victim[s] of patriarchy". Kabeer (1998) noted that participatory approaches that allow development actors to listen to 'women' can provide important insights into their lived experiences, instead of complete reliance on academic theorization of gender issues.

In the case of microfinance, women may aspire to achieve several indicators. Kabeer's (1998) work on *Money can't buy me love?* elaborates on how Bangladesh women involved in microfinance reported that, the small loans had improved their well-being because of several positive experiences, including: the women could afford to put enough food on the table, acquire decent homes, re-invest in their businesses and purchase land and livestock; they were able to make social expenditures (e.g., dowries), felt a sense of worth and received more affection from their husbands; and they saw marriages restored, and a reduction in marital

---

2 The importance of culture in development is largely demonstrated by the United Nations. For example, the General Conference of United Nations Education and Scientific Corporation created an independent World Commission on Culture and Development in 1991. The goal of the commission was to compile a world report on some of the most pressing contemporary cultural issues that have both negative and positive effects on development. The report produced by the Commission, *Our Creative Diversity*, maintains that culture is important for human growth and in order to achieve a sustainable development, economic, environmental and social reforms have to be addressed from a cultural perspective. This notion of cultural development is based on the idea that culture and development are closely interlinked, since all kinds of evolution, including human and economic, are ultimately determined by cultural factors. Culture therefore constitutes the very basis of human development and should be regarded as a source of progress. People have different cultures based on their socio-economic backgrounds so no culture is either inferior or superior to another. However, some cultural practices in developing countries are seen by the West as primitive, which Escobar (1995) maintains should not be the case. But it should also be noted that not all cultural practices aid development.

conflicts and domestic violence against women. Sen (1987) also indicates how a woman being able to fit into the social requirements for modest clothing and going to social places without shame may be important for her well-being.

However, several studies assessing the impacts of development projects, including income-generating initiatives with microfinance loans, are based on 'outsiders' views, making reference to institutionally driven objective indicators of well-being with little or no attention to the subjective indicators of beneficiaries. For example, how improvements in women's incomes and their empowerment from microfinance work meets women's own perceptions of well-being is largely under researched, especially in rural African communities.

This article therefore provides an assessment of the impact of rural women's income-generating work on their perceived well-being. Employing a case study approach, the study sought to determine what rural households in the Bogoso area of Ghana perceive as well-being indicators, and to examine whether and how rural women's microfinance work impacts their perceived well-being indicators.

2. Study Approach

The study was conducted within the concept of Gender and Development (GAD) and methodological frame of critical theory. Fiaseman Rural Bank Microfinance Project was used as a case study. Challenges in data collection were encountered because of the sensitivity of the subject matter.

2.1. Conceptual Framework

Gender perspectives, particularly GAD thinking aims to promote rural development through interventions that contribute in the most favourable way to empower women - as individuals and also as a marginalized group - and to enable both men and women to benefit equitably from development interventions. Within this view women and men are not considered separate entities though each of them may have different needs. This is essentially relevant to rural African communities where the well-being of a couple may be tied to their children's and extended family's. Thus, while well-being may be widely defined to include specific institutionalized objectives, constituting both material and non-material dimensions (e.g., access to food, shelter, personal security, freedom from violence and control over fertility decisions and knowledge of legal and political processes), how married women, for example, can achieve these dimensions without triggering unwanted outcomes for themselves and their children, as well as extended family are crucial. At the same time, a variety of subjective measures of well-being relevant to the particular rural societies to which people belong are considered equally important.

Consequently, this study is approached with the presumption that microfinance projects that target rural women can indirectly and/or directly cause favourable and unfavourable changes in the well-being of household members. Along with the stand point on the vital role of culture in development, this article presents an assessment of the impact of rural women's income generating work on the sensitive subject of household conflict, with reference to what men and women perceive are indicators of their well-being. Also, it is presumed that when

women transition from having little or no incomes of their own to being economically independent, the resulting change in their power and influence levels within the household has a potential to either increase or prevent household conflicts.

2.2. Methodological Theory

Critical theory is also fundamental to this study. This theory is concerned with issues of power and justice and the ways that people's characteristics (e.g., race, class, gender, ethnicity, ideologies, education, religion and other cultural dynamics) interact to construct a social system (Beck-Gernsheim *et al.* 2003). Critical researchers focus on providing meaningful and compelling insights by uncovering existing social structures, discourses, ideologies and epistemologies. They question what appears to be natural, inviolable and obvious (McLaren, 1997; Slaughter, 1989).

Critical researchers also recognize that their own background shapes their interpretation, and therefore position themselves in their research by acknowledging how interpretations flow from their own personal, cultural and historical experiences. Also may be referred to as 'stand-point' theorists`, critical researchers enter into an investigation with assumptions. Upon detailed analysis, they may change their assumptions so that the product of their work could stimulate change (Foley and Valenzuela, 2005; Kincheloe and McLaren, 2005).

In the light of critical theory, the investigators argue that externally pre-conceived objective well-being indicators should not be the sole point of reference in determining the impacts of development interventions, including microfinance projects, on rural households. This stance challenges the notion that evidence of objective standardized measures of well-being of the international community (e.g., income levels and access to education) alone when met would inevitably enhance the well-being of rural households.

2.3. Fiaseman Rural Bank Microfinance

The Fiaseman Rural Bank Microfinance Project (FRBMP) in Bogoso was selected as the case for this study because it assists to generate incomes for women, with the potential to impact the well-being of their households. The Fiaseman Rural Bank is a private financial institution established in 1983, offering savings and credit, including microfinance to clients in the Western Region of Ghana. The Bank's interest in microfinance came from the start-up support from CARE International, a USA-based non-governmental organization (NGO), in 2001. The common problem of lack of collateral and access to capital that have often plagued business start-ups and progress among rural residents may be losing its place with the dawn of microfinance that made capital available to them. CARE offered a loan of 15,000 Ghana cedis (about US$ 15,000) at a low interest rate of 10% per annum, in addition to other logistical support, to the Fiaseman Rural Bank to undertake a pilot microfinance project in 2001.

Using a group lending methodology, which involved lending to a group of five to twenty groups of individuals interested to succeed economically, the Bank observed that not only did microfinance improve the incomes of their clientele, the Bank also found it profitable. As of

2006, the Fiaseman Rural Bank offered microfinance loans up to a maximum of five hundred Ghana cedis (about US$ 500) per a borrower at a time.

2.4. Data Collection and Analysis

The case study approach was considered useful for this study because it is more suitable for exploratory and explanatory investigations of this kind, as well as for investigating contemporary issues and actual behavioural events (Yin, 2003). Communities in the Bogoso area in which residents have accessed microfinance from Fiaseman Rural Bank, for at least two years, were selected to participate in the study. Out of approximately thirty-five communities in the Bogoso area served by the FRBMP, five, namely, Coboldkrom, Adwinpa, Agyeikrom, Ayensukrom No. 2 and Insu, were selected for this study. Each of these communities had one microfinance group or association of borrowers from the Fiaseman Rural Bank.

Couples were the focus of the investigation because it targeted to analyse conflicts in marital and work relationships. More emphasis was on women than men during the data collection because women were the main participants in the microfinance project[3]. Data were collected through focus group discussions, semi-structured and key informant interviews, participant and direct observations and secondary data reviews. Since an objective of this study was to identify respondents' own self-generated well-being indicators, focus group discussions with 'men only' and 'women only' groupings were conducted to allow discussions on a range of issues. Responses from women-only focus group discussions were used to generate a list of well-being indicators, and men were asked to agree or disagree on the well-being indicators generated by women. As well, the focus group discussions with men helped to collate their views on issues identified by women when semi-structured interviews were administered to them concerning any effects of microfinance on their well-being.

From the selected communities, which consisted of varied numbers of women small loan borrowers from the Bank - Coboldkrom (9), Adwinpa (10), Agyeikrom (9), Ayensukrom No. 2 (8) and Insu (4) - there was a total of 40 participating married women who were all chosen as respondents. All the women participated in semi-structured interviews to determine whether and how the microfinance project addressed their own well-being indicators. The semi-structured interviews with the women were also used to collect data on areas such as respondents' age, marital status, level of education and tribal affiliation. Additionally, the bank's personnel, including microfinance field officers were interviewed for data on their historical development of microfinance, loan delivery methodology, microfinance success and related issues.

In order to perceive reality as an insider, the investigators lived in the study communities, particularly within male-headed households of women microfinance borrowers from the FRBMP. Also, they were involved in a variety of activities such as assisting women to produce their wares at home and to sell at the market, and spending time with men and women at their farms.

[3] Although both men and women could borrow from the bank, the majority of the borrowers were women. This is because trading, which is common among borrowers, is primarily considered a woman's job in rural Ghana.

Data were analyzed using Statistical Package for Social Scientists (SPSS) to generate descriptive statistics. Tests of difference were performed on results of respondents' self-generated indicators of well-being, and measures of association using Spearman's correlation were performed to determine if any relationship existed between spousal conflict[4] and children's conflict levels. Qualitative techniques, including open coding were used to analyze open ended questions and focus group discussions' results. Key informant interview responses and participant observations were documented as supporting evidence and/or as facts on their own.

2.5. Study Limitations

Probing a sensitive issue as spousal conflicts posed a difficulty in gathering separate views of men and women. During interviews with some women, their husbands sometimes were present, irrespective of requests to stay away - which could have restricted women from expressing their thoughts in ways that might have affected the findings and conclusions. Also, the conclusiveness of findings on indicators of well-being of households could have been enhanced if men's and children's indicators of well-being were studied separately in greater detail.

3. FINDINGS

This section includes a description of the social and economic demographic characteristics of women respondents, loans amounts and their uses, and how the microfinance work is organized. As well, women's and men's perceptions of indicators of well-being and the effects of microfinance on the incidence of conflicts between spouses, children and parents, and spouses and extended families, which respondents considered important for their well-being, are presented.

3.1. Background of Respondents and Microfinance

Farming and mining are the predominant economic activities in Bogoso. Most of the residents consider agriculture as a livelihood system. Consequently, about 47% of residents engage in subsistence farming, with only 10% in plantation or commercial agriculture. Women comprise 70% of all farmers in the area. Mining plays a significant role in creating both direct mining jobs and support activities (Wassa West District Assembly (2002).

Unlike previously when undermining of girl child education in Ghana progressively created a pool of women with limited career options, increasing numbers of women are becoming actively involved in various aspects of the Ghanaian labour market, as education of girls is encouraged. However, cultural and spatial factors have had a marked impact on the labour process and division among genders. While there is no restrain on what women, including married women, can do for work, child rearing and other traditional roles of women may tend to stand in the way of women desiring to advance into high end jobs. Besides, urban

[4] Reduction in conflicts within households was mentioned in the focus group discussions as a well-being promoter.

and rural disparity in the level and quality of education in favour of urban dwellers means that, few rural women have the qualifications to make them competitive in the modern labour market. Hence, the rural women are more likely to be self-employed in agriculture, trading and the trades (e.g., dress-making and hairdressing).

Of all respondents, approximately 90% belonged to monogamous marriages. Also the majority (90%) of women respondents were in the age group of 35 to 64, and a significant portion (78%) of them have had some formal education. Approximately 68% of the women were from households with 7 to 25 members (including extended families) and 80% of the women have at least four children.

Christianity is the predominant religion among the women, accounting for 90% and most (82.5%) of them belonged to the Akan tribal group, which is the largest of the Ghanaian tribes. Households within the communities are largely matrilineal[5] - children from a marriage are said to belong to the family of the woman and the children inherit from their mothers' lineage.

Women borrowers from the FRBMS obtained between three and six hundred Ghana cedis (between US$ 300 and US$ 600) in loans over an average of two years. The women used their loans to trade and engage in palm and vegetable farming and processing of palm oil (edible oil made from palm fruit). The women reported that they did not use their loans to purchase food since a large portion of food came from their farms; however, they used some of the loan money to pay their children's schooling and apprenticeship costs. Children and husbands provided a significant amount (over 40%) of the labour for women's microfinance work and about 15% of it was provided by extended family members.

3.2. Perception of Indicators of Well-being

When women were asked the indicators that met their own sense of well-being, they mentioned five main indicators. They reported that their well-being is promoted when:

- both spouses are engaged in some income-generating activity;
- there is peace between spouses and among household members;
- household members are engaged in trading;
- children are enrolled in apprenticeship; and
- parents are able to afford food and healthcare for household members, and education for children.

Men were asked in focus group discussions to indicate if the indicators of well-being identified by the women applied to them and/or they have different well-being indicators. The men, in addition to reporting that the indicators indentified by the women pertained to them, also said they did not have differing views.

In semi-structured interviews, the women were asked to rank the indicators according their importance on a scale of one to five (1 = very unimportant, 2 = unimportant, 3 = neither important nor unimportant, 4 = important and 5 = very important). The results of statistical testing - Kolmogorov-Smirnov- revealed that the well-being indicators were either important (values ranging from 3.5 to 4.0) or very important (values ranging from 4.5 to 5) in promoting their well-being (Table 1).

---

[5] Akans are the only matrilineal tribal group in Ghana.

Table 1. Importance of Well-being Indicators

Items	Mean	Order of rank	Significance Level
1. There is peace within household	4.8	1	0.00
2. Husband and wife engage in some income-generating activity	4.1	2	0.00
3. Parents are able to afford food and health care for the household and children's education	3.9	3	0.00
4. Household members are engaged in trading	3.7	4	0.00
5. Children are enrolled in apprenticeship	3.5	5	0.00

(2 tailed) $P \leq 0.01$

Based on a ranking, living within an environment of minimal conflict (between couples, children and extended family) was the indicator with the highest mean value, therefore ranking first. The well-being indicator which was ranked fifth (last) is children being enrolled in apprenticeship. Statistical testing showed that the results in Table 1 are significant because p value for each of the indicators is 0.00[6].

3.3. Microfinance and Intra-household Conflict

Conflict Levels between Spouses

Conflict may occur between different groups within the same household - between spouses, parents and children, and parents and their extended family members. In order to determine the extent to which microfinance promoted peace within households, the levels of conflict and their causes before and during the microfinance were compared.

Table 2. Conflict Levels between Spouses

Categories	Pre-microfinance		During microfinance	
	No. of Respondents	% of Responses	No. of Respondents	% of Responses
Not much conflict	19	47.5	28	70.0
A lot of conflict	14	35.0	3	7.5
No conflict	7	17.5	9	22.5
Total	40	100.0	40	100.0

Changes in conflict levels were measured by their frequency of occurrence. It is evident from Table 2 that conflicts between couples decreased considerably since women participated in microfinance. Thus, unlike the pre-microfinance period, fewer women reported experiencing 'a lot of conflict' while involved in microfinance. Also, 70% of the respondents reported that they experienced 'not much' spousal conflicts as they engaged in microfinance, compared with only 47.5% prior to the microfinance project. The women added that the spousal conflicts occurred less frequently because they could also contribute significantly in financial terms to meet their household needs.

[6] But of course not absolute zero; there is a number above zero at the third or fourth decimal point.

Women discussing the reasons for conflict within their households maintained that customarily, it is the man who marries a woman and not the vice versa in Ghanaian culture. Hence, a husband is responsible for taking care of his wife's and children's needs by providing adequate resources, particularly 'chop money' (e.i., money that a husband gives to his wife to take care of day-to-day needs of the household, especially food and other basic necessities). Consequently, when a husband does not fulfil this expectation, his wife became unhappy. Men on the other hand added that the women compared the amount of 'chop money' they each receive with their peers' and those who have received relatively less were unhappy and got into conflict with them (husbands), until they were able to increase the 'chop money' to match their peers'. A man remarked that:

> For the first two years of our marriage, my wife was very satisfied with the money I gave her for meal preparation. She would often tell me how proud she is of me because I gave her enough money. But since she started going to the market together with a neighbour's wife, she has changed a lot; she has been complaining that the money I give her isn't enough. One day, she told me that my neighbour gives more money to his wife than I give her.

Women also reported that although conflicts were few since their involvement in the FRBMP, the main reason for these conflicts is husbands cutting back their 'chop money' to women. They added that their husbands have deliberately reduced their normal contributions towards household expenses and some of them are reluctant to make large contributions even if they are capable of doing so. According to the women, husbands were of the view that wives earn considerable incomes from their microfinance work and so expect their wives to take care of a sizeable portion of household expenditures. Women, however, maintained that they are extremely careful not to continually spend money on expenditures that may eventually deplete their loans and incomes and prevent them from getting future loans. Both the men and women point out that, conflicts are commonly the consequence of not having adequate financial resources to cater for their household needs.

Moreover, women reported that having large sums of money in their hands encouraged husbands to borrow from them from time to time. Conflicts occurred when husbands either do not repay their debts on time or refuse to pay debts entirely.

Conflict Levels between Parents and their Children

There was a considerable reduction in conflicts between parents and their children after women were involved in microfinance work (Table 3). The women said that they were unable to provide basic needs such as clothing, food and school supplies for their children during the pre-microfinance period when they barely earned any income. Children who lacked these needs were unhappy and often became delinquent towards their parents. However, children were more respectful after women's participation in microfinance work, because their mothers could largely provide their needs. A woman informant, for example, said:

> A few years ago my daughter was so disrespectful; she would refuse to clean the house and do other household chores, no matter how many times I ask her to do so. But now, she cleans the house, collects clean water and washes dishes everyday because I usually buy her earrings and underwear when I go to the market

Table 3. Conflict Levels between Parents and Children

Categories	Pre-microfinance		During microfinance	
	No. of Respondents	% of Responses	No. of Respondents	% of Responses
Not much conflict	11	27.5	27	67.5
A lot of conflict	21	52.5	4	10.0
No conflict	8	20.0	9	22.5
Total	40	100.0	40	100.0

Based on a Spearman's Rank correlation co-efficient (rho), current conflict levels between parents and their children were significantly positively correlated ($r = 0.694$, two-tailed $p \leq 0.01$).

Conflict Levels between Parents and Extended Family

The women reported that the incidence of conflict between spouses and their extended families increased after their participation in microfinance work (Table 4).

Table 4. Levels of Conflict between Spouses and their Extended Family

Category	Pre-microfinance		During microfinance	
	No. of Respondents	% of Responses	No. of Respondents	% of Responses
Not much conflict	26	65.0	3	7.5
A lot of conflict	0	0	20	50.0
No conflict	14	35.0	17	42.5
Total	40	100.0	40	100

They also indicated that increased work load and pressure is the prime cause of the conflicts between these two groups This is because spouses and extended family members, including labourers, have to work harder and for longer hours in order to complete their production targets, given that the loan repayment schedules need to be met to be eligible for future loans. This situation called for job sharing, negotiations and working extra hours, which were not without conflicts.

4. Discussion of Findings

4.1. Indicators of Well-being among Rural People

Well-being is perceived as the outcome of development efforts and a better goal than an improvement in economic terms alone. Several studies have shown that material as well as non-material dimensions of well-being are important in measuring people's well-being (Frey and Shutzer, 2002; Inglehart, 1990). Interestingly, Afshar (2005) also points to the interconnectedness of the two dimensions of well-being by noting that, although material basics are imperative, development out of poverty may also depend on non-material dimensions of well-being. Evidence from findings of men's and women's indicators of well-being highlights the multi-dimensional nature of well-being indicators. Although both men

and women were in agreement with the same indicators, the women indicated that of all the indicators, the most important to their well-being is to have peace, followed by being involved in income-generating activities, and next is to be able to afford needs such as food and healthcare for household members and education for children. The last two were to be involved in trading and to have their children in apprenticeship programs. These indicators suggest that rural people may perceive well-being as comprising both material and non-material components, as they desire to have peace, skills training and employment to promote their well-being.

Another observation is the interrelationships among the indicators of well-being, as illustrated in Figure 1. This figure shows that men and women considered peaceful co-existence as an important well-being indicator after which they linked this to the means to attaining peace by engaging in income-generating opportunities. The outputs of this combination were incomes and assets, which can in turn be used to obtain their needs, including food, education and skill training and healthcare. Thus, peace could be viewed as *a means* and *an end*, both of which improve people's well-being. However, rural people need more than a conflict-free environment to obtain peace, suggesting that income, for example, is essential to their well-being. This thereby reinforces Frey and Shutzer's (2002) position that people want money not for themselves but to make them happy, and in this case, to foster peace.

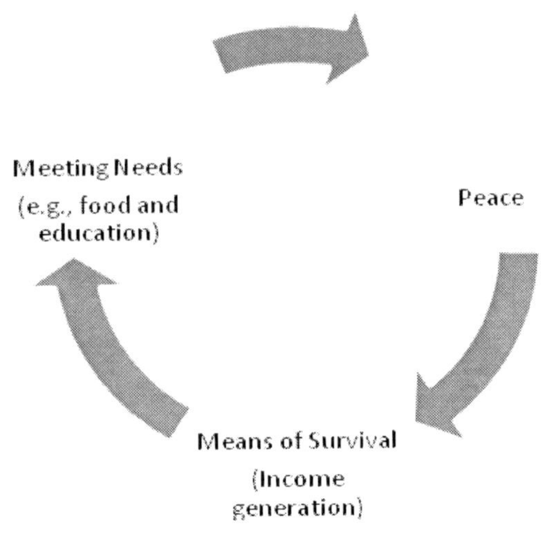

Source: Authors' Fieldwork

Figure 1. Interrelationship among Indicators of Well-being.

It appears that rural people are fundamentally concerned with survival more than wealth (Arku *et al.* 2008). Frey and Shutzer (2002) and Inglehart (1990) noted from their studies of well-being that wealth does not necessarily create well-being; a stance that can be substantiated by the study findings. Both the men and women stayed away from reporting wealth as an indicator of their well-being, while they pointed out access to the means for producing incomes (e.g., trading and skills training for work by apprenticing) as important to their well-being. This situation suggests that winning a lottery, for example, may not be a

preferred source of income for rural people. Perhaps their goal is not to amass wealth, but rather to be involved in a constant pursuit of livelihood opportunities. Consequently, well-being for rural poor could be somewhat interpreted as a condition of having a secure, sustainable means of survival, accompanied by a sense of peace among household members.

4.2. Microfinance, Intra-Household Conflict and Role of Culture for Well-being

In their study of households of Bangladesh Rural Advancement Committee (BRAC) and Grameen Bank members in rural Bangladesh, Schuler *et al.* (1998) observed that husbands became increasingly violent as a social reaction to their wives encroaching into traditional male space to take advantage of opportunities and earn independent incomes. Other studies have showed that women's income-generating work strengthens their economic roles, exposes them to the public and makes them less vulnerable to domestic violence (Hashemi *et al.* 1996; Goetz and Gupta, 1996). Observations from this study is that, in addition to reducing spousal conflicts, income generating work for women promotes a healthy relationship between children and parents. The women experienced fewer spousal conflicts because they produced independent incomes and contributed significantly to their household expenditures. Also, their children showed less delinquent behaviour because mothers could afford most of their needs. This is an indication that women's income-generating work goes beyond enabling rural women to meet the livelihood needs of their households; it can also serve as a remedy to conflicts arising from inadequate resources for household usage. Besides, improved incomes for women through income-generating work can provide a healthy social environment for nurturing children.

Further, although independent incomes for women can reduce conflicts between parents and children, as well as spousal conflicts, it was as well evident that women working with extended family members can be a key contributor to conflicts within the household. As the women in the FRBMP resorted to extended family labour when their husbands' and children's labour is not enough, the incidence of conflicts between spouses and extended family workers increased partly due to the complexities of managing extended relations in the face of increased work load and pressure. However, the couples were not in conflict with each other, suggesting that extended family members may be at a greater risk of conflict than the nuclear family when women operate microfinance ventures.

Also, it is argued that increased income for women improves resources available to the household for nourishment, education of children and dealing with sudden crises (Hashemi e*t al.*, 1996; Hirschland, 2003). Contrarily, Mayoux (1998) noted that an increase in women's income may not imply an increase in resources available for household usage since men may cut back resource contributions for household upkeep. Similarly, the women reported that their incomes were inadequate and therefore relied on some of their husbands' in taking care of the household. Husbands, however, lessened their resource contributions on the assumption that women have reasonably increased incomes. Subsequently, this can worsen women's situation by overburdening them with additional work and yet unable to improve the well-being of their households due to men cutting back their resource contributions. Besides, it is unclear whether men use the withheld parts of their incomes to pursue activities that ultimately improve the well-being of their households, including women and children. In any

case, the amount of resources that men are willing to contribute towards meeting household needs and their income earning opportunities are crucial to the well-being of households in which women engage in income-generating work.

Kabeer (1994) noted in her analysis of the workings of the household that, resources are not always pooled and that a bargaining process is required in determining access to them. Evidence from this study does not only support this claim, but also demonstrates that resource allocation is a heavily negotiated process, and the result is to some extent contingent on exogenous factors. While wives reported experiencing decreasing resource contributions from their husbands since their involvement in microfinance, the husbands on the other hand indicated that their wives got upset and asked for more money, if they realized that their 'chop money' was less than their peers'. This observation suggests that whereas back and forth negotiations between men and women around resource contributions exist, at the same time, non-household members, including peers may influence the process and outcomes of negotiations. In effect, this rather comparative approach to organizing resources between men and women can do two things: encourage conflicts and/or an even distribution of resources among rural women.

On the institutional side, it is apparent that women microfinance borrowers are becoming 'mini banks', offering loans to other members of their household. Nonetheless, it is uncertain why husbands borrowed money at an interest-free rate from their working wives and refused to either repay or repay on time, especially when husbands expect their wives to make significant money contributions towards household upkeep. This situation questions how sustainable women's income-generating work and benefits can be, in the light of women's interest-free loans to men and conflicts arising from men defaulting repayments. Conversely, Khan's (1999) study of BRAC members in Bangladesh showed that some of the women gave parts of their loans to their husbands and other family members or friends to work with, and the women got a share of the income generated through an informal contract.

Moreover, the role of culture in making resource allocation decisions within the household cannot be overemphasized. Becker (1965, 1976, 1985), explaining the theory of New Household Economics with reference to the goal of maximizing joint utility, argued that conflicts of interest and welfare inequality within the household are eliminated because household members subordinate their individual tastes and preferences in pursuit of common goals - pure altruism. And that this is also due to the influence of the household head who sets goals in the interest of all. This analysis has faced objection on the basis that, household heads do not know enough about the needs of women and children, and their interest may not necessarily coincide with those of the immediate household unit (Whitehead, 1981). Hence, Moser (1993) maintains that economic and cultural determinants have created both equality and inequality in intra-household resources allocation. The role of culture in such outcomes was evident from this investigation. Particularly when in spite of the matrilineal system of inheritance which limited fathers from investing significantly in their children's welfare within the study communities, couples felt obligated to adequately care for their children because of their religious belief of dual ownership of children. This finding implies that aside the influence of the household head and pure altruism by household members; belief systems within cultures are pertinent to creating or eliminating household inequalities.

4.3. Ways forward in Promoting the Well-being of Rural Households

Knowing what matters to people and how development interventions meet their perceptions of well-being is vital to reducing poverty. As evident from this study, when women are economically independent, the peace of the nuclear household is largely secured and the well-being of the household can be said to have improved. This may be so especially in cultures where separation or divorce is rarely an option for a challenging marriage - perhaps due to wives' dependency on husbands and religious values. Also, spousal conflicts and child or juvenile delinquency could stem from women's poverty in certain contexts. Women and other members of the household dynamically interact, co-operatively to achieve common and individual goals, and a woman's deprived condition that may lead to despair and conflict is the result of various forms of human deprivation, usually emerging from factors such as social exclusion, lack of human capital and productive assets that affect the entire household. Thus, a closer attention to the link between parents' poverty and children's delinquency can be helpful in strategizing effective development interventions. And efforts that establish and enhance the overall goal of attaining and maintaining peace within rural households of Bogoso may be pursued as this remains central to their well-being.

As well, to facilitate a conflict-free environment, household members who may assist with women's microfinance work, would require training in business and conflict management, to help them to better manage their work load and pressure. In the same way, husbands of women to be involved in microfinance may be encouraged to avoid defaulting payment of loans from women and to obtain loans from existing borrowing institutions when they have a need for loans. Also, negotiations between couples on a fair and reasonable contribution from each party for household maintenance may be necessary to limit conflicts and to keep women's income generating work viable.

Finally, since perceptions of well-being are subjective and dynamic, measuring a combination of objective and subjective well-being dimensions is recommended, if meeting the well-being of beneficiaries of development interventions is a priority. A good insight of what is important to beneficiaries can ensure effective targeting of what really matters to them; an element which becomes even more important in the face of limited resources. Also, knowledge of subjective indicators when applied to development policies, programs and projects can promote not only well-being, but also a more accurate measurement of well-being of target groups.

5. Conclusion

This article revealed that both material and non-material aspects of well-being are important to the general well-being of rural households, noting that rural people's well-being primarily may rely on the skills training and continuous pursuit of economic opportunities that provide incomes for meeting their needs, ultimately promoting peace within their households. Undoubtedly, the self-generated indicators of well-being compared to the impacts of microfinance on conflict within the households of women participants in the FRBMP showed that, women's income-generating work complements the well-being of rural households. Thus, women improve their resource contribution towards meeting household needs when they are financially sound, which helps to keep conflicts down between couples, and children

and parents. However, husbands lessening resource contributions to the household due to wives' increased incomes and husbands borrowing money from wives and defaulting payment, were the reasons for any conflicts among spouses since women's involvement in microfinance. At the same time, conflicts may go up between spouses and their extended family members working for the women because of increased work load and issues with managing it. Nevertheless, rural women's microfinance work will advance their households' well-being more effectively, if the men can maintain reasonable contributions to the household and do not borrow women's money, and conflicts from increased work load are mitigated.

REFERENCES

Afshar, F. (2005). Exploring the frontiers of international development: Countries of the north, well-being, spirituality, and contemplation. *Canadian Journal of Development Studies* XXVI (3): 527-545.

Arku, F. S., Filson, G. and Shute, J. (2008). Empirical approach to the study of well-being among rural men and women in Ghana. *Social Indicators Research* 88: 365-387.

Bastelaer, T.V. (1999). *Does Social Capital Facilitate the Poor's Access to Credit? A Review of the Microeconomic Literature*. The World Bank, Washington DC.

Becker, G. (1965). A theory of the allocation of time. *Economic Journal* LXXX: 493-517.

Becker, G. (1976). *The Economic Approach to Human Behaviour*. Chicago: University of Chicago Press.

Becker, G. (1985). *Treatise on the Family*. Cambridge, MA: Harvard University Press.

Beck-Gernsheim, E., Butler, E. J. and Puigvert, L. (2003). *Women Social Transformation*. New York: Peter Lang.

Copestake, J. (2008). Wellbeing in international development: What's new? *Journal of International Development* 20: 577-597.

Diener, E. and Suh, M. E. (2000). Measuring subjective well-being to compare quality of life of cultures. In E. Diener and I. Suh (Eds.), *Culture and Subjective Well-being* (2-12). London: MIT Press.

Escobar, A. (1995). *Encountering Development: The Making and the Unmaking of the Third World*. Princeton, New Jersey: Princeton University Press.

Foley, G. and Valenzuela, A. (2005). Critical ethnography: The politics of collaboration. In N. K. Denzin and Y. S. Lincoln (Eds.), *The Sage Handbook of Qualitative Research* (Third Edition, 217-234). London: Sage.

Frey, B. S. and Shutzer, A. (2002). *Happiness and Economics*. New Jersey: Princeton University Press.

Goetz, A. M. and Gupta, S. R. (1996). Who takes the credit? Gender, power, and control over loan use in rural credit Programs in Bangladesh. *World Development* 24(1): 45-63.

Gross, R. and Schafer, B. (2001). *GTZ guidelines for impact monitoring and Assessment in micro-finance programmes*. Berlin: GTZ.

Guérin, I. (2006). Women and money: Lessons from Senegal. *Development and Change* 37(3): 549-570.
Harris, O. (1981). Households in Natural Units. In K. Young, C. Wolkowitz, and C. McCullagh (Eds.), *Of Marriage and the Market*. London: CSE.
Hashemi, S., Schuler, S. and Riley, A. (1996). Rural credit programs and women empowerment in Bangladesh. *World Development* 24(4): 635-653.
Hirschland, M. (2003). Serving small depositors: Overcoming the obstacles, recognizing the tradeoffs. *The Microbanking Bulletin* 9.
Inglehart, R. (1990). *Culture shift in Advanced Industrial Society*. Princeton, New Jersey: Princeton University Press.
Kabeer, N. (1994). *Reversed Realities: Gender Hierarchies in Development Thought*. London: Verso.
Kabeer, N. (1998). Money can't buy me love: Re-evaluating gender, credit and empowerment in rural Bangladesh. *IDS Discussion Paper* 363. Brighton: University of Sussex.
Kerr, J. (1998). Women's rights in the global economy: Can feminists transform development. *Sixth annual Hopper Lecture*. Guelph: University of Guelph.
Kincheloe, L. J. and McLaren, P. (2005). Rethinking critical theory and qualitative Research. In N. K. Denzin and S. Y. Lincoln (Eds.), *The Sage Handbook of Qualitative Research* (Third Edition, 303-342). London: Sage.
Khan, R. M. (1999). Micro-finance, wage employment and housework: A gender analysis. *Development in Practice* 9(4): 424-436.
Mayoux, L. (1998). Women's empowerment and micro-finance programmes: approaches, evidence and ways forward. *Unpublished report*, Milton Keynes: The Open University.
Mayoux, L. (2001). Tackling the down side: Social capital, women's empowerment and micro-finance in Cameroon. *Development and Change* 32(3): 435-464.
Mayoux, L. (2005). *Gender and empowerment concepts*. Retrieved on December 10, 2008, from http://www.genfinance.info/Documents/GenderConcepts.pdf
McLaren, P. (1997). *Revolutionary Multiculturalism: Pedagogies of Dissent for the New Millennium*. New York: Routledge.
Moser, C. O. (1989). Gender planning in the Third World: Meeting practical and strategic needs. *World Development* 17: 1799-1825.
Moser, C. O. (1993). *Gender Planning and Development: Theory Practice and Training*. London: Routledge.
Narayan, D., Chambers, R., Shah, M. K. and Petesch, P. (2000). *Voices of the Poor Crying Out for Change*. New York: The World Bank.
Porter, F. and Sweetman, C. (2005). Editorial. In F. Porter and C. Sweetman (Eds.), *Mainstreaming Gender in Development: A Critical Review* (2-10). Oxford: Oxfam.
Schuler, R. S., Hashemi, M. S and Badal, H. S. (1998). Men's violence against women in rural Bangladesh: Undermined or exacerbated by microcredit programmes. *Development in Practice* 8 (2): 148-157.
Sen, A. (1983). Poor, relatively speaking. *Oxford Journals* 35 (2): 153-169.
Sen, A. (1987). *The standard of living*. Cambridge: Cambridge University Press.
Shah, M. K. (1998). Gendered perceptions of well-being and social change in Darko, Ghana. In I. Guijt, and M. K. Shah (Eds.), *The Myth of Community: Gender Issues in Participatory Development* (141-151). London: Intermediate Technology Publications.

Shek, T. L., Chan, Y. K. and Lee, P. S. N. (2005). Quality of life in the global context: A Chinese response. *Social Indicators Research* 71(1): 1-10.

Slaughter, R. (1989). Cultural reconstruction in the post-modern world. *Journal of Curriculum Studies* 3: 255-270.

Townsend, P. (1985). A sociological approach to the measurement of poverty – A rejoinder to Professor Amartya Sen. *Oxford Economic Papers* 37: 659-668.

Veenhoven, R. (2005). Apparent quality-of-life in nations: How long and happy people live. *Social Indicators Research* 71(1): 61-86

Veenhoven, R. (2008). Sociological theories of subjective well-being. In M. Eid and R. J. Larsen (Eds.), *The Science of Subjective Well-being*, New York: The Guilford Press. 44-61.

Ver Beek, K. (2000). Spirituality: A development taboo. *Development in Practice* 10 (1): 31-43.

Wassa West District Assembly (2002). *Wassa West District Medium Term Plan* (WWDMTP) 2002-2004. Tarkwa, Ghana: Wassa West District Assembly.

Whitehead, A. (1981). I'm hungry, mum the politics of domestic budgeting. In K. Young, C. Wolkowitz and C. McCullagh (Eds.), *Of Marriage and the Market: Women's Subordination in International Perspective* (88-111). London: CSE.

Yin, K. R. (2003). *Case Study Research Design and Methods, Third edition.* London: Sage.

In: Business and Finance: Performance and Management ISBN: 978-1-61122-936-3
Editors: R. Morland and A. Gagglione

Chapter 9

MARKOVIAN APPROACHES IN MODELING WORKFORCE SYSTEMS

Marie-Anne Guerry [1,*] ***and Tim De Feyter*** [2,**]

[1]Centre for Manpower Planning, Vrije Universiteit Brussel, Pleinlaan 2, B-1050 Brussels, Belgium

[2]Centre for Corporate Sustainability, Hogeschool-Universiteit Brussel, K.U.Leuven Association, Stormstraat 2, B-1000 Brussels, Belgium

ABSTRACT

Manpower planning is a fundamental aspect of Human Resource Management which is to a great extent based on statistical techniques and focused on quantitative models for workforce systems. Aggregated Markov models are defined by transition probabilities between homogeneous subgroups of personnel of the workforce system. The analytical Markovian approach in manpower planning allows identifying interesting characteristics of the workforce system, allows predicting the evolution of the workforce and controlling it by setting the organization's human resource policies (e.g. recruitment, promotion, training). There is a rich variety of publications on Markov manpower models, in which properties of workforce systems are investigated under very specific assumptions. This paper offers a review of the different types of Markov manpower models. Hereby attention has been paid to the successive stages of the Markov manpower planning methodology in real-world applications, from model building and selection, parameter estimation, model validation to prediction and control. The paper covers the latest advances in the field.

Keywords: Manpower Planning, Stochastic models, Markov models, Homogeneity, Attainability

* E-mail address: marie-anne.guerry@vub.ac.be, Tel: +32 2 6292049, Fax: +32 2 6292054
** E-mail address: tim.defeyter@hubrussel.be, Tel: +32 2 6098274, Fax: +32 2 2101619

INTRODUCTION

While the term manpower planning originates from the 1960s (Walker, 1992; Smith and Bartholomew, 1988), the first applications of quantitative techniques for personnel management go back until 1779. The British Marine used a mathematical model to plan military careers and to analyze turnover (McClean, 1991). It concerned an application of a model from actuarial sciences. The techniques originally developed to analyze demography, were suitable to study workforce systems: recruitments, turnover and promotions were studied in the same way as respectively births, deaths and changes in socio-economic characteristics (Bartholomew, 1971). This allowed predicting the internal personnel availability. Dill, Graver and Weber (1966) refer to the use of the replacement table before World War II. This was an early version of the skills inventory (Ivancevich, 2003; Mondy, Noe and Premeaux, 1999), which had the objective to predict turnover by actuarial methods and to assure succession from within the organization. The largest problem with applications of actuarial methods in personnel management was the lack of accuracy. The estimation of birth-, death- and transition probabilities in demography is based on large datasets, while populations within organizations are much smaller. Therefore, other stochastic methods for personnel management were developed since the 1940s (Bartholomew, 1971). While previously manpower planning was mainly applied in the army, during World War II, because of a large personnel shortage at national level, individual American companies were obligated to estimate their future personnel needs (Dill, Graver and Weber, 1966).

Young and Almond (1961) were the first to introduce the application of Markov theory in manpower planning (Smith and Bartholomew, 1988; Verbeek 1991). They hereby laid the foundations for decades of ongoing research on Markovian approaches for modeling the dynamics in workforce systems. The main objective of those Markov models is predicting and controlling an organization's internal personnel supply (Verhoeven, 1980). In practice, workforce systems can also be analyzed by other operations research techniques as there are computer simulation models, optimization models and models based on system dynamics (Wang, 2005; Parker and Cain, 1996; Purkiss, 1981). In general those alternative models are much more complex. While complex models have the objective to improve the accuracy of results, they often require very specific data which are difficult to collect. Especially when a large number of parameters have to be estimated, this just could harm the reliability of the results. At the cost of simplicity, simpler and more robust models (like Markov manpower models) are therefore often much more attractive (Skulj, Vehovar and Stamfelj, 2008). Moreover, for real-world practitioners, the use of very complex models might be too costly and time-consuming. Finally, unlike other more complex models, the analytical Markovian approach allows identifying interesting characteristics of the workforce system which influence its future dynamics.

This paper offers a review of the current state-of-the-art in research on Markovian approaches for modeling workforce system dynamics. In the first section, an overview is given of the basic concepts and assumptions underlying those models. We discuss their interesting possibilities for prediction and control. However, the adequacy of the model depends on some strict assumptions. In Section 2, we consider a framework for building an adequate Markov manpower model. Additional alternative hypotheses on the workforce system result in Markov models with special characteristics. This allows examining

prediction, control and asymptotic behavior in a very specific manner, which is described in Section 3. Finally some possibilities for future research are discussed in Section 4.

1. Modeling the Dynamics in a Workforce System: General Concepts

The evolution of personnel availability fully depends on the future dynamics of the workforce. To study this dynamics, Markov manpower planning models consider organizations as workforce systems of stocks and flows.

Stocks and Flows

The workforce system is classified into k exclusive subgroups, resulting in the states of the system $S_1,\ldots,S_k$. Those states form a partition of the total population. The number of members in state S_i at time t is called the stock of S_i and is denoted as $n_i(t)$. The stock vector is the ($1 \times k$) vector $n(t)=(n_i(t))$ and is called the personnel distribution at time t. The total number of members at time t, can be expressed as $N(t)=\sum_{i=1}^{k} n_i(t)$. Sometimes it is useful to express stocks as a proportion of the total number of members in the workforce system, resulting in a stochastic vector $q(t)=(q_i(t))$ with:

$$q_i(t)=\frac{n_i(t)}{\sum_{i=1}^{k} n_i(t)}.$$

The stock vector provides a snapshot of the system, but gives no information about changes in the personnel distribution over time. The number of individuals moving from state S_i to state S_j in the time interval [t-1,t) is denoted by $n_{ij}(t-1,t)$. For time interval [t-1,t), the flows are denoted in a square matrix $N(t-1,t)=(n_{ij}(t-1,t))$. It is much more common to express the flows as transition rates:

$$p_{ij}(t-1,t)=\frac{n_{ij}(t-1,t)}{n_i(t-1)}.$$

The transition matrix $P(t-1,t)=(p_{ij}(t-1,t))$ characterizes the internal flows within the workforce system. Depending on the definition of the states, a transition could be interpreted as e.g. getting experience, acquiring specific qualifications, developing a broader range of skills or simply a promotion. To model the future manpower dynamics, external flows should also be taken into consideration. External flows refer to incoming or outgoing employees, in other words recruitments and wastage. The total number $R(t)$ of persons recruited in the time interval $(t-1,t]$ and who have not left the system before time t is divided over the k states

according to the distribution $r(t-1,t)=(r_i(t-1,t))$, with $r_i(t-1,t)$ being the proportion of the recruits assigned to state S_i. The flow rates from state S_i out of the workforce system can be obtained by $w_i(t-1,t)=1-\sum_{j=1}^{k} p_{ij}(t-1,t)$. The dynamics in a workforce system can be expressed as a relation between stocks and flows in terms of a system of difference equations: $n(t)=n(t-1)\,P(t-1,t)+R(t)\,r(t-1,t)$.

Assumptions in Markovian Approaches

The functional relation between stocks and flows is very convenient for predicting and controlling the internal personnel supply. To allow this, Markov manpower models simplify this relation by making the following assumptions:

- Markov manpower models are discrete-time models. Stocks and flows are only studied over equal time intervals. Consequently, the model ignores multiple sequential flows during [*t*-1,*t*). Only the flow between the state at *t*-1 and the state at *t* is considered.
- The system is memory-less, meaning that future transitions happen with a probability only depending on the present state and independent from previous transitions (e.g. previous promotions, length of service).
- The flow rates are time-independent. In every time interval, the transition rates $p_{ij}(t-1,t)$ are the same. The time-independent transition rates are denoted by p_{ij}, and the time-independent transition matrix is then $P=(p_{ij})$. The time-independent recruitment vector is $r=(r_i)$.
- The states are homogeneous personnel groups with respect to the transition rates.

Under the Markov manpower model assumptions, the relation between stocks and flows is given by: $n(t)=n(t-1)\,P+R(t)\,r$.

Although it falls beyond the scope of this paper, we mention other Markovian approaches in manpower planning that relax the restrictive assumptions of the Markov manpower model. Vassiliou and his research team focused on non-homogeneous Markov models. Those models are characterized by transition rates that are not time-homogeneous (Georgiou 1992; Georgiou and Vassiliou, 1997; Tsantas, 1995; Vassiliou, 1982b; Vassiliou, 1984; Vassiliou, 1986; Vassiliou, 1992; Vassiliou, 1998; Young, 1974). More recently, results on non-homogeneous Markov models can also be found in Yadavalli et al. (2002). Semi-Markov models on the other hand relax the assumptions of homogeneous subgroups, by assuming conditional transition rates, depending on the duration in the grade. Indeed, the longer a person stays in a particular state, the less likely it might be for him to leave the organization. The probability of leaving may therefore vary substantially with duration and destination. A semi-Markov manpower model combines a transition matrix of probabilities of moving between grades with a conditional distribution of duration in a grade (e.g. Yadavalli and Natarajan, 2001; McClean and Montgomery, 2000; Vassiliou, 1992). Some researchers

combine those two alternatives in non-homogeneous semi-Markov models (e.g. Janssen and Manca, 2002; McClean, Montgomery and Ugwuowo, 1998). Although those alternative approaches have the objective to improve accuracy in forecasting the workforce system dynamics, they suffer the same bottlenecks as other complex models (cfr. introduction). For real-world applications, practitioners might therefore be better off with strict Markov manpower models. In Section 2, some guidelines are given to build models conform to the strict Markov manpower model assumptions.

Deterministic and Stochastic Models

Markov theory is by definition a stochastic approach. Nevertheless, in Markov manpower planning research, stochastic as well as deterministic models can be distinguished. The stochastic nature of Markov theory is inconvenient for extensive workforce system investigation and therefore many researchers ignore it. They take the model assumptions for granted. Firstly, they assume a given personnel classification in homogeneous groups, mostly called grades. Consequently, internal transitions are referred to by the term promotions. Secondly, deterministic models assume a known transition matrix and recruitment distribution (e.g. Georgiou and Tsantas, 2002; Davies, 1975). This might be reasonable in some real-world applications, for example when the transitions are completely under management control.

In most cases however, there is no functional but a statistical relation between successive stocks. According to the Markov philosophy, the stock is considered to be a random variable. It is well known that $n(t)$ follows a multinomial distribution, for which the parameters (i.e. the flow rates) should be estimated. In this case, the flow rates are transition probabilities and the model can be used for predicting future stocks and flows. Of course, prediction in stochastic models incorporates uncertainty which can not be ignored in real-world applications. Three sources of error can be distinguished: Firstly, a statistical error arises from the fact that stocks are associated with a probability distribution. Secondly, an estimation error occurs because the transition probabilities have to be estimated (De Feyter and Guerry, 2009; Vassiliou and Gerontidis, 1985). Finally, if the model assumptions are not satisfied, prediction involves a specification error. Bartholomew (1975) provides estimators for the prediction error in stochastic Markov manpower models under specific alternative hypotheses, i.e. Markov cohort analysis, Markov census analysis with given or estimated recruitment and Markov census analysis with known total size (cfr. Section 3).

Besides the manpower models in which the flows are considered as deterministic and the models in which the flows are treated as stochastic, manpower planning has paid attention to partially stochastic models in which some flows are deterministic and others are stochastic. In practice on the one hand the number of promotions is usually largely in hands of the management and on the other hand the natural wastage, for example, is uncontrollable. For these reasons manpower models have been discussed in which the description of promotions is deterministic and the wastage variable is considered as stochastic (Davies, 1982; Davies, 1983; Guerry, 1993; McClean, 1991).

Prediction and Control

Whether the Markov manpower model is applied from a deterministic or a stochastic approach, the relation between stocks and flows allows forecasting internal personnel supply. Moreover, it offers insights in possible actions to match future personnel demand and supply. Therefore, research on Markov manpower models is concerned with several specific problems, briefly described further in this section. In Section 3 a current state-of-the-art is given on the answers offered by scientific research.

In a Markov manpower model the flows (internal, incoming and outgoing) are characterized by transition probabilities. The values of these parameters of the model reflect the personnel strategy of the workforce system. In fact the parameters of the model are a quantification of aspects as promotion and recruitment policy. An interesting question that can be stated concerns the predictions of the stocks, i.e. how the system would evolve in case the currently considered strategy remains unchanged for the future. In case the model assumptions as well as the values of the parameters of the model remain relevant for the future, the (expected) stocks can be forecasted: Starting from the current stocks and based on the model, predictions for the stocks can be computed in an iterative way. In fact, the forecasting procedure can be repeated for alternative personnel strategies. An alternative strategy can be characterized by modified values of the parameters of the model. The forecast of the stocks under these conditions give an answer to the question ***what*** the evolution of the personnel system would be ***if*** the strategy would be characterized by those modified values of the parameters. Such what-if-analyses give insights in the effect of a particular change in the strategy on the evolution of the stocks. Moreover those analyses allow comparing the quality of different strategies in terms of certain goals to be achieved in the system.

For reasons of efficiency and effectiveness it is desirable to have the right number of employees at the right places in the organization at any time. Therefore in manpower planning it is important to deal with the problem of controlling parameters in order to maintain or to attain a desired stock vector. In control problems, first of all, it has to be clarified which aspects are under control of the management in order to have an evolution of the personnel system in a desired direction. The control actions that can be taken into consideration depend on the set of parameters of the model that can be controlled and on the direction(s) the control of these parameters is acceptable in order to minimize the discrepancy between the desired and the actual stocks in the future. The aspects that are under control of the management will determine the list of parameters of the model that can be controlled. Moreover the direction in which these aspects are controllable and to what degree, determine restrictions that result in realistic values for these parameters of the manpower model (Skulj, Vehovar and Stamfelj, 2008). These insights can be translated into a characterization of the personnel strategies that are acceptable for the company. In case alternative recruitment strategies are under consideration for the workforce system, the system is under control by recruitment (Davies, 1975; Davies, 1976; Davies, 1982). Similar, the system is under control by promotion in case alternative internal transition probabilities can be considered for the personnel strategy (Bartholomew, Forbes and McClean, 1991).

Maintainabilty and Attainability

Postulated objectives of a company can be of different kind. In case the current stock vector is a desirable one for the future, the goal is to maintain the stocks. In case there is a desirable stock vector for the future, not corresponding with the current one, the goal is to attain these preferred stocks. Maintainability and attainability are studied, among under other conditions, control by promotion and control by recruitment (Abdallaoui, 1987; Bartholomew, 1977; Bartholomew, Forbes and McClean, 1991; Davies, 1975; Davies, 1981; Guerry, 1991; Haigh, 1983; Haigh, 1983; Nilikantan and Raghavendra, 2005; Tsantas and Georgiou, 1998).

- Maintainability refers to the fact that the stock vector is wanted to be kept constant in time. Besides the discussion on maintainability (after one period of time), in manpower studies there has also been attention for the more generalized concept of maintainability after *n* steps (Davies, 1973).
- In quasi-maintainability the goal is less restrictive than in maintainability since the proportional personnel structure is maintained constant in time, although the stocks can vary in time because of a change in the total size (Nilikantan, 2005).
- The objective of a workforce system can also be formulated in terms of the asymptotic behavior of the stock vector. The limiting structure of the system reflects properties of the evolution in the long run (Keenay 1975; Vassiliou 1982a).

Within the set of strategies that are acceptable for the company, preferences for the strategy in achieving the goal(s) can be taken into account. By doing this it can be reflected whether some way of achieving the goal(s) may be preferable to others. It can be for example that a personnel strategy is more preferred as the corresponding cost is less (Vajda, 1978; Glenn and Yang, 1996; Georgiou and Vassiliou, 1997), as the speed of converging is faster (Keenay, 1975), or as the strategy is at the same time efficient in reaching the goal(s) and deviates as little as possible from a preferred strategy (Mehlmann, 1980). Besides, in case a desired stock vector is not attainable, a preferred strategy can be selected based on the concept of the grade of attainability, i.e. the degree of similarity between attainable stock vectors and the desired vector (Guerry, 1999).

2. A Framework for Building a Markovian Manpower Model

Markov manpower models can be used for prediction and control in various ways. In the simplest case, practitioners are only interested in the future available personnel of the organization in its entirety. In other cases, the interest is in the future supply of employees with a certain characteristic, e.g. grade, salary, qualifications or experience level (Wijngaard, 1983). The description of the nature of the problem defines the states in the personnel system under study and the data necessary for model estimation. However, to meet the Markovian model assumption of homogeneous personnel groups, those preliminary groups might need further division in the model-building process. In this section, we consider a framework for building an adequate Markov manpower model which estimates its parameters and minimizes the specification error.

Data Collection

A historical dataset of (former and current) employee transitions between (preliminary) states is necessary to investigate the dynamics of a personnel system. But this might not be enough to build a Markov manpower model that satisfies the assumption of homogenous groups. Therefore, building a Markov manpower model requires data on personnel characteristics which might have a direct or indirect influence on the employee's transition behavior (e.g. gender, number of children, full-time equivalent). The dataset should include all changes in the considered states and in the influential factors.

The most natural way for collecting data to model the dynamics of a personnel system is to observe a group of entrants. Such a group, joining the personnel system in the same time interval, is called a cohort. In practice, it is often only possible to have data on stocks and flows for recent time periods. This means that the available cohort-information is related to a restrictive period. In case a personnel dataset consists of incomplete data of different cohorts, the data are called transversal data (Bartholomew, Forbes and McClean, 1991).

Identification of Homogeneous Groups

In a Markov manpower model the states are homogeneous groups of personnel for which the transition probabilities are assumed to be equal for each of the individuals within a group. Once the data have been collected, homogeneous groups can be identified. The problem description defines a preliminary group classification. In De Feyter (2006) a general framework is presented to determine homogeneous subgroups in a personnel system:

- For every state, a multinomial logistic regression analysis is suggested to investigate the relation between personal characteristics and the transition probabilities. This identifies the significant variables for further division of the preliminary groups into more homogenous subgroups. Guerry (2008) offers an alternative recursive partitioning algorithm to determine homogeneous subgroups of personnel profiles under time-discrete Markov assumptions. In the final definition of the states of the Markov manpower model, one can decide to aggregate subgroups that have comparable transition probabilities (Wijngaard, 1983). An aggregation of subgroups results in personnel groups with a greater number of members that leads to better estimations of the parameters.
- A matrix of observed flows (n_{ij}) can be tested for the presence of a Markov-memory based on a χ^2-test (Hiscott, 1981). This test indicates to what extent the probability for a member to be in state j at time t depends on the state i at time t-1 and not on the states at t-2, t-3, … .
- Another consideration in this stage of the model-building process is the assumption of time-homogeneous transition probabilities. The heterogeneity in the preliminary states most often causes a problem with time-homogeneity. Since the preliminary groups consist of subgroups with different transition probabilities, the composition of the overall preliminary group would change over time. This way, it is unlikely that the preliminary groups satisfy the assumption of time-homogeneity. However, the

possibility exists that the transition probabilities of homogeneous subgroups also suffer from time-dependency. Therefore, De Feyter (2006) suggests, besides other personal variables, to also enter time as an explanatory variable in the multivariate regression analysis, as well as the interaction effect between time and the other variables. For this, two approaches can be used complementary: by considering time as a continuous variable, a functional relation with transition probabilities is tested. In case of a significant relation, by a transformation, this could be incorporated in the model (Bartholomew, 1975). By considering time as a discrete variable, less predictive time-heterogeneity can be tested. In case of time-dependent transition probabilities which are difficult to incorporate in the model, the practitioner might still prefer non-homogeneous Markov models (cfr. Section 1). However, at the cost of accuracy, the practitioner might be better off with accepting this specification error (cfr. introduction). In this case, the best subset of explanatory variables without the variable time is chosen. Alternatively, Sales (1971) offers a Goodness of Fit Statistic for testing time-homogeneity of transition probabilities in state i:

$$\chi^2(i) = \sum_t \sum_{J(i)} n_i(t-1) \frac{(\hat{p}_{ij}(t-1,t) - \hat{p}_{ij})^2}{\hat{p}_{ij}}$$

which follows a χ^2-distribution with $(T-1)(m(i)-1)$ degrees of freedom,

with: $J(i)$ = all values of j for which $\hat{p}_{ij} > 0$

$\hat{p}_{ij}(t-1,t)$ = transition rate during interval $[t\text{-}1,t)$

$\hat{p}_{ij}$ = the estimated transition probability based on the whole historical dataset

T = number of observed time-periods in the historical dataset

$m(i)$ = number of possible flows originating from state S_i.

The general framework suggested above determines homogeneous groups in a personnel system based on observable variables available in the historical dataset. Nevertheless in practice, some flows depend on individual traits even within such a homogeneous group. In case there is a lack of observations on these sources of heterogeneity, parameter estimation is not possible for these subgroups in a Markov model. Earlier work (Ugwuowo and McClean, 2000) concerning manpower models points to the importance of making a distinction between two types of sources of heterogeneity, namely observable sources and latent sources. Guerry (2005) dealt with the problem of latent sources of heterogeneity by introducing a hidden Markov manpower model. This specifies a technique to improve homogeneity of the subgroups of the workforce system. When latent sources are considered in the model-building process, the statistical relation between stocks and flows needs further specification to allow prediction and control (Guerry, 2005).

Model Estimation

Once the homogeneous groups are determined, the transition probabilities have to be estimated. During the identification of homogeneous groups, the relations between the individual's characteristics and transition probabilities are investigated. Consequently, the fitted response functions could be used to estimate the parameters of the Markov manpower model. However, a closed-form solution exists for the values of the transition parameters. Already in 1957, Anderson and Goodman developed a maximum likelihood estimator for the transition probabilities under the strict Markov assumptions:

$$\hat{p}_{ij} = \frac{N_{ij}}{N_i} \text{ with } N_{ij} = \sum_{t=0}^{T-1} n_{ij}(t) \text{ and } N_i = \sum_{t=0}^{T-1} n_i(t).$$

$n_i(t)$ and $n_{ij}(t)$ are the observed stocks and flows in the historical dataset. This estimator is shown to be a minimum variance unbiased estimator.

Model Validation

In validating the manpower model, the goal is to measure the extent to which the model is able to reproduce the data on the observed stock vectors. According to validity, in most previous work in manpower planning a distinction was made between internal and predictive validity (Bartholomew, Forbes and McClean, 1991). For the internal validation the parameters of the model are estimated based on the available observations for all time periods $[t,t+1)$ $t = 0,...,T-1$ of the stocks and flows. Based on the estimated parameters and the initial stock vector at time $t = 0$, projections are computed for the stock vectors at the subsequent time points. In comparing these predicted stocks with the observed ones, it becomes clear to what extent the model is able to reproduce the observations. For the predictive validity the observations are divided into two sets. The observations of the stocks and flows available for the time periods $[t, t+1)$ $t = 0,...,\tau-1$ with $\tau < T$ are used to estimate the parameters of the model. Based on these estimated parameters and the observed stock vector at time τ, projections for the stocks at time $\tau+1,...,T$ are computed and compared with the actual observed stocks. In fact in the predictive validation method the quality of the model is tested by treating the time τ as the present and the time points $\tau+1,...,T$ as the future (for observations are available). Moreover an n-fold cross validation approach can be useful in testing the goodness of fit of a manpower model.

Since the flows from a state S_i are multinomial the validity of the Markov model can be discussed based on a χ^2-test. In previous work a goodness of fit test is expressed in terms of the observed stocks and their estimated values (Sales, 1971). Alternatively the validity can be examined by a χ^2-test based on the observed flows and their estimations.

3. Some Markovian Manpower Models

The model-building process, as discussed in Section 2, ensures the acceptability of the Markov model assumptions. It will result into well-defined states. These states are personnel subgroups that are homogeneous with respect to the transition probabilities (estimated based on observable variables). Under the Markov model assumptions, additional alternative hypotheses on the workforce system result in different models. In each of these models, the aspects prediction, control and asymptotic behavior can be examined in a very specific manner.

Markov Cohort Analysis

In modelling a cohort and under the assumption that nobody can join the cohort in a later stage, no incoming flows are considered for the workforce system. The personnel system can be described by an absorbing Markov chain in which the transient states are corresponding with the homogeneous categories of the personnel system and the absorbing states are corresponding with the different types of wastage flows (retiring, accepting a job in another organisation ...).

Based on the matrix $P=(p_{ij})$ of the internal transition probabilities from a personnel category S_i $(1 \leq i \leq k)$ to a personnel category S_j $(1 \leq j \leq k)$, the evolution of the stock vector can be described as:

$$n(t)=n(t-1).P=n(0).P^t \; .$$

The fact that there are no recruitments at a later stage results in stocks evolving towards zero, under the condition that there is wastage out of each of the personnel categories:

$$\lim_{t\to\infty} n\,(t) = (0,....,0) \; .$$

The fundamental matrix $N=(n_{ij})=(I-P)^{-1}$ of the absorbing Markov chain provides information on the (expected) total number of times n_{ij} that the process, starting from category S_i, is in category S_j (Bartholomew, 1982). Consequently for members starting from category S_i, the average seniority at the moment of leaving the workforce system is given by $\sum_j n_{ij}$.

Markov Census Model

In general, a workforce system is not composed only by the members of one cohort: staff members will leave the system and others will join the system. Based on census personnel

data the transition matrix, the wastage vector and the recruitment vector can be estimated (cfr. Section 2). For some workforce systems prognoses or assumptions on the trend of the total number of recruitments in the future will be made based on efficiency and effectiveness considerations (Gallisch, 1989). For other systems it is more obvious to formulate targets for the evolution of the total number of employees (Zanakis, 1980). Depending on the aspects on which insights are available for the future and depending on the assumptions that are realistic for the workforce system, the evolution of the stock vector will be described in a different way. In what follows Markov census models are built and discussed under several hypotheses.

Markov Census Model with Known Recruitment

In a manpower model with known recruitment, at any time t a known targeted number $R(t)$ of staff members is recruited. The incoming flow can therefore be considered starting from an additional state of which the stock at time t equals $R(t)$. The probability that a new recruit will enter into state S_i is given by r_i, the i-th component of the recruitment vector. The evolution of the stock vector can be discribed as:

$$n(t) = n(t-1)P + R(t)r$$

with P the matrix of the internal transition probabilities.

Although the hypotheses of this model are corresponding with the Markov properties, in general the manpower model is no Markov chain model.

Under the more restrictive hypothesis of a constant total number R of recruitments at any time, the asymptotical behavior is characterized by the limiting stock vector:

$$\lim_{t\to\infty} n(t) = R.r.(I-P)^{-1}$$

that is also a fixed point for the strategy characterized by P, R and r (Bartholomew, Forbes and McClean, 1991).

Markov Models with Known Total Size

At time t the stocks in the different states are the coordinates of the stock vector $n(t)$, with which one can calculate the total size of the system at that moment as:

$$N(t) = \sum_i n_i(t) .$$

The probability that a member of the personnel category S_i has left the system after one period of time is $w_i = 1 - \sum_j p_{ij}$. The vector $w = (w_i)$ is the wastage vector.

The evolution of the stock vector can be described as:

$$n(t) = n(t-1).\left(P + w'r\right) + \left[N(t) - N(t-1)\right].r$$

in which the matrix $Q = P + w'r$ is a row-stochastic matrix.

If the evolution of the size of the system is of this nature that after each time interval the size has increased/decreased with a fixed proportion α , i.e. the expanding/contracting rate, then $N(t) = (1+\alpha)N(t-1)$. And the proportional personnel structure $q(t) = \dfrac{n(t)}{N(t)}$ can be forecasted based on:

$$q(t) = \frac{1}{1+\alpha}q(t-1).\,Q + \frac{\alpha}{1+\alpha}.r.$$

According to Bartholomew, Forbes and McClean (1991), for a system with expansion rate α and that is under control by recruitment, the proportional personnel structure $q(t)$ is attainable from $q(t-1)$ iff

$$q(t-1).P \le (1+\alpha)q(t).$$

And in the context of quasi-maintainability, there can be stated that the proportional personnel structure q is maintainable iff $q.P \le (1+\alpha)q$.

In the more restrictive situation of a workforce system with a constant total size, the evolution of $q(t)$ is characterized by the Markov chain with transition matrix Q:

$$q(t) = q(t-1).Q.$$

In case the matrix Q is the transition matrix of a regular Markov chain, the Fixed point theorem for regular Markov chains provides a characterization of the asymptotic behavior of the proportional personnel structure (Seneta, 1973). Namely independent of the initial distribution $q(0)$ the limiting proportional personnel structure:

$$\lim_{t\to\infty} q(0).Q^t = q^*$$

is equal to the unique probability vector q^* that is a fixed point of Q.

It is possible that a particular structure is not maintainable/attainable after one period of time but that it is after n steps. The set of n-step maintainable structures and the set of n-step attainable structures are discussed in Davies (1973) for both systems with constant total size and systems with constant expanding/contracting rate. In Davies (1975), for a constant size system with k states and controllable by recruitment, the set M_n of n-step maintainable structures is described geometrically as the convex hull of k^n points of $\mathbb{R}^k$.

In order to attain a preferred proportional structure, Vajda (1978) introduced an optimization algorithm to find a preferred strategy as the result of minimizing the corresponding cost by taking into account the cost of supporting a state as well as the cost of recruiting. Hereby the cost may differ from state to state and may vary from step to step.

Mehlmann (1980) deals with the problem of attainability for a system with known total size by introducing a dynamic programming approach to determine optimal strategies. Hereby the goal is to get from the initial structure to the desired proportional personnel distribution in a reasonably short time and to hold deviations from the preferred recruitment distribution and transition matrix as small as possible. Another criterion in selecting the most preferred strategy can be for example efficiency (Keenay 1975). In case a desired stock vector is attainable by several acceptable strategies, a strategy resulting in the desired stocks after a minimum number of time periods is the most efficient in achieving the goal. In Keenay (1975) convergence properties, such as the speed of convergence, are studied for systems with expanding/contracting rate α .

In Bartholomew (1982) the set of attainable structures is described for constant size systems under control by recruitment and for systems under control by promotion. In this approach a structure is attainable in case it is attainable in a finite number of steps from at least one other structure. The interest of the study lies in the complement of the set, since for a structure not belonging to the set of attainable structures it is known that it is not attainable from whatever starting structure. In case a desired stock vector is not attainable, a preferred strategy can be selected based on the degree of similarity between attainable stock vectors and the desired vector, resulting in a strategy with an attainable stock vector that is very similar to the desired one. This concept of the grade of attainability is studied for constant size systems under control by recruitment in Guerry (1999).

Markov Models Applied to Age and Length of Service Distributions

In general, wastage probabilities are to an important degree depending on the age and/or the length of service of the members (Forbes, 1971). For this reason in several Markov manpower models the states are defined based on age and length of service (e.g. Bartholomew, 1977; Keenay, 1975; Nilikantan and Raghavendra, 2008). For example in Woodward (1983) a Markov manpower model in which the states are defined by grade, age and length of service provides projections of age and grade distributions of academics in UK Universities. The discussed model is equispaced: the prediction intervals are all equal and the personnel are classified in age and length of service classes of the same size as the prediction intervals.

Proportionality in Markov Manpower Models

More recently Nilakantan and Raghavendra (2005) introduced the concept of proportionality into the Markov manpower models. The condition of proportionality refers to the fact that in the same time interval the recruitment inflow into a personnel category S_j equals a prespecified proportion of the promotion inflow into the category S_j. Under the assumption of proportionality the incoming flows and the internal flows are not considered as independent, as it is the situation in general manpower models. In Nilikantan (2005)

maintainability, quasi-maintainability and attainability is examined for proportionality policies.

Mixed Push-pull Models

The Human Resource Management literature distinguishes two recruitment approaches, in function of the firm's competitive strategy (Sonnenfeld et al. 1989; Schuler and Jackson, 1987). Firstly, vacancies could be filled by external recruitment. Once hired, employees grow in terms of skills, knowledge and abilities. In this case, Markov manpower models are suitable to investigate personnel dynamics. Therefore, Markov manpower models are also often called push models, because in each time interval $[t\text{-}1, t)$ a certain number of employees is expected to make a transition from state S_i to state S_j, independent from vacancies in state S_j. Secondly, vacancies could be filled by internal recruitment. Therefore, the manpower planning literature offers a pull approach, based on Renewal models (Bartholomew, Forbes and McClean, 1991; Sirvanci, 1984). In such systems, transitions from state S_i to state S_j are only possible in case of vacancies in state S_j. Vacancies are assumed to follow a binomial distribution, based on the wastage probability in state S_j. More recently, the consensus has grown that firms seldom apply one unique competitive or recruitment strategy, but mix several strategies to enable success on several separate markets (Ferris et al., 1999). Consequently, a mix of push and pull promotions might occur in the same personnel systems at the same time. Georgiou and Tsantas (2002) and De Feyter (2007) therefore introduced mixed push-pull models for prediction, control and investigation of asymptotic behavior.

Georgiou and Tsantas (2002) introduced the Augmented Mobility Model, which allows modeling push as well as pull flows within the system. Besides the push flows between the active classes in the system, a trainee class is introduced from which individuals can be pulled towards the active classes S_j in case vacancies arrive in the active states. However, the discussion in Georgiou and Tsantas (2002) is restricted to an embedded Markov model, assuming known total size (cfr. above), implying that the total number of individuals in the system is fixed or at least known and the vacancies are calculated at an aggregated level. For some companies however, it might be more interesting to model vacancies at the level of individual states. De Feyter (2007) weakened the assumptions of the Augmented Mobility Model, by modeling push and pull flows between all states in the personnel system and by estimating vacancies in all individual states using a binomial distribution.

4. Conclusion

A Markov manpower model implicitly assumes several hypotheses that might not be realistic for any organisation. This aspect can be experienced as a disadvantage of the Markov manpower models. Nevertheless a Markov manpower model anyway is an interesting tool for gaining insights by, e.g. what-if-analyses. What-if-analyses based on a manpower model with Markov assumptions result in properties of the evolution of the workforce system under the

assumption that the actual promotion rates, wastage rates and recruitment vector would be applied in the future. These insights can be helpful in deciding whether the actual personnel strategy is a preferable one for the future.

Moreover an analysis based on a Markov manpower model does have the advantage that the results can be easily communicated in terms of rates and/or numbers of employees in well-defined personnel categories. As a consequence of its simplicity, there are no advanced quantitative concepts to know to understand a report on the results from a Markov analysis.

This paper offers a review on Markov manpower models. First of all, it clarified the interesting characteristics of those models in comparison with other Operations Research techniques. This explains the ongoing efforts of researchers in the field. Moreover, this paper offers an overview of all steps during a real-world application and explained the specific problems dealt with by academic researchers. Therefore, it is very useful for the scientific community to place further research in the current state-of-the-art. Important elements in the operationalisation of these models (finding homogenous groups, estimating the model parameters and model validation) are discussed. Under specific characteristics of the workforce system, attention was paid to the main aspects prediction, asymptotic behavior and control. An overview is given of properties with respect to maintainability and attainability.

The validity of the Markov models is to a great extent determined by the degree of homogeneity of the states. One of the challenges for further research is to get an integrated approach in which the definition of the states of the manpower model takes into account observable as well as hidden heterogeneity in order to end up with more homogeneous states.

In this context, another point that has to be clarified is in what way a good balance can be found between the level of the subdivision of the personnel system on the one hand and the quality of the estimated parameters with respect to the corresponding states on the other hand. A division of the personnel system into more subgroups can result in states of the Markov model that are more homogeneous but not necessarily in parameter estimations that are of a better quality.

In summary, manpower planning involves long term strategic management decisions. Besides this, strong Operations Research efforts have been taken to solve problems at the short term tactical level of personnel management. Personnel Scheduling and Rostering assigns the available employees to specific tasks or shifts that should be performed by the company (Ernst et al., 2004; Burke et al., 2004). While in personnel scheduling the available personnel is more or less fixed, manpower planning tries to adapt the long term availability of employees in the company and/or the forecasted long-term needs. Of course, in real-world applications, a strong interaction exists between manpower planning and Personnel Scheduling. Decisions about future personnel availability, taken at the long term planning level, will have an impact on the conditions which short term planning should take into account. On the other hand, Personnel Scheduling and Rostering might incorporate some specific needs about future personnel characteristics (e.g. willingness to work flexible hours) which long term planning should consider. Operations Research models that integrate both long and short term problems (to obtain an optimal solution at both levels) are still quite rare. This forms an interesting but rather complex challenge for future research in Operations Research (Petrovic and Vanden Berghe 2007).

REFERENCES

Abdallaoui G., Probability of maintaining or attaining a structure in one step, *Journal of applied probability,* 24 (1987), 1006-1011.

Anderson, T. W. and Goodman, L. A. Statistical inferences about Markov chains, *Annals of mathematical statistics,* 28(1) (1957), 89-110.

Bartholomew, D. J. The statistical approach to manpower planning, *The Statistician,* 20(1) (1971), 3-26.

Bartholomew, D. J. Errors of prediction for Markov chain models, *Journal of the Royal Statistical Society, Series B,* 3 (1975), 444-456.

Bartholomew, D. J. Maintaining a grade or age structure in a stochastic environment, *Advances in Applied Probability,* 9 (1977), 1-17

Bartholomew, D. J. *Stochastic models for social processes* (3rd ed), John Wiley & Sons, New York, 1982.

Bartholomew, D. J., Forbes, A.F. and McClean, S. I. *Statistical techniques for manpower planning,* Chichester: Wiley publishers, 1991.

Burke, E. K., De Causmaecker, P., Vanden Berghe, G. and H. Van Landeghem. The state of the art of nurse rostering, *Journal of Scheduling*, 7 (2004), 441-499.

Davies, G. S. Structural control in a graded manpower system, *Management Science,* 20 (1973), 76-84.

Davies, G. S. Maintainability of structures in Markov chain models under recruitment control, *Journal of Applied Probability*, 12 (1975), 376-382.

Davies, G. S. Consistent recruitment in a graded manpower system, *Management Science*, 22 (1976), 1215-1220.

Davies, G. S. Maintainable regions in a Markov manpower model, *Journal of Applied Probability,* 18 (1981), 738-742.

Davies, G. S. Control of grade sizes in partially stochastic Markov manpower model, *Journal of Applied Probability*, 19 (1982), 439-443.

Davies, G. S. A note on the geometric/probabilistic relationship in a Markov manpower model, *Journal of Applied Probability,* 20 (1983), 423-428.

De Feyter, T. Modeling heterogeneity in Manpower Planning: dividing the personnel system in more homogeneous subgroups, *Applied Stochastic Models in Business and Industry,* 22(4) (2006), 321-334.

De Feyter, T. Modeling mixed push and pull promotion flows in Manpower Planning, *Annals of Operations Research*, 155(1) (2007), 25-39.

De Feyter, T. and Guerry, M. A. Evaluating recruitment strategies using fuzzy set theory in stochastic manpower planning, *Stochastic analysis and applications*, 27(6) (2009), 1148-1162.

Dill, W., Graver, D. P. and Weber, W. L. Models and Modelling for Manpower Planning, *Management Science*, 13(4) (1966), 142-167.

Ernst, A. T., Jiang, H., Krishnamoorthy, M. and Sier, D. Staff scheduling and rostering: A review of applications, methods and models, *European Journal of Operational Research,* 153 (2004), 3-27.

Ferris, G., Hochwarter, W., Buckley, R. et al, Human Resources Management: Some new directions, *Journal of Management*, 25(3) (1999), 385-415.

Forbes, A. F. Non-Parametric Methods of Estimating the Survivor Function, *Statistician*, 20 (1971), 27-52.

Gallisch, E. On the development of manpower number and recruitment in the civil services, *Methods and Models of Operations Research*, 33 (1989), 267-286.

Georgiou, A. C. Partial maintainability and control in nonhomogeneous Markov manpower systems, *European Journal of Operational Research*, 62(2) (1992), 241-251.

Georgiou, A. C. and Vassiliou, P.-C. G. Cost models in nonhomogeneous Markov systems, *European Journal of Operations research*, 100 (1997), 81-96.

Georgio, A. C. and Tsantas, N. Modelling recruitment training in mathematical human resource planning, *Applied Stochastic Models in Business and Industry*, 18 (2002), 53-74.

Glenn, J. J. and Yang, C.L. A model for promotion rate control in hierarchical manpower systems, *IMA Journal of Management Mathematics*, 7(3) (1996), 197-206.

Guerry, M. A. Monotonicity property of t-step maintainable structures in three-grade manpower systems: a counterexample, *Journal of Applied Probability,* 28 (1991), 221-224.

Guerry, M. A. The probability of attaining a structure in a partially stochastic model, *Advances in Applied Probability*, 25(4) (1993), 818-824.

Guerry, M. A. Using fuzzy sets in manpower planning, *Journal of Applied Probability,* 36(1) (1999), 155-162.

Guerry, M. A. Hidden Markov chains as a modelisation tool in manpower planning, *Working paper* MOSI/18, (2005).

Guerry, M. A. Profile based push models in manpower planning, *Applied Stochastic Models in Business and Industry*, 24(1) (2008), 13-20.

Haigh, J. Maintainability of manpower structures – counterexamples, results and conjectures, *Journal of Applied Probability*, 20 (1983), 700-705.

Haigh, J. Further counterexamples to the monotonicity property of t-step maintainable structures, *Journal of Applied Probability*, 29(2) (1992), 441-447.

Ivancevich, J. M. *Human Resource Management* (9th edition), McGraw-Hill, New York, 2003.

Janssen, J. and Manca, R. Salary cost evaluation by means of nonhomogeneous Semi-Markov processes, *Stochastic models*, 18(1) (2002), 7-23.

Keenay, G. Convergence properties of age distributions, *Journal of Applied Probability,* 12 (1975), 684-691.

McClean, S., Montgomery, E. and Ugwuowo, F. Non-homogeneous continuous-time Markov and semi-Markov manpower models, *Applied Stochastic Models and Data Analysis* 13 (1998), 191-198.

McClean, S. I. and Montgomery E. J. Estimation for Semi-Markov Manpower Models in a Stochastic Environment, in: *Semi-Markov Models and Applications.* Eds. J. Janssen and N. Limnios, Kluwer Academic Publishers, (2000), 219-227.

McClean, S. Manpower planning models and their estimation, *European Journal of Operational Research,* 51 (1991), 179-187.

Mehlmann, A. An approach to optimal recruitment and transition strategies for manpower systems using dynamic programming, *Journal of the Operational Research Society*, 31 (11) (1980), 1009- 1015.

Mondy, R. W., Noe, R. M. and Premeaux, S.R. *Human resource management* (7^e ed), Prentice Hall, Upper Saddle River, N.J., 1999.
Nilikantan, K. and Raghavendra, B. G. Control aspects in proportionality Markov manpower systems, *Applied Mathematical Modelling*, 29 (2005), 85-116.
Nilikantan, K. and Raghavendra, B. G. Length of service and age characteristics in proportionality Markov manpower systems, *IMA Journal of Management Mathematics,* 19 (2008), 245-268.
Parker, B. and Caine, D. Holonic modeling: human resource planning and the two faces of Janus, *International Journal of Manpower,* 17(8) (1996), 30-45.
Petrovic, S. and Vanden Berghe, G. Preface Special Issue on Personnel Planning and Scheduling, *Annals of Operations Research*, 155(1) (2007), 1-4.
Purkiss, C. Corporate manpower planning: a review of models, *European Journal of Operational Research,* 8 (1981), 315-323.
Sales, P. The validity of the Markov chain model for a class of the civil service, *The statistician,* 20(1) (1971), 85-110.
Schuler, R. S. and Jackson, S. E. Linking competitive strategies with human resource management practices, *The Academy of Management Executive*, 3 (1987), 207-219.
Seneta, E. *Non-negative Matrices. An Introduction to Theory and Applications*. George Allen and Unwin, London, 1973.
Sirvanci, M. Forecasting manpower losses by the use of renewal models, *European Journal of Operational Research*, 16(1) (1984), 13-18.
Smith, A. R. and Bartholomew, D. J. Manpower planning in the United Kingdom: An historical review, *Journal of the operational research society,* 39(3) (1988), 235-248.
Skulj, D., Vehovar, V. and Stamfelj, D. The modelling of manpower by Markov chains – A case study of the Slovenian armed forces, *Informatica*, 32 (2008), 289-297.
Sonnenfeld, J., Peiperl, M. A. and Kotter, J. P. Strategic determinants of managerial labour markets: a career systems view, *Human Resource Management*, 4 (1988), 369-388.
Tsantas, N. Stochastic analysis of a non-homogeneous Markov system, *European Journal of Operational Research,* 85 (1995), 670-685.
Tsantas N. and Georgio, A. C. Partial maintainability of a population model in a stochastic environment, *Applied stochastic Models and Data Analysis*, 13 (1998), 183-189.
Tsantas, N. Ergodic behavior of a Markov chain model in a stochastic environment, *Mathematical Methods of Operations Research*, 54(1) (2001), 101-118.
Ugwuowo, F. I. and McClean, S. I. Modelling heterogeneity in a manpower system: a review, *Applied stochastic models in business and industry*, 16 (2000), 99-110.
Vajda, S. *Mathematics of manpower planning*, John Wiley, London, 1978.
Vassiliou, P. Asymptotic behavior of Markov system, *Journal of Applied Probability,* 19 (1982a), 851-857.
Vassiliou, P. On the limiting behaviour of a non-homogeneous Markovian manpower model with independent Poisson input, *Journal of Applied Probability,* 19 (1982b), 433-438.
Vassiliou, P. Cyclic behaviour and asymptotic stability of non-homogeneous Markov system, *Journal of Applied Probability,* 21 (1984), 315-325.
Vassiliou, P. and Gerontidis, I. Variances and covariances of the grade sizes in manpower systems, *Journal of Applied Probability*, 22(3) (1985), 583-597.
Vassiliou, P. Asymptotic variability of nonhomogeneous Markov systems under cyclic behaviour, *European Journal of Operational Research,* 27(2) (1986), 215-228.

Vassiliou, P. Non-homogeneous semi-Markov systems and maintainability of the state sizes, *Journal of Applied Probability*, 29 (1992), 519-534.

Vassiliou, P. The evolution of the theory of non-homogeneous Markov systems, *Applied stochastic Models and Data Analysis*, 13 (1998), 159-176.

Verbeek, P. J. *Learning about Decision Support Systems: two case studies on Manpower Planning in an airline*, Tinbergen Institute Research Series, (1991).

Verhoeven, C. J. *Instruments for corporate manpower planning. Applicability and applications,* (PhD) Technische Universiteit Eindhoven, Nederland, 1980.

Walker, J. W. *Human Resource Strategy*. McGraw-Hill, New-York, 1992.

Wang, J. *A review of operations research applications in workforce planning and potential modelling of military training*. DSTO Systems Science Laboratory. Australia, 2005.

Wijngaard, J. Aggregation in manpower planning, *Management Science*, 29 (1983), 1427-1435.

Woodward, M. On forecasting grade, age and length of service distributions in manpower systems, *Journal of Royal Statistical Society,* 146 (1983), 74-84.

Yadavalli, V. S. S. and R. Natarajan, A semi-markov model of a manpower system, Stochastic analysis and applications, 19(6) (2001), 1077-1086.

Yadavalli, V. S. S., Natarajan, R. and Udayabhaskaran, S. Time dependent behavior of stochastic models of manpower system – impact of pressure on promotion, *Stochastic analysis and applications*, 20(4) (2002), 863-882.

Young, A. and Almond, G. Predicting Distributions of Staff, *The Computer Journal,* 3(4) (1961), 246-250.

Young, A. and Vassiliou, P. A non-linear model on the promotion of staff, *J.R. Statist. Soc., A* 137 (1974), 584-595.

Zanakis, S. A. and Maret, M. W. A Markov chain application to manpower supply planning, *Journal of the Operational Research Society,* 31 (1980), 1095-1102.

Reviewed by Prof. Dr. Ir. Greet Vanden Berghe, KaHo Sint-Lieven and K.U. Leuven.

In: Business and Finance: Performance and Management ISBN: 978-1-61122-936-3
Editors: R. Morland and A. Gagglione

Chapter 10

CAN CORPORATE TAXATION BE EXPLAINED BY LIMITED LIABILITY?*

Anton Miglo†
University of Guelph, Department of Economics,
Guelph, Ontario, Canada

Abstract

We consider a model where wealth-constrained entrepreneurs have private information about the qualities of available investment projects. We show that some "high risk-high return" projects will receive external financing even if they are not socially profitable. Some "low risk-low return" projects will not be funded even if they are socially profitable. Government interventions can improve equilibrium. Optimal government policy may include corporate taxation, subsidies or other instruments. A universal tax on all entrepreneurs with limited liability is not optimal.

1. Introduction

Traditional "folk" opinion is that corporate tax is the price corporations pay for the right of limited liability. However, there is no formal proof of this argument. Musgrave and Musgrave (1980) and Rosen (2004) noticed that it is hard to believe in the link between the real amount of benefits corporations receive from limited liability and the magnitude of corporate taxation.

We turn to asymmetric information to address the issue. We consider an environment where entrepreneurs choose between risky projects, with high potential profitability, and safe projects, with minimal profitability. An entrepreneur's incentive depends on the financing contracts. There are two contracts available: one with limited liability and one with unlimited liability. The entrepreneurs choose contracts based on a trade-off between interest rates (unlimited liability contracts have a lower interest rate) and a loss in the bad state (limited liability contracts do not imply a loss for the entrepreneur in the bad state). If

*I thank James Amegashie, Henry Thille, and the seminar participants at the University of Guelph for useful suggestions and comments.

†E-mail address: amiglo@uoguelph.ca, tel. (519) 824-4120, ext. 53054.

the project fails and an entrepreneur faces unlimited limited liability, then in addition to be forced to cover a firm's loss the entrepreneur sustains additional costs such as, for example, relocation costs (in case he has to sell his house) and reputation costs. [1] We argue that the equilibrium is inefficient: some entrepreneurs use limited liability contracts and invest inefficiently (*overinvestment problem*) and some of them do not undertake socially efficient projects (*underinvestment*). Although corporate taxation reduces the incentive to overinvest it does not mitigate the underinvestment problem. Optimal government policy includes a combination of corporate taxation, subsidies and other instruments.

2. The Model

Consider a set of entrepreneurs, indexed by j, with investment projects available. Projects require the same amount of external financing equal to 1. In the case of success a project generates a cash flow F_j and a cash flow of zero otherwise.[2] The probability of success is p_j. There is also a risk-free investment project with cash flow $I < F_j - 1$. There are two types of financing available for the risky project. One is a limited liability contract (LLC). Here, an entrepreneur borrows an amount 1 from a bank. In the case of success, the entrepreneur pays D to the bank. If the project fails the parties have no returns. Alternatively, the entrepreneur can use an unlimited liability contract (ULC). It is assumed that each entrepreneur has sufficient collateral, equal to 1. Hence, ULC represents a risk-free debt for the bank and thus has a face value of 1. If an entrepreneur has ULC and the project fails then in addition to losing collateral there is cost r for entrepreneur, $r > 0$. For instance, if the entrepreneur has to sell his house there is cost of new house search and moving cost. There might also be additional costs for family members due to moving to a new location. F_j and p_j are the private information of each entrepreneur. Banks do not have this information. Entrepreneurs and banks are risk-neutral.

3. Underinvestment and Overinvestment

The following equation separates socially efficient risky projects from socially inefficient projects:

$$p_jF_j - 1 = I \tag{1}$$

If the left side is greater, the project is socially efficient and vice versa. For marginal entrepreneurs (marginal entrepreneurs' projects satisfy (1)) $\partial p_j/\partial F_j = -(1+I)/F_j^2 < 0$ and $\partial^2 p_j/\partial F_j^2 = 2(1+I)/F_j^3 > 0$.

We have the following set of equations which determine an equilibrium. The choice between the LLC and the risk-free project is given by:

$$p_j(F_j - D) = I \tag{2}$$

[1] Becker and Fuest (2007) explore a different approach based on entrepreneur's opportunities to off-set losses and come to a different conclusion regarding optimal government policy. See comment in footnote 2 regarding the model in their paper.

[2] The present model is more general than one in Becker and Fuest (2007) where the cash flows are the same across the projects in the case of project's success.

where $D = 1/p^*$ and p^* is the average probability of success among the entrepreneurs with a LLC. For this equation we also have $\partial p_j/\partial F_j < 0$ and $\partial^2 p_j/\partial F_j^2 > 0$. If an entrepreneur's project satisfies (2) he is indifferent between the LLC and the risk-free project. If the left side is greater, the entrepreneur chooses the LLC and vice versa.

The choice between the LLC and the ULC is given by:

$$p_j(F_j - 1/p^*) = p_j(F_j - 1) - (1 - p_j)(1 + r)$$

This equation can be rewritten as:

$$p_j = \frac{1+r}{r+1/p^*} \tag{3}$$

and the choice between the ULC and the risk-free project is given by:

$$p_j(F_j - 1) - (1 - p_j)(1 + r) = I \tag{4}$$

The analysis of equations (1)-(4) reveals the following. (a) From (1) and (2) the marginal entrepreneur with $p_j = p^*$ is indifferent between the LLC and the risk-free project. (b) From (1) and (3) marginal entrepreneurs with $p_j = p^*$ prefer the LLC to the ULC. This is because the right side of (3) is greater than p^* since $r > 0$. (c) Marginal entrepreneurs prefer the risk-free project to the ULC. To see this let us rewrite (1) and (4) as follows:

$$p_j = (1 + I)/F_j \tag{5}$$

$$p_j = (I + 1 + r)/(F_j + r) \tag{6}$$

The right side of (6) is greater than that of (5) because $F_j > 1 + I$.

Figure 1 illustrates the equilibrium decision-making for the entrepreneurs. The thick lines represent equations (1)-(4). Letters f, l and u denote the areas where the entrepreneurs choose the risk-free contract, the limited liability contract, or the unlimited liability contract respectively.

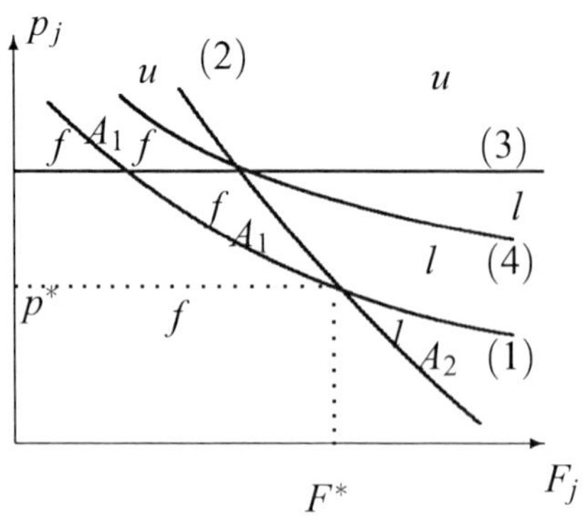

Figure 1. Overinvestment and underinvestment.

From the remark (a) above the point of intersection of (1) and (2) has the probability of success $p_j = p^*$. The intersection is unique since the slope of (1) is greater than that of (2): $-\frac{1+I}{F_j^2} = -\frac{p^2}{1+I} > -\frac{I}{(F_j-D)^2} = -\frac{p^2}{I}$. From (b) the line corresponding to (3) lies above the line $p_j = p^*$. From (c) the line corresponding to (4) lies above the line corresponding to (1).

As follows from Figure 1, there are two areas of inefficiency. Firms in area A_1 underinvest and firms in area A_2 overinvest (and use the LLC). What explains these results?

First, consider entrepreneurs with unlimited liability. Suppose $C = 0$. The unlimited liability contract is a risk-free debt for the bank. Thus, the entrepreneur's expected earnings equal the project's expected earnings (p_jF_j) reduced by the payment to the bank (which equals the investment cost 1). This means that under unlimited liability, entrepreneurs will not invest in socially inefficient projects because they are always better-off with the risk-free investment (eq. (1)). The same holds if $C > 0$ because in this case entrepreneurs earn even less than when $C = 0$ (line (4) lies above the line (1)).

Secondly, consider entrepreneurs with limited liability. From (1) marginal entrepreneurs have projects with equal expected values. In area A_2 marginal entrepreneurs have lower probabilities of success than p^* (the average probability of success among entrepreneurs with limited liability contracts). A higher probability of default is detrimental for creditors. Thus, marginal entrepreneurs in area A_2 make a positive surplus compared to the symmetric information case. This implies that there are some entrepreneurs with a lower probability of success than marginal entrepreneurs which will choose limited liability investment in risky projects (similar to the asset substitution effect).[3] On the other hand, marginal entrepreneurs in area A_1 have a higher probability of success which is beneficial for creditors and harmful for shareholders because they receive a lower return in the good state. Thus, some entrepreneurs with a high probability of success will not invest in socially efficient risky projects. Optimal government policy will include a tax on entrepreneurs with limited liability contracts and high earnings (high F_j) and subsidies for entrepreneurs with limited or unlimited liability contracts and low earnings (low F_j).[4] This will move line (2) toward line (1) reducing areas A_1 and A_2.[5] A universal tax on all entrepreneurs with limited liability is never optimal because it will move line (2) up and to the right, increasing area A_1.

References

[1] Becker, J., and C. Fuest, 2007, Why is there corporate taxation? The role of limited liability revisited, *Journal of Economics* **92**(1), 1-10.

[2] DeMeza, D., and D. Webb, 1987, Two much investment: a problem of asymmetric information, *Quarterly Journal of Economics* **102**, 281-92.

[3] DeMeza and Webb (1987).

[4] Mathematical calculations of the optimal tax rate and the amount of subsidies are omitted for brevity. Note that they depend on whether the government is able to observe (ex-post) the type of entrepreneur or only the amount of earnings.

[5] It is assumed that all entrepreneurs have sufficient collateral (that makes debt risk-free for banks). It can be shown that if this assumption is relaxed one can have an equilibrium where some entrepreneurs with unlimited liability overinvest. Thus, optimal policy may include taxes on some entrepreneurs with unlimited liability.

[3] Musgrave, R., and P. Musgrave, 1980, *Public finance in theory and practice*, McGraw-Tokyo.

[4] Rosen, H. *Public Finance.* McGraw-Hill/Irwin; 7 edition, 2004.

In: Business and Finance: Performance and Management ISBN: 978-1-61122-936-3
Editors: R. Morland and A. Gagglione

Chapter 11

"EMPIRE-BUILDING", UNDERINVESTMENT AND CAPITAL GAIN TAXATION

Anton Miglo*
University of Guelph, Department of Economics,
Guelph, Ontario, Canada

Abstract

This note provides an explanation for why tax rates on capital gains are usually lower than ordinary income tax rates based on manager's agency problem related to "empire-building" and the underinvestment problem.

JEL codes: D86, G35, H24, H32, J33

Keywords: capital gains tax, moral hazard, underinvestment, empire-building

1. Introduction

In many countries (Canada, Australia, United Kingdom, France, etc.) capital gains are taxed at a lower rate than ordinary income, but there is no unanimously supported theorectical explanation for this phenomenon. Some argue that capital gains occur unexpectedly, and thus it is unfair to tax them at the same tax rate as ordinary income because capital gains require taking on additional risk. In addition to that, there is disutility from abstaining from current consumption. Opponents of lower capital gains tax rates argue that other kinds of income have a risk component as well. Furthermore, disutility from taking on a job is not necessarily less sacrificing than disutility from investing.

Another justification for reduced capital gains tax rates is that preferential tax treatment is needed in order to stimulate more investment and capital growth. However, a reduction in the dividend tax rate reduces the cost of equity financing and thus can also increase investments. The debate between these two policy alternatives is particularly relevant since the introduction of the Job Growth and Taxpayer Relief Reconciliation act of 2003 in the United States, that introduced dividend and capital gain tax changes (see, for example,

*E-mail address: amiglo@uoguelph.ca

Poterba, 2004). One result of these debates is that without taking other factors into consideration rather than taxes it is difficult to give an advantage to either point of view given that both dividends and capital gain represent returns on equity investments and both are important for equityholders. In addition note that a social planner is not concerned about increasing investments as much as possible but rather about attaining an optimal level of investments. It is not clear why the latter cannot be achieved when dividends and capital gains are taxed equally.

This paper does not rely on fairness or temporary policy objectives. It builds on Chetty and Saez (2005) who argue that more Principal-Agent models are needed in order to understand how a difference in capital gain taxation and dividend taxation affect the firm investment policy. We argue that if capital gains and dividends are taxed equally firms underinvest due to managers' moral hazard problem in using available free cash. Reducing the tax rate on capital gains may improve societal welfare by increasing the equilibrium level of investments.

2. Model

Consider a firm with an investment project available. The amount of earnings generated by the project depends on the amount of investment. If the firm invests i, the project will return a cash flow of $r(i)$, $r' \geq 0$, $r'' \leq 0$, $r(0) = 0$. Initially, the firm pocesses an amount c of cash available. The firm belongs to an entrepreneur who owns 100% of the firm's equity. The entrepreneur hires a manager who makes the investment decision. Everybody is assumed to be risk-neutral and the risk-free interest rate is normalized to zero. The manager's reservation payoff is w_0. Besides investment in the project, the manager can decide to invest in other (inefficient from the firm's point of view) projects. This moral hazard problem or agency problem (in this case it can also be called the free cash flow problem) is well documented in existing theoretical and empirical literature (see, among others, Jensen (1986) and Dittmar, Mahrt-Smith and Servaes (2003)). More specifically we assume that if the manager has an amount of funds e available he has a choice between i and b such that $e = i + b$ and b is the amount of funds invested inefficiently. For simplicity it is assumed that b increases the manager's utility by the same amount. This can represent utility from giving the job to family members, friends and other benefits from investment in socially inefficient projects. A direct control of manager's actions is impossible so the entrepreneur cannot prevent the manager from investing inefficiently. The manager's decision depends on its contract. We assume that the entrepreneur and manager should determine a fixed initial payment w to the manager, $w \leq c$ and a fraction a of earnings generated by the main project belonging to the manager. The higher a is, the more incentive the manager has to invest efficiently.

The firm exists for two years. In the first year the firm makes all decisions about the project (the sequence of events is described below) and earnings from the project are generated in year 2. After the project is completed and earnings are generated the entrepreneur may either sell their shares in the firm or to liquidate the firm and distribute dividends. Also, the entrepreneur may sell his shares at the end of period 1 before investment is made. Dividends will be taxed with the ordinary tax rate and capital gain (in case the entrepreneur decides to sell shares) are taxed with capital gain tax rate. Let t_d be the ordinary income tax rate and t_c be the tax rate on capital gains.

The entrepreneur faces the following trade-off. High dividends in year 1 may reduce the manager's "entrenchment" problem (since it reduces the amount of cash on which the manager has discretion) but, on the other hand, it can also reduce the amount of investments in the efficient project.

The sequence of events is as follows. Year 1. The firm gets cash c and an investment project. The entrepreneur offers a contract (w,a) to the manager. The game is over if the manager rejects the offer (the manager's gets his reservation utility w_0; the firm does not undertake the project; the entrepreneur is stuck with initial cash c). Otherwise the manager is hired and gets w. The entrepreneur determines the year 1 dividends d_1 (an alternative sequence can be considered where dividends are determined before the manager is hired. Although this is technically plausible because the manager's role is limited to making the investment, in reality the manager exists all the time. This changes nothing in the solution). The manager determines i and b, $i+b=c-w-d_1$. Year 2. Project generates earnings $r(i)$; the manager gets $ar(i)$; the entrepreneur determines the year 2 dividends d_2 and sells the firm's shares.

The first-best choice of i maximizes $r(i)-i$. Thus socially optimal investments i^* is determined by:

$$r'(i^*)=1 \tag{1}$$

We assume

$$r(i^*)>c>i^*+w_0 \tag{2}$$

meaning that firstly the firm has sufficient funds to cover the optimal investment needs and secondly the project's net present value is positive.

Before beginning the formal solution let us present the outline of the major ideas. If there is no moral hazard and the manager invests only in the efficient project (b is always equal to 0) then the entrepreneur should retain an amount of earnings i^* and distribute the rest as dividends. An optimal contract for the manager is just fixed initial payment w_0. Since the entrepreneur holds 100% of the project earnings he does not have any incentive to retain an amount of earnings different from i^*. In the model with moral hazard the key problem is the entrepreneur's year 1 dividend decision. When the capital gain tax equals the ordinary income tax rate, the entrepreneur will anticipate the manager's moral hazard problem, and will react by distributing more dividends than is socially optimal. Reducing the capital gains tax may improve the entrepreneur's incentive and improve the dividends decision.

We solve the model by backward induction.

Year 2 dividend. The entrepreneur's decision depends on whether the capital gains tax rate is higher or lower than then ordinary income rate. If it is higher then the entrepreneur will prefer dividends; otherwise he prefers capital gain (it is assumed for simplicity that assets can be freely sold without value loss so the dividends can be as high as the firm's value).

Let V_2 be the firm's value at the beginning of year 2 (after earnings from the project are realized but before dividends are determined). Let V_1 be the cost of shares for the entrepreneur (it affects the capital gains tax). If the entrepreneur holds shares until year 2 then $V_1=0$. If the entrepreneur sells shares at the end of year 1 then V_1 is the firm's value at that moment. In the latter case the firm has a new decision-maker at year 2 (new shareholders)

because the shares were sold at year 1 end (this fact does not affect the derivations below). When making year 2 dividend decision, the entrepreneur (or new shareholders) maximizes: $W_2 = d_2(1-t_d)+(V_2-d_2)-\max\{(V_2-d_2-V_1),0\}t_c$. This means that dividends are taxed with the rate t_d, the remained value of the firm is V_2-d_2. The entrepreneur's capital gain is $V_2-d_2-V_1$ and this amount will be taxed with tax rate t_c.

Lemma 1. *If $V_2 > V_1$, and $t_c \geq t_d$, $d_2 = V_2 - V_1$, $W_2 = (V_2-V_1)(1-t_d)+V_1$. If $t_c < t_d$, then $d_2 = 0$ and $W_2 = V_2-(V_2-V_1)t_c$. If $V_2 < V_1$, $d_2 = 0$, $W_2 = V_2-(V_2-V_1)t_c$.*
Proof. The proof is rather technical so it is delegated to the Appendix.

Now consider the manager's investment decision. Let $e = c-w-d_1$ (retained cash after year 1 equal initial cash minus dividend payment and salary payment). The manager maximizes the sum of private benefits and bonus paid at year 2: $W_M = b+ar(c-d_1-b)$.

$$\frac{\partial W_M}{\partial b} = 1-ar'(i) \tag{3}$$

It follows from (1) and (3) that if $a = 1$, the manager retains 100% of earnings from the socially efficient project and hence the first-best level of investment is achieved. In this case however, the manager has positive rent (i.e. his budget constraint is not binding) by (2) because $r(i^*) > w_0$. If $a < 1$, the manager underinvests because from (3) $r'(i) = 1/a > 1$. Thus $i < i^*$. The following lemma summarizes the above analysis.

Lemma 2. *If $a = 1$, $i = i^*$. If $a < 1$ and $r'(e) \geq 1/a$, $r'(i) = 1/a$. If $r'(e) < 1/a$, $i = e$.*

Next let us analyze the entrepreneur' decision about selling shares at the end of year 1 (after the year 1 dividends are paid and before managers make investment decision). This depends on whether the dividend tax rate is higher or lower than the capital gain(**s**) tax rate. Without formal proof, the entrepreneur's decision can be described as follows. If the entrepreneur does not sell shares then by Lemma 1 (given that $V_1 = 0$), the entrepreneur earnings are either $(1-a)r(i)(1-t_d)$ or $(1-a)r(i)(1-t_c)$, depending on whether t_c is greater or less than t_d (i is determined by Lemma 2). If the entrepreneur sells shares at the end of year 1. The firm's value at the end of year 1 is $(1-a)r(i)$ (again i is determined by Lemma 2). Outside investor will be willing to pay this amount since the firm's value in year 2 after completing the project will be equal to the same amount so they can resell the firm for this amount without incurring any capital gain tax. The entrepreneur selling shares get thus $(1-a)r(i)(1-t_c)$. Comparing this with the case when he retains shares until year 2 we conclude that if dividend tax is lower then the entrepreneur earnings are $(1-a)r(i)(1-t_d)$ (the entrepreneur does not sell shares). Otherwise it is $(1-a)r(i)(1-t_c)$ (he is indifferent between either decision).

Thus we have the following result.

Lemma 3. *If $t_c \geq t_d$, the entrepreneur does not sell shares and $W_2 = (1-a)r(i)(1-t_d)$. If $t_c < t_d$, the entrepreneur sells shares and $V_1 = (1-a)r(i)(1-t_c)$.*

Proof. See Appendix.

Let us now turn to the first-period dividend decision.

if $t_c > t_d$ then the entrepreneur's earnings W equal $W_1+W_2 = d_1(1-t_d)+(1-a)r(i)(1-$

t_d).

$$\frac{\partial W}{\partial d_1} = 1 + (1-a)r'(i)\frac{\partial i}{\partial d_1} \tag{4}$$

if $t_c \le t_d$ then $W = d_1(1-t_d) + (1-a)r(i)(1-t_c)$.

$$\frac{\partial W}{\partial d_1} = 1 - t_d + (1-a)r'(i)\frac{\partial i}{\partial d_1}(1-t_c) \tag{5}$$

Note that in the first case the manager's objective function does not depend on t_c and from (4) and (5) the first case is equivalent to the second case when $t_c = t_d$. So we just ignore the first case and analyze the second case.

Two situations may exist. 1. When $d_1 < c - w - i^{**}$, where $i^{**} \equiv i^{**}(a)$ is such that

$$r'(i^{**}) = 1/a \tag{6}$$

we have by Lemma 2 $\frac{\partial i}{\partial d_1} = 0$. This means that if the manager's has enough funds to cover investment i^{**} he will invest this amount in the efficient project (by Lemma 2). Anticipating this, the entrepreneur distributes as much dividends as possible just to leave the amount i^{**} for investment and not leaving any private benefits for the manager: $d_1^{**} = c - w - i^{**}$ ($\frac{\partial i}{\partial d_1} = 0$ implies by (5) that $\frac{\partial W}{\partial d_1} = 1 - t_d > 0$) and hence $b = 0$.

2. When $d_1 > c - w - i^{**}$, we have by Lemma 2 $i = e$ or $i = c - w - d_1$. Thus $\frac{\partial i}{\partial d_1} = -1$; $\frac{\partial W}{\partial d_1} = 1 - t_d - (1-a)r'(i)(1-t_c)$ and $b = 0$. Let $i^{***} \equiv i^{***}(a)$ such that

$$r'(i^{***}) = \frac{1-t_d}{(1-a)(1-t_c)} \tag{7}$$

and let $d_1^{***} = c - w - i^{***}$.

If $1/a > \frac{1-t_d}{(1-a)(1-t_c)}$ then $i^{***} > i^{**}$, $d_1^{***} < d_1^{**} = c - w - i^{**}$. We thus have $\frac{\partial W}{\partial d_1} < 0$, $\forall d_1 > c - w - i^{**}$ implying corner solution $d_1 = c - w - i^{**}$. If $1/a < \frac{1-t_d}{(1-a)(1-t_c)}$ then $i^{***} < i^{**}$, $d_1^{***} > d_1^{**} = c - w - i^{**}$ and we thus have an interior optimum $d_1 = c - w - i^{***}$.

Lemma 4. *If* $1/a \ge \frac{1-t_d}{(1-a)(1-t_c)}$ *then* $d_1 = c - w - i^{**}$. *If* $1/a < \frac{1-t_d}{(1-a)(1-t_c)}$ *then* $d_1 = c - w - i^{***}$.

The intuition behind this result is following. The manager's contract shapes not only the manager's incentive but also those of entrepreneur. According to (5), the entrepreneur preference point for investments is i^{***}. This however cannot be implemented directly since the decision is taken by a self-interested manager. The manager prefers i^{**} if it has funds or he will invests as much as possible. If $i^{***} > i^{**}$, the entrepreneur cannot induce i^{***} and thus he will stick with i^{**}. Otherwise he will induce i^{***}.

Now consider optimal contract for the manager.

The entrepreneur's problem is to design the manager's contract and to choose d to maximize his expected payoff.

$$\max_{w,a} W \tag{8}$$

where

$$W = \begin{cases} (c - w - i^{**}(a))(1-t_d) + (1-a)r(i^{**})(1-t_c), & \text{if } 1/a \ge \frac{1-t_d}{(1-a)(1-t_c)} \\ (c - w - i^{***}(a))(1-t_d) + (1-a)r(i^{***})(1-t_c), & \text{if } 1/a < \frac{1-t_d}{(1-a)(1-t_c)} \end{cases} \tag{9}$$

subject to

$$
\begin{array}{c}
w + ar(i^{**}) \geq w_0, \text{ if } 1/a \geq \frac{1-t_d}{(1-a)(1-t_c)} \\
w + ar(i^{***}) \geq w_0, \text{ if } 1/a < \frac{1-t_d}{(1-a)(1-t_c)}
\end{array}
\tag{10}
$$

Note that in (9) the first-period dividend (by Lemma 4) is either $c - w - i^{**}(a)$ or $c - w - i^{***}(a)$. From (9):

$$
\frac{\partial W}{\partial a} = \begin{cases} -i_a^{**}(a)(1-t_d) + (1-a)r'(i^{**})i_a^{**}(a)(1-t_c) - r(i^{**})(1-t_c), \\ \qquad \text{if } 1/a \geq \frac{1-t_d}{(1-a)(1-t_c)} \\ -i_a^{***}(a)(1-t_d) + (1-a)r'(i^{***})i_a^{***}(a)(1-t_c) - r(i^{***})(1-t_c), \\ \qquad \text{if } 1/a < \frac{1-t_d}{(1-a)(1-t_c)} \end{cases}
$$

Using (7):

$$
\frac{\partial W}{\partial a} = \begin{cases} -i_a^{**}(a)(1-t_d) + (1-a)r'(i^{**})i_a^{**}(a)(1-t_c) - r(i^{**})(1-t_c), \\ \qquad \text{if } 1/a \geq \frac{1-t_d}{(1-a)(1-t_c)} \\ -r(i^{***})(1-t_c), \text{ if } 1/a < \frac{1-t_d}{(1-a)(1-t_c)} \end{cases}
\tag{11}
$$

The only candidate for optimal a is $a \leq \frac{1-t_c}{2-t_d-t_c}$ (this is equivalent to $1/a \geq \frac{1-t_d}{(1-a)(1-t_c)}$). Proof by contradiction. Suppose that optimal $a > \frac{1-t_c}{2-t_d-t_c}$. Two cases are possible. If the manager's budget constraint is not binding, one can reduce a that improves the entrepreneur's earnings by (11). If it's binding then a reduction in a increases investment by Lemma 4 and (7) and taking into account the concavity of $r(i)$. This increases the total payoff of entrepreneur and manager. The entrepreneur will adjust w to satisfy the manager's budget constraint.

Thus only the case $a \leq \frac{1-t_c}{2-t_d-t_c}$ can be a candidate for optimal a (by continuity). We have (see, for instance, Varian (1992), ch.27)):

$$
sign\frac{\partial a}{\partial t_d} = sign\frac{\partial^2 W}{\partial a \partial t_d} = sign\{i_a^{**}(a)\}
$$

The latter is positive by (6). Indeed, by differentiating both parts of (6) in a we get

$$
r''(i \mid i = i^{**})i_a^{**}(a) = -1/a^2
$$

The concavity of $r(i)$ implies that $i^{**}(a)$ is increasing. This inturn implies that $\frac{\partial a}{\partial t_d} > 0$. Since an increase in t_d increases a, this leads to higher i^{**} and higher amount of investment by Lemma 4. This leads to the following proposition.

Proposition 1. *An increase in t_d is socially efficient.*

3. Conclusion

This note has analyzed optimal dividend policy and investment decision in a model where a firm's manager is subject to moral hazard and has ability to invest in socially inefficient projects. It is shown that equilibrium level of investment is below socially optimally since the entrepreneur distributes too much dividends to reduce the manager's entrenchment problem. By increasing the dividend tax rate over capital gain tax rate, social planner can improve the equilibrium level of investment by giving more incentive to entrepreneur to retain funds inside the firm.

Appendix

Proof of Lemma 1. Two cases are possible. Case 1: $V_2 - d_2 > V_1$. Then

$$\frac{\partial W_2}{\partial d_2} = t_c - t_d$$

If $t_c > t_d$ then $d_2 = V_2 - V_1$. Otherwise $d_2 = 0$. High dividends will be paid if dividend tax rate is smaller than capital tax rate and no dividends will be paid otherwise. Case 2. $V_2 - d_2 < V_1$. Then

$$\frac{\partial W_2}{\partial d_2} = -t_d$$

Then $d_2 = \max\{0, V_2 - V_1\}$. Finally we have. If $V_2 > V_1$, and $t_c > t_d$, $d_2 = V_2 - V_1$. If $t_c < t_d$, then compare $d_2 = 0$ and $d_2 = V_2 - V_1$. In the first case $W_2 = V_2 - (V_2 - V_1)t_c$. In the second case $W_2 = (V_2 - V_1)(1 - t_d) + V_1$. First case is better for the entrepreneur. Finally, if $V_2 < V_1$, $d_2 = 0$. *End proof.*

Proof of Lemma 3. First suppose that the entrepreneur does not sell shares. Then by Lemma 1 (given that $V_1 = 0$), if $t_c > t_d$ the entrepreneur's earnings are $W_2 = (1-a)r(i)(1-t_d)$. Otherwise it is $(1-a)r(i)(1-t_c)$, where i is determined by Lemma 2.

Now suppose that the entrepreneur sells shares at the end of year 1. What is the value of the firm then?

Recall that V_1 is the value of the firm in this case. We have $V_2 = (1-a)r(i)$, where i is determined by Lemma 2. Suppose $V_1 \leq V_2$. If $t_c > t_d$, then by Lemma 1 $d_2 = V_2 - V_1$ and the new shareholders' payoff (buying shares from the entrepreneur) is $W_n = V_1 + (V_2 - V_1)(1 - t_d)$. This should be equal to V_1. Thus we have $V_1 = V_2 = (1-a)r(i)$. If $t_c < t_d$ then $d_2 = 0$ and $W_n = V_2 - (V_2 - V_1)t_c$. Thus $V_1 = V_2 - (V_2 - V_1)t_c$ or $V_1 = \frac{V_2(1-t_c)}{1-t_c} = V_2$. Now suppose that $V_1 > V_2$. This situation is impossible because no one will be willing to buy the shares of the firm at the end of year 1. To summarize: at the end of year 1 the firm's value is $(1-a)r(i)$, where $i = c - d_1 - w - b$.

If the entrepreneur sells shares at the end of year 1 he gets $(1-a)r(i)(1-t_c)$. *End proof.*

References

[1] Chetty , R., Saez, E. (2005). Dividend Taxes and Corporate Behavior: Evidence From the 2003 Dividend Tax Cut. *Quarterly Journal of Economics,* **120** (3), 791-833.

[2] Dittmar, A., Mahrt-Smith, J., Servaes, H. (2003). International Corporate Governance and Corporate Cash Holdings. *Journal of Financial and Quantitative Analysis,* **38** (1), 111-133.

[3] Jensen, M. C. (1986). Agency Cost of Free Cash-flow, Corporate Finance and Takeovers. *American Economic Review,* **76** (2), 323-329.

[4] Poterba, J. (2004). Taxation and Corporate Payout Policy. *American Economic Review,* **94** (2), 171-175.

[5] Varian, H. (1992). *Microeconomic Analysis.* W. W. Norton, 3rd edition.

In: Business and Finance: Performance and Management ISBN: 978-1-61122-936-3
Editors: R. Morland and A. Gagglione

Chapter 12

ARE THE HIGH-ORDER MOMENTS OF THE ASSETS RETURNS DISTRIBUTION FORECASTABLE?

Trino Manuel Ñíguez[1]*
University of Westminster, UK

Abstract

This paper analyzes the out-of-sample ability of different parametric and semi-parametric GARCH-type models to forecast the conditional variance and the conditional and unconditional kurtosis of three types of financial assets (stock index, exchange rate and Treasury Note). For this purpose, we consider the Gaussian and Student-t GARCH models by Bollerslev (1986, 1987), and two different time-varying conditional kurtosis GARCH models based on the Student-t and a transformed Gram-Charlier density.

Key words: Gram-Charlier densities; Financial data; High-order moments; Out-of-sample forecasting.

JEL classification: C16, G1.

1. Introduction

The literature related to financial econometrics and asset pricing has shown that the conditional distribution of high-frequency returns exhibits stylized features that include excess of kurtosis, negative skewness, and temporal persistence in conditional moments. Remarkably, time dependency may be a characteristic that not only is present in the dynamics of the expected return and the conditional variance, but also in higher-order moments $E_t\left(r_{t+1}^s\right)$, $s \geq 3$; see, Nelson (1996). Among these, the conditional skewness and kurtosis (related to

*E-mail address: T.M.Niguez@wmin.ac.uk. Phone: +44 (0) 22 7911 5000. Fax: +44 (0) 22 7911 5839. Department of Economics and Quantitative Methods, Westminster Business School, University of Westminster, 35 Marylebone Road, NW1 5LS London, UK.

the third- and fourth-order conditional central moments, respectively) are particularly relevant for their implications in risk management, asset pricing, and optimal portfolio selection, as pointed out by Chunhachinda, Dandapani, Hamid and Prakash (1997), Harvey and Siddique (2000), Christie-David and Chaudhry (2001) and Schmidt (2002). For instance, rational investors concerned with the non-Gaussian properties of returns would be averse to negative skewness and high kurtosis. As a result, the composition of their optimal portfolio would change (everything else being equal) whenever they expect changes in any of those characteristics. In this regard, Fang and Lai (1997) have reported empirical evidence of positive risk premiums for conditional skewness and conditional kurtosis in the US market. All this has given rise to a string of recent articles which have gone beyond the traditional modelling and forecasting of the conditional volatility to also focus on the time-varying properties of higher-order moments. The models proposed in this literature include both parametric (see, among others, Hansen 1994, Dueker 1997, Harvey and Siddique 1999, and Brooks, Burke, Heravi and Persand 2005) and semi-parametric approaches, such as entropy distributions (Rockinger and Jondeau 2002), and Gram-Charlier densities (Le ́on, Rubio and Serna 2005).

The econometric modelling of high-order moments attempts to exploit time dependency to improve the forecasts which are typically needed in financial applications. In this paper, we analyze the out-of-sample ability of different parametric and semi-parametric GARCH-type models to forecast the conditional variance as well as the conditional and unconditional kurtosis of several classes of financial assets. We do not focus on asymmetric distributions (*i.e.*, we do not consider skewness in this paper) so that we can specifically isolate the gains from modelling kurtosis, which is widely considered as the most representative non-Gaussian stylized feature of financial data. We compare four different approaches in our study with increasing degree of complexity, going from the standard GARCH model to more sophisticated specifications. The starting point in our analysis is the simple Gaussian GARCH model by Bollerslev (1986), which implies the same degree of constant conditional kurtosis as the Normal distribution. Second, we consider the straightforward generalization of this model suggested by Bollerslev (1987) which, on the basis of the conditional Student-t distribution, is able to capture the underlying conditional kurtosis in the data, still assuming constant kurtosis. Next, we consider a further generalization, the so-called Student-t GARCHK model, suggested in Brooks *et al.* (2005). This is intended to fit the time-varying dynamics of the conditional variance and the kurtosis separately via a Student-t distribution with a degrees of freedom parameter that is allowed to vary over time. Finally, we consider a restricted version of the semi-parametric GARCH model with time-varying conditional kurtosis proposed in León et al. (2005) as an alternative to the Student- t GARCHK model. The semi-parametric approach relies upon a Gram-Charlier type polynomial expansion so that the resulting probability density function is flexible enough to approximate any unknown density, without imposing any assumption on the underlying conditional distribution.

The main questions we try to solve refer to *i*) whether conditional kurtosis models are able to yield better out-of-sample forecasts, and *ii*) which conditional kurtosis approach (parametric or semi-parametric) is more appropriate for applied purposes. These are ultimately empirical questions that we shall address statistically in this paper by means of an out-of-sample forecasting analysis. In particular, we compute one-day ahead forecasts

of the conditional variances and the conditional and unconditional kurtosis implied by the different models, and compare their forecasting ability in terms of the Mean Square Error (MSE) loss-function. Patton (2006) has recently argued that only few of the volatility loss functions are not affected by the choice of the proxy used, showing that the MSE loss-function is robust. The same arguments may hold when analyzing higher-order conditional moments for which the true values are not directly observable and must be proxied with sampling error. We use the procedure in Diebold and Mariano (1995) to test statistically whether the differences observed across the different GARCH models are truly significant.

The remainder of this paper is organized as follows. Section 2 describes the conditional models that we use to fit and forecast conditional variance and kurtosis. Section 3 discusses the main features of the empirical analysis. Finally, Section 4 summarizes and concludes.

2. Modelling Forecasting Conditional Variance and Higher-Order Moments

Let us first introduce the basic data generating process and the general notation used throughout the paper. We observe a sample of (daily) asset prices from which we compute the series of returns $r_t = 100\log\left(P_t/P_{t-1}\right),\ t = 1, ..., T$. We assume that the returns follow the dynamics,

$$\begin{aligned} r_t &= E_{t-1}(r_t) + \varepsilon_t, \\ \varepsilon_t &= h_t^{1/2}\eta_t; \end{aligned} \tag{1}$$

where the conditional expectation $E_{t-1}(\cdot) = E\left(\cdot|I_{t-1}\right)$ is taken on the observable set of information available up to time $t-1$, denoted as I_{t-1}. The set of random innovations η_t are conditionally distributed according to certain density function $f\left(\eta_t|I_{t-1}\right)$ that satisfies $E_{t-1}\left(\eta_t\right) = 0$ and $E_{t-1}\left(\eta_t^2\right) = 1$, with $E\left(\eta_t^s\right) < \infty$ for some $s > 2$.

The expected return in the model is given by $E_{t-1}(r_t)$. We shall use a simple AR(1) model, $E_{t-1}(r_t) = c + \rho r_{t-1}$, to filter out any predictable component in the conditional mean of the series. The conditional variance of the process is given by $h_t = E_{t-1}(\varepsilon_t^2)$, which is the main object of interest in many papers that specifically focus on volatility modelling. In this regard, one of the most widely used models is the GARCH(1,1) process of Bollerslev (1986), which assumes a linear functional form,

$$h_t = \omega + \alpha\varepsilon_{t-1}^2 + \beta h_{t-1} \tag{2}$$

with the parameter restrictions $\omega > 0,\ \alpha, \beta \geq 0$ ensuring almost sure positiveness in the conditional variance process. The additional restriction $\alpha + \beta < 1$ is sufficient and necessary for $E\left(\varepsilon_t^2\right) < \infty$, whereas the existence of higher-order moments imply further restrictions on the driving parameters (α, β) as well as the existence of suitable moments of η_t (e.g., the unconditional fourth-order moment is well defined when $\kappa_\eta\alpha^2 + \beta^2 + 2\alpha\beta < 1$, with κ_η denoting the kurtosis of η_t).

The enormous success of the GARCH(1,1) model strives in its appealing interpretation, large degree of statistical parsimony, and computational tractability. The main GARCH equation describes the conditional variance forecast h_t as a weighted average of a constant

term (long-run variance), ω, the previous variance forecast, h_{t-1}, and a proxy for the conditional variance given the information which was not available when the previous forecast was made (related to new information arrivals), ε_{t-1}^2. As a result, the model is able to capture the main stylized feature in the conditional variance (namely, clustering and persistence) by resorting to a small number of parameters in a fairly simple representation, from which one-step and multi-step forecasts can easily be obtained.[1] Further generalizations that conform the broad GARCH family arise by readily extending this basic structure (for instance, towards including leverage and other non-linear effects), and/or by considering different assumptions on the conditional distribution $f(\eta_t|I_{t-1})$. We shall discuss in more detail the basic model and several of its extensions intended to capture excess of kurtosis and time dependence in higher-order moments in the following subsections.

2.1. GARCH Modelling

2.1.1. Gaussian GARCH

The simplest approach in GARCH-type modelling is the Gaussian GARCH(1,1) model of Bollerslev (1986). In addition, to the basic data generating process (1)-(2), it is assumed that the conditional shocks $\{\eta_t\}$ are independent and identically normally distributed with mean 0 and variance 1, *i.e.*, it is imposed the particularly strong restriction

$$\eta_t \sim iid\mathcal{N}(0,1), \tag{3}$$

or $f(\eta_t|I_{t-1}) = f(\eta_t) = (2\pi)^{-1/2}\exp\left(-\eta_t^2/2\right)$. The model is fully specified with this assumption, and the relevant parameters $\xi_0 := (c,\rho,\omega,\alpha,\beta)'$ can then be estimated from the sample by Maximum Likelihood [ML henceforth]. Under conventional assumptions on the pre-sample observations which do not play any relevant role when the sample is large enough, the log-likelihood function of the t-th observation, after dropping a constant term, can be written as:

$$l_t(\xi_0) = -\frac{1}{2}\log h_t - \frac{\varepsilon_t^2}{2h_t}; \quad t = 1,...,T, \tag{4}$$

Since the information matrix related to the two sets of parameters involved (conditional mean and conditional variance) is block-diagonal, the respective parameter vectors, say $\xi_{0m} := (c,\rho)'$ and $\xi_{0v} := (\omega,\alpha,\beta)'$, can be estimated separately. We shall proceed in this way, computing first the demeaned series $\hat{\varepsilon}_t = r_t - \hat{c}_T - \hat{\rho}_T r_{t-1}$, and then estimating the remaining parameters given $\{\hat{\varepsilon}_t\}$.[2]

Conditional normality is a fairly restrictive assumption which is widely accepted not to hold in the majority of applications involving real financial data. This fact is observed even when the data are sampled on a relatively low frequency basis which implies a high

[1] The empirical analysis in Hansen and Lunde (2005) makes an out-of-sample comparison of over 300 different volatility models using daily exchange rate data. They find that none of these models is able to provide a significantly better forecast than the GARCH(1,1) model.

[2] The orthogonality condition $E\left(\partial l_t(\xi_0)/\partial\xi_{0m}\xi_{0v}\right) = 0$ holds for all the models considered in this paper. It is usual to estimate the parameters in the AR(1) model by Least Squares, whereas the parameters related to the conditional variance (and higher-order moments) must be estimated by ML.

degree of aggregation. Fortunately, it is also widely accepted that the Normal assumption does not play a critical role when the main purpose is model fitting and/or volatility forecasting and, in fact, there are both computational and statistical reasons that have supported the wide use of the Gaussian GARCH in applied settings. First, the Gaussian log-likelihood function, $\mathcal{L}(\xi_0) = \sum_{t=1}^{T} l_t(\xi_0)$, is very tractable and typically does not pose any computational problems in order to be optimized numerically – hence, the GARCH model is directly implemented in most statistical packages, and can be estimated even with a spreadsheet. Second, and more importantly, the resultant estimation, namely $\hat{\xi}_T = \arg\max_{\xi_0} \mathcal{L}(\xi_0)$, is known to be $\sqrt{T}$–consistent and asymptotically normally distributed under certain regularity conditions even if η_t are not really Gaussian distributed (in this case $\hat{\xi}_T$ is referred to as the quasi maximum likelihood estimator [QML]); see Weiss (1986), Bollerslev and Wooldridge (1992), Lee and Hansen (1994), and Newey and Steigerwald (1997). These properties ensure tractability and accuracy for many applications in which the main aim is to obtain consistent estimates of ξ_0, and/or forecasts of the conditional variance process, which are simply determined as $\hat{h}_{T+s} = \hat{\omega}_T + \hat{\alpha}_T\hat{\varepsilon}_T^2 + \hat{\beta}_T\hat{h}_{T-1}$ for $s = 1$, and $\hat{h}_{T+s} = \hat{\omega}_T + \left(\hat{\alpha}_T + \hat{\beta}_T\right)\hat{h}_{T+s-1}$ for $s > 1$.

2.1.2. Student-*t* GARCH

The Normal assumption may be convenient, but it turns out to be too restrictive for applications on risk management and asset pricing, because these require the conditional density of η_t, and not just volatility estimations.[3] The failure of the Normal assumption is mainly due to the large degree of kurtosis that is typically observable in real data, which in turn is related to the magnitude and the frequency of extreme values that characterize almost any financial time series. Although the unconditional distribution implied by the Gaussian GARCH(1,1) model is leptokurtic (Bollerslev, 1986), often this model cannot generate large enough values to match the range which is observed in practice owing to limitations in its statistical properties; see Carnero, Peña and Ruiz (2004) for a discussion on this topic. Furthermore, the empirical distribution of the estimates $\hat{\eta}_t$, given the ML estimates $\hat{\xi}_T$, also suggest an excess of conditional kurtosis over the theoretical level which is implied by the Normal distribution.[4] Overall, the empirical evidence largely supports the existence of strong leptokurtosis in both the unconditional and conditional distributions of returns, thereby suggesting model misspecification in the Gaussian GARCH approach.

This observation motivated further extensions aiming to capture extreme movements through heavy-tailed distributions. A very simple, yet useful extension, was early suggested by Bollerslev (1987), who proposed a transformed Student t-distribution with v degrees of freedom to accommodate the excess of kurtosis, *i.e.*,

$$\eta_t \sim iidt_v(0,1), \tag{5}$$

[3] A leading example is the Value at Risk methodology. The percentiles of η_t, together with the forecasts of the future conditional variance, jointly determine the maximum expected loss of an asset at a certain significance level.

[4] For instance, the standardized residuals of the Gaussian GARCH model studied in Section 3 below have a kurtosis of nearly 6 in the in-sample period considered for the S&P index. The Jarque-Bera test for normality (JB=444.56) rejects the hypothesis of normality. Similar results are obtained for the remaining time-series.

where the degrees of freedom parameter, v, is directly characterized by the shape of the underlying distribution, and can be estimated by ML from the available data (subject to the restriction $v > 2$ so that the variance process is well defined). Apart from a constant term, the relevant log-likelihood function is given by,

$$l_t(\xi_1) = \log\left(\frac{\Gamma((\nu+1)/2)]}{\Gamma(\nu/2)}\right) - \frac{1}{2}\log((v-2)\,h_t) - \frac{v+1}{2}\log\left[1 + \frac{\varepsilon_t^2}{(v-2)\,h_t}\right], \tag{6}$$

with $\xi_1 = (v, \xi_0')'$, and $\Gamma(\cdot)$ denoting the Gamma function. When $1/\hat{v}_T \to 0$, the conditional distribution approaches a Normal distribution and the Gaussian restriction may be acceptable. However, for small values such that $1/\hat{v}_T > 0$, the empirical distribution has fatter tails than the corresponding Normal distribution. For many empirical applications related to risk-management, such as Value at Risk, the Student-*t* GARCH model tends to provide a superior performance over the Gaussian GARCH model; see, for instance, Alexander (1998).

2.2. Further Approaches: Modelling Higher-Order Conditional Moments

2.2.1. The Student-*t* GARCHK Model

The Student-*t* GARCH model provides further flexibility to capture constant unconditional leptokurtosis. Obviously, there is no prior reason to believe that higher-order conditional moments should remain unchanged, other than for model simplicity and computational tractability. Consequently, Brooks et al., (2005) proposed a further extension of this model, the so-called Student-*t* GARCHK, by allowing the possibility of heterogeneity in the conditional distribution $f(\eta_t|I_{t-1})$ due to time-varying kurtosis.

Considering the basic GARCH model, the key assumption now is that $\{\eta_t\}$ are conditionally distributed according to a Student-*t* distribution with a time-varying number of degrees of freedom, say v_t, which evolves independently of the dynamics followed by the conditional variance. In particular, the characteristic restriction is given by

$$f(\eta_t|I_{t-1}) \sim t_{v_t}(0,1); \;\; \nu_t = \frac{2(2k_t-3)}{k_t-3}, \tag{7}$$

where k_t is the conditional kurtosis of the process at time t. In the same spirit of the structural GARCH modelling, an autoregressive moving average process is used to capture the dynamics of the conditional kurtosis:

$$k_t = \kappa + \delta\left(\frac{\varepsilon_{t-1}^4}{h_{t-1}^2}\right) + \theta k_{t-1}. \tag{8}$$

As in equation (2), the parameter restrictions $\kappa > 0$, $\delta, \theta \geq 0$, are sufficient for ensuring positiveness in the resultant process. Note that k_t arises as a weighted combination of a long-run constant value, the previous kurtosis forecast, and a term with updated information of the conditional kurtosis as proxied by $(\varepsilon_{t-1}^2/h_{t-1})^2$. Under the restriction $\delta = \theta = 0$, the model reduces to the constant kurtosis model studied in the previous subsection, which suggests an easy way to statistically test for the suitability of the time-varying specification. It is

important to remark that the conditional variance process, h_t, and the conditional kurtosis process, k_t, are not contemporaneously functionally related, so they may be parameterized individually as desired by using different specifications than those discussed above, for instance, introducing nonlinearities or dependence upon other variables. The log-likelihood of the model, apart from a constant term, is given by,

$$l_t(\xi_2) = \log\left(\frac{\Gamma[(\nu_t+1)/2]}{\Gamma(\nu_t/2)}\right) - \frac{1}{2}\log((\nu_t-2)h_t) - \frac{\nu_t+1}{2}\log\left[1+\frac{\varepsilon_t^2}{h_t(\nu_t-2)}\right], \tag{9}$$

with $\xi_2 = (\kappa, \delta, \theta, \xi_0')'$, and $v_t > 4$ to ensure the existence of the first fourth-order moments. The similitudes between (9) are (6) are obvious, since the time-varying kurtosis generalizes the constant kurtosis model by simply allowing time variability in the degrees of freedom parameter.

The empirical in-sample evidence discussed in Brooks et al., (2005, Section 3) for several US and UK equities and bonds supports the hypothesis of heterogeneity in the conditional kurtosis, largely outperforming the specification with constant kurtosis.

2.2.2. The Gram-Charlier GARCHK Model

Let us start this section by recalling the dynamics of the conditional variance-kurtosis models which have been discussed thus far:

$$\begin{aligned} r_t &= E_{t-1}(r_t) + \varepsilon_t;\ \varepsilon_t = h_t^{1/2}\eta_t, \\ h_t &= \omega + \alpha\varepsilon_{t-1}^2 + \beta h_{t-1}, \\ k_t &= \kappa + \delta\left(\frac{\varepsilon_{t-1}^4}{h_{t-1}^2}\right) + \theta k_{t-1}, \end{aligned} \tag{10}$$

given the set of unknown parameter $\xi_2 = (\kappa, \delta, \theta, \xi_0')'$. Instead of imposing a particular assumption on the conditional distribution of η_t as we did in the previous sections (Normal, Student-t, or Student-t with time-varying degrees of freedom), we may use a Gram-Charlier type of expansion to fit semi-parametrically the unknown density function $f(\eta_t|I_{t-1})$. This is the central point discussed in the model proposed in León et al. (2005), which we summarize below.

Under certain regularity conditions, any probability density function (pdf henceforth) can be expanded in an infinite series of derivatives of the standard Normal density, $\phi(\eta_t)$, as follows,

$$f(\eta_t|I_{t-1}) = \phi(\eta_t)\sum_{s=0}^{\infty} d_{st}H_s(\eta_t), \tag{11}$$

where $H_s(\eta_t)$ is the sth order Hermite polynomial defined in terms of the sth order derivative of the Gaussian pdf:

$$\frac{d^s\phi(\eta_t)}{d\eta_t^s} = (-1)^s\phi(\eta_t)H_s(\eta_t). \tag{12}$$

For applied purposes, the infinite expansion is not operative and has to be truncated. Thus, considering the finite expansion (approximation) of $f(\eta_t|I_{t-1})$ in (11) with a truncation

factor up to the fourth-order moment, we obtain:

$$f(\eta_t|I_{t-1}) \simeq \phi(\eta_t)\left[1+\frac{s_t}{3!}(\eta_t^3-3\eta_t)+\frac{k_t-3}{4!}(\eta_t^4-6\eta_t^2+3)\right]=\phi(\eta_t)\psi(\eta_t), \qquad (13)$$

where the polynomial $\psi(\eta_t)$ is defined implicitly, and the terms s_t and k_t correspond to the conditional skewness and kurtosis, respectively. Note that the resulting approximation, $\phi(\eta_t)\psi(\eta_t)$, is characterized by the underlying dynamics of the conditional moments up to the fourth-order moment and the set of unknown parameters ξ_2. We do not overload unnecessarily the notation by remarking the latter feature as this is completely clear at this point.

Since the approximation based on a finite polynomial expansion of $f(\eta_t|I_{t-1})$ implies certain amount of truncation error, the right-hand side of (13) cannot be seen as a proper density function. The main reason is that $\phi(\eta_t)\psi(\eta_t)$ is not ensured to be almost surely positive uniformly on the parameter space of ξ_2. This unappealing feature does not only suppose a major shortcoming from a theoretical viewpoint, but also may cause the failure of the ML estimation in empirical settings. León et al. (2005) propose a solution building on the same methodology as Gallant and Nychka (1987), Gallant and Tauchen (1989) and Gallant Nychka and Fenton (1996). In essence, they achieved a well-defined pdf by first using a simple positive transformation of $\psi(\eta_t)$ that ensures almost-surely positiveness (namely, squaring $\psi(\eta_t)$, although other transformation in similar spirit are possible as well), and then re-normalizing the resulting function by a suitable scaling factor such that the resulting function intregates up to one. More specifically, given the normalizing factor,

$$\Delta_t=\int_{-\infty}^{\infty}\phi(\eta_t)\psi^2(\eta_t)\,d\eta_t=1+\frac{s_t^2}{3!}+\frac{(k_t-3)^2}{4!} \qquad (14)$$

the transformed Gram-Charlier probability density function, denoted $f^*(\eta_t|I_{t-1})$, can readily be written as

$$f^*(\eta_t|I_{t-1})=\left(\frac{1}{\Delta_t}\right)\phi(\eta_t)\psi^2(\eta_t). \qquad (15)$$

Note that the Hermite polynomial that characterize $\psi(\eta_t)$ convey information about the empirical degree of conditional moments, and so does $f^*(\eta_t|I_{t-1})$, from which ξ_2 can be identified from the observable data. However, the terms s_t and k_t no longer admit the interpretation of conditional moments, and further adjustments to forecast the conditional moments given $f^*(\eta_t|I_{t-1})$ are necessary; see Section 3.2.2 for further details. Since we are restricting ourselves to symmetric conditional distributions, we set $s_t=0$ in (13) for all t, and denote as $\overline{\psi}(\eta_t)$ the restricted version of the model. Hence, the normalizing factor reduces accordingly to $\overline{\Delta}_t=1+(k_t-3)^2/4!$, and the corresponding log-likelihood function, apart from a constant term, is given by

$$l_t(\xi_2)=-\frac{1}{2}\ln h_t-\frac{\varepsilon_t^2}{2h_t}-\ln\overline{\Delta}_t+\ln\left[\overline{\psi}^2(\eta_t)\right]. \qquad (16)$$

It is worth remarking at this point the similitudes between this function and the Gaussian log-likelihood function (4) used in the basic GARCH model: The Gram-Charlier

log-likelihood function simply adds two adjustment terms to the latter in order to capture the non-Gaussian features of the data, in our case, conditional kurtosis dynamics. In fact, the Gaussian likelihood (4) is nested as a particular case by setting constant kurtosis ($\delta = \theta = 0$), equal to that of the Normal distribution (*i.e.*, $k_t = \kappa = 3$). As in Brooks et al. (2005), the empirical results in León et al. (2005) indicate a significant presence of time-variability in the higher-order moments which support the suitability of conditional kurtosis.

3. Empirical Analysis

3.1. The Data

The data used in this study are daily returns (scaled by a factor of 100) of the S&P500 index (SP), the GBP(£)/US Dollar($) exchange rate (FX), and the 10 years Treasury Notes (TN). The series are sampled over the period June 9, 1993 to June 8, 2008 for a total of $T = 3,912$ observations obtained from Datastream. Table 1 displays some descriptive information for the total sample. As expected, stock returns are much more volatile (as measured by the unconditional volatility) than the other series. The unconditional distribution of any of these series shows clearly non-Gaussian features, such as a (mild) skewness in the case of the SP and FX series, and a remarked excess of kurtosis over the Normal distribution due to outliers in the three time series considered. The Jarque-Bera tests for normality are easily rejected, particularly in the case of the stock index time-series.[5] The analysis of dependence through the Ljung-Box portmanteau test statists shows some form of weak dependence in the level of the returns, and a strong, persistent correlation in higher-order moments.

3.2. Modelling and Out-of-Sample Forecasting

We split the total sample into an in-sample period to estimate the models, and an out-the-sample window to make a total of $N = 500$ one-step predictions of the conditional variance and kurtosis by means of a rolling-window procedure. To assess the ability of the different GARCH models involved, we need a time-varying measure of the actual conditional moments. In both cases, the main problem for addressing forecasting ability is that the true conditional variance and kurtosis are not observable and have to be approached by means of statistical proxies which often can only provide a crude measure.

In the context of volatility forecasting, the empirical proxies considered in most papers are based on measurable transformations of the absolute-valued unexpected returns $|\varepsilon_t|$, most frequently ε_t^2. Following this literature, we shall consider ε_{T+1}^2 as a proxy for variance in this paper.[6] Although there exists an agreement (at least empirically) on how conditional variance could be proxied, to the best of our knowledge there is no obvious guidance on

[5]The Jarque-Bera test for normality uses the test statistic $JB = T\left[\frac{s^2}{3!} + \frac{(k-3)^2}{4!}\right]$, where s and k are the sample skewness and kurtosis, respectively. The test is asymptotically distributed as $\chi^2(2)$, and is rejected for non-zero values of the sampled skewness and/or excess of kurtosis.

[6]The availability of intraday data has motivated the use of a new strand of proxies for volatility which provide a more accurate measure based on realized volatility.

Table 1. Descriptive statistics for daily returns

Statistic	SP	FX	TN
Sample		9/06/1993 - 8/06/2008	
Observations		3913	
Mean	0.0561	-0.0067	-0.0093
Median	0.1186	0.0000	0.0000
Maximum	16.107	3.4233	6.1278
Minimum	-15.419	-4.2211	-5.1238
St. Dev.	1.8624	0.5112	1.1807
Skewness	-0.1033	-0.0131	0.3568
Kurtosis	11.01	5.8469	5.4564
Jarque-Bera	10470 (0.00)	1324 (0.00)	1066.8 (0.00)
Ljung-Box Q(1)-r_t	17.29 (0.00)	16.65 (0.00)	4.0521 (0.04)
Ljung-Box Q(20)-r_t^2	1047.1 (0.00)	229.4 (0.00)	1322.2 (0.00)
Ljung-Box Q(20)-r_t^3	93.50 (0.00)	399.7 (0.00)	73.28 (0.00)
Ljung-Box Q(20)-r_t^4	120.7 (0.00)	459.7 (0.00)	297.1 (0.00)
LR: $(\kappa, \delta, \theta) = 0$	146.9 (0.00)	154.4 (0.00)	153.2 (0.00)
LR: $(\delta, \theta) = 0$	77.70 (0.00)	9.43 (0.00)	14.1 (0.00)

The Jarque-Bera normality test is asymptotically distributed as a $\chi^2(2)$ under the null of normality, the Ljung-Box is asymptotically distributed as a $\chi^2(\varsigma)$, ς being the autocorrelation order, the Likelihood Ratio test (LR) is asymptotically distributed as a $\chi^2(q)$ being q the number of restrictions under the null, (asymptotic p-values in parenthesis).The critical values of $\chi^2(1)$, $\chi^2(2)$, $\chi^2(3)$ and $\chi^2(20)$ are 3.84, 5.99, 7.81, 31.41, at 5% level, respectively.

how to approach conditional kurtosis. Given that the estimation bias may be more significant when considering higher-order moments, and that the choice of the proxy necessarily conditions the results, we consider different proxies for the conditional kurtosis. In particular, we take the sample kurtosis in the m days immediately following the last in-sample observation, namely

$$\bar{k}_{T+1,m} = \left(\frac{\frac{1}{m}\sum_{j=1}^{m} \left(\varepsilon_{T+j} - \bar{\varepsilon}_m\right)^4}{\left[\frac{1}{m}\sum_{j=1}^{m} \left(\varepsilon_{T+j} - \bar{\varepsilon}_m\right)^2\right]^2} \right); \quad \bar{\varepsilon}_m = \sum_{j=1}^{m} \varepsilon_{T+j}/m, \tag{17}$$

with $m = \{5, 50, 500\}$.[7] The choice of m here seeks a compromise between the tautological notion of *conditional* and the statistical problems related to measurement errors in the relevant statistic when using a few number of observations. As $m \to 1$, the proxy is more erratic and extremely noisy, and can severely be influenced by a few large observations, whereas the largest window in our analysis ($m = 500$ observations) is related to the out-of-sample unconditional kurtosis.

We consider the MSE as a loss function for any of the conditional variance and kurtosis

[7] We also used othe values for m, noting no qualitative difference with the results reported in the main text.

forecasts series, *i.e.*, we compute the statistic $N^{-1}\sum_{i=1}^{N}\left(\hat{\pi}_{T+1,i}-\bar{\pi}_{T+1,i}\right)^2$ for each model and time-series, where $\hat{\pi}_{T+1,i}$ is the i-th prediction (either conditional variance or kurtosis) and $\bar{\pi}_{T+1,i}$ the proxy for the actual value. The forecasting performance is compared in statistical terms by means of the test proposed by Diebold and Mariano (1995). This test assumes no differences between the loss functions of two alternative models under the null hypothesis. The null is rejected for large values of the statistic $DM = \bar{x}/\sqrt{2\pi f_x\left(w=0\right)/N}$, where $\bar{x}$ denotes the sample mean of the differences in the forecasting errors of the two alternative models, $f_x\left(w=0\right)$ is the spectral density function of the forecasting error differences evaluated at the zero frequency (long-run variance), and N is the total number of forecasts. The statistic is asymptotically distributed as a standard Normal random variable under the null.

3.2.1. In-sample Analysis

The slight (positive) autocorrelation pattern in the conditional mean of the returns is filtered out by fitting an AR(1) process estimated by Least-Squares. Given the demeaned series, $\hat{\varepsilon}_t$, all the conditional variance-kurtosis models are then estimated by optimizing the corresponding log-likelihood functions using the Newton-Raphson method, and initializing the conditional variance and kurtosis dynamics with values equal to the corresponding unconditional moments. Convergence in the optimization process to the global extremes is easily obtained in the case of the simplest Gaussian and Student-t GARCH models. Similarly, the estimation of the Student-t and Gram-Charlier GARCHK models is not computationally troublesome providing that the starting values are chosen properly.[8] The main results from the estimation in the in-sample period are displayed in Table 2 below.

The estimates of the conditional variance for the three series show the usual degree of high persistence and low sensitivity to shocks which is commonly observed in daily asset returns. Persistence is related to the magnitude of the coefficient $\hat{\alpha}_T+\hat{\beta}_T$, which tends to be slightly smaller than unity, while sensitivity to new information arrivals is measured through $\hat{\alpha}_T$, which takes small values empirically. Owing to the large degree of unconditional kurtosis in the data, the Student-t GARCH model determines a degrees of freedom parameter around 6 for all the series. This result confirms that extreme observations in real data are much more likely to occur in relation to the Normal distribution. Assuming that the true distribution is a Student-t, higher-order moments larger than 6 would not be well-defined. The models that allow for time-varying kurtosis reject the hypothesis of constant kurtosis, since the restriction $\delta=\theta=0$ is easily rejected by a standard Likelihood Ratio test in the three time series considered. Overall, the empirical evidence we observe perfectly agrees with the results in Brooks et al. (2005) and León et al. (2005), showing that extending GARCH models toward accounting for time-varying kurtosis leads to a better in-sample fitting.

There are two further interesting features that arise when comparing the results observed across the different types of estimation techniques involving time-varying kurtosis, and the different classes of financial assets considered. First, whereas the estimates of the GARCH equation remain virtually unaltered given the different models, the estimates of the driving

[8]Also, in order to avoid convergence to local extremes, the optimization routine is monitored using a grid of different starting values. Normal convergence is obtained in all the cases.

Table 2. GARCH in-sample estimation results

		GARCH-*n*	GARCH-*t*	GARCHK-*t*	GARCHK-GC
		Panel 1: SP			
Mean equation	μ	0.056 (1.73)			
	ϕ	0.083 (5.26)			
Variance equation	ω	0.118 (3.05)	0.107 (2.76)	0.107 (2.96)	0.113 (3.49)
	α	0.159 (5.36)	0.139 (4.94)	0.155 (5.66)	0.155 (6.01)
	β	0.809 (22.7)	0.832 (23.3)	0.819 (24.2)	0.807 (25.9)
Kurtosis equation	κ			0.801 (1.49)	1.887 (4.12)
	δ			0.024 (1.07)	0.008 (0.64)
	θ			0.842 (8.87)	0.448 (3.39)
DoF	ν		6.202 (9.60)	[5.977]	
AIC		3.731	3.704	3.681	3.687
		Panel 2: FX			
Mean equation	μ	-0.007 (-0.89)			
	ϕ	-0.065 (-4.08)			
Variance equation	ω	0.007 (1.96)	0.003 (1.89)	0.004 (1.83)	0.003 (2.22)
	α	0.036 (3.30)	0.031 (3.96)	0.032 (3.59)	0.038 (5.83)
	β	0.937 (44.1)	0.967 (80.4)	0.955 (69.6)	0.944 (93.9)
Kurtosis equation	κ			2.883 (1.63)	2.684 (2.66)
	δ			0.049 (0.28)	0.008 (5.82)
	θ			0.599 (2.61)	0.223 (0.77)*
DoF	ν		5.319 (10.7)	[5.344]	
AIC		1.478	1.424	1.422	1.432
		Panel 3: TN			
Mean equation	μ	-0.0091 (-0.46)			
	ϕ	0.0322 (2.01)			
Variance equation	ω	0.012 (2.45)	0.007 (2.11)	0.007 (2.13)	0.009 (2.49)
	α	0.039 (5.16)	0.038 (5.71)	0.041 (4.87)	0.037 (5.73)
	β	0.951 (96.8)	0.958 (126)	0.954 (104)	0.953 (117)
Kurtosis equation	κ			4.197 (2.11)	0.671 (3.73)
	δ			0.665 (1.38)	0.001 (0.28)
	θ			0.216 (0.72)	0.806 (15.8)
DoF	ν		5.685 (10.3)	[4.695]	
AIC		3.009	2.969	2.956	2.963

Estimation results (robust QML t -statistics in brackets) for the Gaussian GARCH (GARCH-n), the Student-t GARCH (GARCH-t), the Student-t GARCHK (GARCHK-t) and the Gram-Charlier GARCHK models (GARCHK-GC). AIC denotes the Akaike Information Criterion statistic. The row DoF shows the estimated degrees of freedom parameter in the Student-t distribution under the GARCH-t model, $\widehat{\nu}_T$, and the unconditional kurtosis implied by the estimated parameters, $\kappa/(1-\delta-\theta)$, in case of the GARCHK-t model.

parameters of the conditional kurtosis, say $\xi_{2k} = (\kappa, \delta, \theta)'$, reveal very different dynamics depending on whether a Student-t or a transformed Gram-Charlier densities is used. In particular, the dynamics of the conditional kurtosis tend to be much more persistent under the assumption of the Student-t distribution, whereas the parameter related to the arrivals of new information, δ, tend to be not significant under the Gram-Charlier fitting. This feature shows that the driving parameters of the kurtosis are particularly sensitive to the model assumptions that must capture the actual tail-behavior of the underlying distribution. Second, the estimated dynamics of the conditional kurtosis of the Treasure Notes time series differ remarkably from those estimated for the SP and the FX series. This evidence is in sharp contrast to the dynamics followed by the variance, which tend to show the same type of pattern across fairly different classes of financial assets.

Both features seem to suggest that, whereas the dynamics of the conditional variance can always be characterized by 'stylized features' (a small estimated α coefficient, and high persistence as measured by the estimated term $\alpha+\beta$), the dynamics of the conditional kurtosis may exhibit a much more idiosyncratic behavior and vary across the class of financial asset and sample period considered. This empirical observation should not be very surprising, since the dynamics of the conditional kurtosis are strongly related to the likelihood and the magnitude of extreme observations (*i.e.*, outliers), which in turn are known to show a large degree of heterogeneity and irregular behavior. The main implication is that, whereas GARCH models tend to yield similar estimation outcomes regardless the financial time-series and the market considered, conditional-kurtosis modelling may yield quite different results depending on the asset considered, and the relevant assumption about the tail-behaviour of the conditional distribution.

3.2.2. Out-of-sample Analysis

One-step forecasts of conditional variance from the Gaussian GARCH, Student-t GARCH, and Student-t GARCHK models are easily obtained as

$$\widehat{h}_{T+1} = \widehat{E}_T(h_{T+1}) = \widehat{\omega}_T + \widehat{\alpha}_T \hat{\varepsilon}_T^2 + \widehat{\beta}_T \widehat{h}_T. \tag{18}$$

For the Gram-Charlier GARCHK model, the forecast $\widehat{h}_{T+1}$ is obtained as

$$\widehat{h}_{T+1} = \left(\widehat{\omega}_T + \widehat{\alpha}_T \hat{\varepsilon}_T^2 + \widehat{\beta}_T \widehat{h}_T\right) \left[\frac{1+216\widehat{d}_4^2}{1+24\widehat{d}_4^2}\right]; \ \widehat{d}_4^2 = \frac{\widehat{k}_{T+1}-3}{4!}. \tag{19}$$

For the Gaussian GARCH model, the kurtosis is constant and equals 3, whilst for the Student-t GARCH model the kurtosis forecast is given by $\widehat{k}_{T+1} = 3(\widehat{\nu}_T - 2)/(\widehat{\nu}_T - 4)$, being $\widehat{\nu}_T$ the degrees of freedom parameter estimated in the in-sample period. The forecasts of the conditional kurtosis of the Student-t GARCH models are simply given by

$$\widehat{k}_{T+1} = \widehat{E}_T(k_{T+1}) = \widehat{\tau}_T + \widehat{\delta}_T \left(\frac{\hat{\varepsilon}_T^2}{\widehat{h}_T}\right)^2 + \widehat{\theta}_T \widehat{k}_T \tag{20}$$

while the Gram-Charlier GARCHK determines a conditional forecast given by:

$$\widehat{k}_{T+1} = \frac{(3+2952\widehat{d}_4^2+12\widehat{d}_4^2)(1+24\widehat{d}_4^2)}{(1+216\widehat{d}_4^2)^2} \tag{21}$$

The MSEs for the GARCH models used to forecast conditional variance and kurtosis are presented in Table 3, while Table 4 shows the p-values related to the Diebold-Mariano test (a value smaller than 0.05 implies that the model with smallest MSE in the comparison yields a significant improvement at the 95% confidence level). Some comments follow. We note that the differences in the MSE loss functions for volatility forecasting are not generally significant across the different GARCH models considered in all the series analyzed. This is not surprising, since Gaussian GARCH forecasts are known to be accurate in mean from the property of consistency (discussed in Section 2), and because the dynamics of the conditional kurtosis are modelled independently of the dynamics followed by the conditional variance, we should expect no interaction between them. Therefore, considering further dynamics in the higher-order moments, or allowing for excess of kurtosis in the conditional distribution, would hardly improve empirically the on-average accuracy of the variance forecasts made by a simple Gaussian GARCH model.

In relation to (un)conditional kurtosis, the main results of our analysis are the following. First, the model that yields better out-of-sample forecast of the unconditional kurtosis given the proxy $\overline{k}_{T+1}^{(500)}$, consistently across the three series considered, is the Gram-Charlier GARCHK model. Owing to its semi-parametric nature, the Gram-Charlier type modelling does not rely upon a specific assumption on the underlying distribution of the data, which provides robustness against potential departures over the parametric models (which, on the other hand, would be consistent and more efficient under correct specification). As we have seen from the empirical results for the conditional variance, robustness turns out to be a precious property when making predictions, and of course this property also applies when considering higher-order moments. Second, and related to the previous consideration, we observe that the Gram-Charlier GARCHK model largely overperforms the Student-t GARCHK model in forecasting conditional kurtosis, as proxied for small values of m in $\overline{k}_{T+1}^{(m)}$. Overall, these findings suggest that the assumption of a Student-t distribution with time-varying degrees of freedom may not be appropriate for applied purposes related to conditional-kurtosis forecasting.

Finally, we can only observe mixed and somewhat inconclusive evidence regarding the empirical importance of modelling time-varying kurtosis, since only in the case of the TN time series there seems to be statistical improvements over the simplest Gaussian GARCH model, and only when using the Gram-Charlier GARCHK specification. There are several reasons that may explain, at least partially, the seeming failure of the conditional-kurtosis GARCH models in the SP and FX time series. First, the presence of measurement errors in the proxy considered $\overline{k}_{T+1}^{(m)}$ may end up playing a significant role in the MSE loss-function (particularly as $m \to 1$) given the particularities of the time-series involved, and leading to distorted empirical conclusions. Second, although the conditional-kurtosis GARCH models may provide a better fit in the in-sample period, this does not necessarily imply that these models have to improve the out-of-sample forecast performance. There are two different reasons supporting this statement, both of them being rooted in the high degree of heterogeneity and idiosyncratic behavior of the (conditional) kurtosis. On the one hand, Korkie, Sivakumar and Turtle (2006) have argued that the persistence in the higher-order moments of financial returns may be a statistical artifact related to variance spillovers, so there would not be any gain from forecasting these dynamics. If this pervasive effect exists, it may be more important for some variables than for others, as we have documented statistical gains

from modelling kurtosis in the case of the TN time series. On the other hand, even if the conditional kurtosis does really change over time, its dynamics are necessarily linked to the particularities of the data generating process that drives extreme observations and irregular outliers. This feature brings up further statistical concerns, because the time-varying kurtosis process has to be characterized empirically by finite-sample ML estimates that are strongly conditioned by the assumption on the underlying distribution (as we have seen in the previous section) and which, furthermore, may suffer from important biases related to the occurrence and magnitude of outliers in the in-sample period. A few irregular, large enough outliers are perfectly able to strongly bias the ML estimates of the conditional kurtosis in the attempt to provide the best possible in-sample fit, given the underlying assumption that determines the theoretical likelihood and magnitude of extreme observations, but at the logical cost of poorly forecasting on-average the out-of-sample dynamics in which such extreme observations do not occur.

Table 3. Out-of-sample volatility and kurtosis MSE forecasting performance

	A: Gaussian GARCH				C: Student-t GARCHK			
		$\overline{k}_{T+1}^{(m)}$				$\overline{k}_{T+1}^{(m)}$		
	h_{T+1}	5	50	500	h_{T+1}	5	50	500
SP	37.88	5.627	0.221	2.177	37.81	14.08	7.662	1.698
FX	0.133	22.17	1.266	0.771	0.133	34.74	19.31	10.75
TN	0.719	5.321	0.717	5.847	0.717	31.06	24.46	13.19

	B: Student-t GARCH				D: Gram-Charlier GARCHK			
		$\overline{k}_{T+1}^{(m)}$				$\overline{k}_{T+1}^{(m)}$		
	h_{T+1}	5	50	500	h_{T+1}	5	50	500
SP	37.53	14.60	8.201	1.937	37.97	6.305	0.149	0.643
FX	0.133	34.64	19.07	10.56	0.133	21.90	1.229	0.011
TN	0.715	17.97	10.52	1.653	0.717	6.184	0.552	3.017

This table shows the Mean Square Error (MSE) for the one-step ahead conditional variance and kurtosis forecasts from the different GARCH models used in the analysis. The proxies considered for the kurtosis, $\overline{k}_{T+1,m}$, are estimated from the sample kurtosis of the first $m = 5, 50$ and 500 days immediately following the last day in the in-sample window.

4. Concluding Remarks

Several papers have argued that the kurtosis of returns may exhibit clusters and time dependency similar to the characteristic patterns which are observable in the proxies of conditional variance. The modelling of the conditional third- and fourth-order moments tend to improve the in-sample goodness of fit over the simplest GARCH models that assume constant higher-order moments. The main aim of this paper is to provide better insight on whether accounting for time-varying kurtosis is valuable for out-of-sample forecasting of

Table 4. Diebold and Mariano statistics

	GARCH-*t*				GARCHK-*t*				GARCHK-GC			
		$\bar{k}_{T+1}^{(m)}$				$\bar{k}_{T+1}^{(m)}$				$\bar{k}_{T+1}^{(m)}$		
	h_{T+1}	5	50	500	h_{T+1}	5	50	500	h_{T+1}	5	50	500
					SP							
GARCH-*n*	0.05	0.00	0.00	0.00	0.32	0.00	0.00	0.00	0.22	0.00	0.00	0.00
GARCH-*t*					0.00	0.00	0.00	0.00	0.01	0.00	0.00	0.00
GARCHK-*t*									0.07	0.00	0.00	0.00
					FX							
GARCH-*n*	0.28	0.00	0.00	0.00	0.21	0.00	0.00	0.00	0.06	0.29	0.00	0.00
GARCH-*t*					0.34	0.13	0.09	0.08	0.49	0.00	0.00	0.00
GARCHK-*t*									0.44	0.00	0.00	0.00
					TN							
GARCH-*n*	0.03	0.00	0.00	0.00	0.09	0.00	0.00	0.07	0.01	0.00	0.00	0.00
GARCH-*t*					0.13	0.02	0.01	0.01	0.09	0.00	0.00	0.00
GARCHK-*t*									0.35	0.00	0.00	0.02

This table reports the results of the DM test for the difference of the MSE loss function from the GARCH models under analysis (see notation in Table 2). The entries are DM test p -values for the predictive ability of the model in the row versus the model in the column.

both conditional variance and conditional kurtosis, and which procedure (among several of the parametric and semi-parametric alternatives that have been suggested in the literature) is better suited for empirical purposes.

As in the previous literature, our empirical results on three different classes of financial assets confirm that the semi-parametric Gram-Charlier and the Student-t GARCHK models that allow for time-varying kurtosis provide a better in-sample goodness-of-fit over the constant-kurtosis GARCH models, with the parametric Student-t distribution slightly overperforming the Gram-Charlier type distribution. For forecasting purposes, the best procedure to forecast the unconditional kurtosis seems to be the Gram-Charlier GARCHK model, as the semi-parametric nature of this approach provides robust properties against model misspecification which may ruin the out-of-sample forecasting ability of the model. Similarly, this methodology largely overperforms the Student-t distribution with time-varying degrees of freedom parameter in forecasting conditional kurtosis, which overall suggests that the semi-parametric approximation may be better indicated in practice. Unfortunately, the Gram-Charlier GARCHK model does not always achieve a significant success in beating the forecasts made by the simplest Gaussian GARCH model, at least given the proxies for conditional kurtosis considered in this paper. The lack of conclusive results for some of the time series analyzed may be, at least partially, a statistical artifact due to the sizeable measurement errors in the proxies used in the analysis. However, it is also possible that the empirical success of forecasting higher-order moments strongly depends on the class of asset and the sample period considered, given that the data generating process of the conditional kurtosis does not seem to exhibit the same degree of parameter uniformity as, for instance, the conditional variance does: whereas we always observe the same sort of

stylized features in the GARCH-type estimates of the conditional variance, the conditional kurtosis exhibits a large degree of idiosyncratic behavior. Hence, the econometric modelling allowing for time-varying kurtosis may not generally necessarily enhance the out-of-sample forecasting performance of the models, even if in-sample results seem to suggest the opposite. More research on the empirical role of the dynamics of the conditional kurtosis seems deserved.

Acknowledgment

Financial support from the Spanish Ministry of Education through projects SEJ2006-06104/ECON and ECO2008-02599 is gratefully acknowledged.

References

[1] Alexander CO. 1998. *Volatility and correlation: methods, models and applications*. In Risk Management and Analysis: Measuring and Modelling Financial Risk (C.O. Alexander, Ed.) Wiley.

[2] Bollerslev T. 1986. Generalized autoregressive conditional heteroscedasticity. *Journal of Econometrics* **31**, 307-327.

[3] Bollerslev T. 1987. A conditional heteroskedastic time series model for speculative prices and rates of return. *Review of Economics and Statistics* **69**, 542-547.

[4] Bollerslev T, Wooldridge JM. 1992. Quasi-Maximum likelihood estimation and inference in dynamics models with time-varying covariances. *Econometrics Reviews* **11**, 143-172.

[5] Carnero MA, Peña D, Ruiz E. 2007. Effects of outliers on the identification and estimation of GARCH models. *Journal of Time Series Analysis* **4**, 471-497.

[6] Christie-David R, Chaudhry M. 2001. Coskewness and cokurtosis in futures markets. *Journal of Empirical Finance* **8**, 55-81.

[7] Chunhachinda P, Dandapani K, Hamid S, Prakash A. 1997. Portfolio selection and skewness: evidence from international stock markets. *Journal of Banking and Finance* **21**, 143–167.

[8] Diebold FX, Mariano R. 1995. Comparing predictive accuracy. *Journal of Business and Economics Statistics* **13**, 253-264.

[9] Dueker MJ. 1997. Markov switching in GARCH processes and mean-reverting stock-market volatility. *Journal of Business and Economic Statistics* **15**, 26-34.

[10] Fang H, Lai TY. 1997. Co-kurtosis and capital asset pricing. *The Financial Review* **32**, 293-307.

[11] Gallant AR, Nychka DW. 1987. Seminonparametric maximum likelihood estimation. *Econometrica* **55**, 363-390.

[12] Gallant AR, Tauchen G. 1989. Seminonparametric estimation of conditionally constrained heterogeneous processes: asset pricing applications. *Econometrica* **57**, 5, 1091-1120.

[13] Gallant AR, Nychka DW, Fenton V. 1996. Convergence rates of SNP density estimators. *Econometrica* **64**, 719-727.

[14] Hansen BE. 1994. Autoregressive conditional density estimation. *International Economic Review* **35**, 705-730.

[15] Hansen PR, Lunde A. 2005. A forecast comparison of volatility models: does anything beat a GARCH(1,1)? *Journal of Applied Econometrics* **20**, 873-889.

[16] Harvey CR, Siddique A. 1999. Autoregressive conditional skewness. *Journal of Financial and Quantitative Analysis* **34**, 465–487.

[17] Harvey CR, Siddique A. 2000. Conditional Skewness in Asset Pricing Tests. *Journal of Finance* **55**, 1263-1295.

[18] Jondeau E, Rockinger M. 2000. Conditional volatility, skewness and kurtosis: existence and persistence. *Working Paper* **77**. Banque de France & *HEC School of Management*.

[19] Jondeau E, Rockinger M. 2001. Gram-Charlier Densities. *Journal of Economic Dynamics and Control*, **25**, 1457-1483.

[20] Korkie B, Sivakumar R, Turtle HJ. 2006. Variance spillover and skewness in financial asset returns. *The Financial Review* **41**, 139-156.

[21] Lee SW, Hansen BE. 1994. Asymptotic properties of the maximum likelihood estimator and test of the stability of parameters of the GARCH and IGARCH models. *Econometric Theory* **10**, 29-52.

[22] León A, Rubio G, Serna G. 2005. Autoregressive conditional volatility, skewness and kurtosis. *Quarterly Review of Economics and Finance* **45**, 599-618.

[23] Nelson D. 1996. Asymptotic filtering theory for multivariate ARCH models. *Journal of Econometrics* **71**, 1–47.

[24] Newey W, Steigerwald D. 1997. Asymptotic bias for quai-maximum-likelihood estimators in conditional heteroskedasticity models. *Econometrica* **65**, 587-599.

[25] Patton A. 2006. Volatility forecast comparison using imperfect volatility proxies. Research Paper 175. Quantitative Finance Research Centre. *University of Technology Sydney*.

[26] Sargan JD. 1976. Econometric estimators and the Edgeworth approximation. *Econometrica* **44**, 421-448.

[27] Schmidt R. 2002. Tail dependence for elliptically contoured distributions. *Mathematical Methods of Operations Research* **55** (2), 301-327.

[28] Weiss AA. 1986. Asymptotic theory of ARCH models: Estimation and testing. *Econometric Theory* **2**, 107-131.

Reviewer's Name and Afiliation

Professor Tibor Neugebauer
Faculty of Law, Economics and Finance
University of Luxembourg
Campus Kirchberg 4, rue Albert Borschette (Room K2B2 2.13)
L-1246 Luxembourg
Telephone: +352466644-6285
Fax: +3524666446835
Email: Tibor.Neugebauer@uni.lu

In: Business and Finance: Performance and Management ISBN: 978-1-61122-936-3
Editors: R. Morland and A. Gagglione

Chapter 13

MISERY AS CORPORATE MISSION: USER IMAGERY AT THE NIGHTCLUB THE SPY BAR

***Niklas Egels-Zandén*[1,*] *and Ulf Ågerup*[2,†]**
[1] Centre for Business in Society, School of Business, Economics and Law at Göteborg University, Göteborg, Sweden
[2] Marketing Group, School of Business, Economics and Law at Göteborg University,Göteborg, Sweden

ABSTRACT

Despite extensive corporate responsibility research into both *what* products firm produce and *how* they produce them, research is lacking in one product category in which the *what* and *how* linkage create questionable corporate practice – luxury products. Luxury is in some cases created by companies controlling the so-called user imagery of their customers, i.e., by companies encouraging 'desirable' individuals to consume their products and obstructing 'undesirable' individuals from consumption. This chapter critically analyses the implications of this corporate practice based on a study of Sweden's most luxurious nightclub. The study's results show that the nightclub has organised its activities to allow categorisations of individuals into 'desirable' and 'undesirable' customers. Furthermore, the study shows that a creation of 'misery' for the vast majority of individuals (the 'undesirable') is essential for creating 'enjoyment' for the selected few (the 'desirable'). The chapter concludes by discussing implications for practitioners interesting in altering this situation.

INTRODUCTION

When discussing a firm's corporate responsibility, two main issues arise. *What* products does the firm produce, and *how* does it produce these products? Researchers, as well as practitioners, have given much attention to the idea that some products are 'irresponsible' – most notably cigarettes, weapons, alcohol, and gambling products (e.g., Newton, 1993;

---

* E-mail address: Niklas.Egels-Zanden@handels.gu.se; Tel: +46-31-7862729.
† E-mail address: Ulf.Agerup@handels.gu.se; Tel: +46-31-932329.

Kinder and Domini, 1997; Elm, 1998; Havemann, 1998; Maitland, 1998; Brenkert, 2000; Green, 2000). For example, firms producing these products are excluded often from 'ethical' funds (e.g., Kinder and Domini, 1997). Similarly, much attention has been given to *how* products are produced. Lately, this debate has mainly been focused on human and workers' rights in production in developing countries. Hot research topics include: the corporate embracement of codes of conduct (e.g., Frenkel, 2001; van Tulder and Kolk, 2001; Graafland, 2002; Winstanley *et al.*, 2002; Egels-Zandén, 2007), the signing of global collective agreements (e.g., Wills, 2002; Carley, 2005; Fairbrother and Hammer, 2005; Riisgaard, 2005; Anner *et al.*, 2006; Egels-Zandén and Hyllman, 2006, 2007), and corporate operations in controversial markets (e.g., Donaldson 1989, 1996; De George 1990, 1993; Donaldson and Dunfee, 1994; Carroll and Gannon, 1997; Schermerhorn, 1999). Despite the ample research into both *what* products firm produce and *how* they produce them, research is lacking in one product category in which the *what* and *how* linkage create questionable corporate practice – luxury products.

A review of the last years of international publications into corporate responsibility clearly shows that luxury products are a neglected area of research. This lack is likely due to that luxury products generally are not of 'irresponsible' nature (compared to cigarettes, alcohol, weapons, etc.), and that the quality demands and high price range often limit the abuse of human and workers' rights in production (cf. McWilliam and Siegel, 2001). Hence, since previous research has treated the *what* and *how* questions separately, luxury products have escaped its radar. However, this chapter argues that when treated together the *what* in luxury products (i.e., their exclusiveness) leads to problematic aspects in *how* the products are produced and marketed.

The purpose of this chapter is to address this gap in previous research by analysing the intersection between *what* and *how*. More specifically, we focus on the corporate practice of customer base management aimed at influencing the user imagery of the product, and critically analyse the implications of this practice. This is much needed, since previous marketing research into user imagery and luxury products has neglected the corporate responsibility aspects of this practice. Hence, corporate responsibility researchers have neglected the area of luxury products and user imagery, while marketing researchers have studied both luxury products and user imagery but ignored their corporate responsibility aspects. We base our analysis of user imagery on a study of Sweden's most luxurious nightclub – The Spy Bar – and our results show that corporate responsibility as well as marketing researchers be well advised to recognise the corporate responsibility aspects of luxury products and user imagery in future research since the corporate practice entails critical issues for further academic and practitioner discussions.

Luxury Products and User Imagery

The core idea of 'luxury' is that the product is only attainable for a limited range of consumers (e.g., Berry, 1994; Twitchell, 2002). However, recently there has been a shift in the clientele for luxury products with more affordable, although still expensive, alternatives for 'normal' people being launched (e.g., Twitchell, 2002; Allères, 2005). It is problematic to precisely define 'luxury' (e.g., Dubois *et al.*, 1995; Vigneron and Johnson, 1999), although most people in practice can categorise products into 'luxury' and 'non-luxury' products. In

this chapter, luxury is defined as products that are widely desired and more expensive than what their utility motivates (cf. Berry, 1994; Twitchell, 2002). Hence, luxury products are primarily consumed because of their meaning to us rather than because of their utility. Consequently, brand meaning creation is central to the creation of luxury.

Brand meaning is created partly through product design, market communication, but also through the communication between stakeholders in society (Balmer and Gray, 2000) in the form of, for example, public speech and print (Twitchell, 2002), word-of-mouth (Keller, 2003), and user imagery (Aaker, 1996). The idea of *user imagery* is that values are transferred to a brand through the people that are associated with it, i.e., that the brand meaning is dependent on those associated with the brand (cf. McCracken, 1989). This includes both companies' employees and the users of the product (Keller, 2000). Hence, consumers' perceptions of the brand users affect their perception of the meaning of the brand (Aaker, 1996; Schroeder, 2005; Brioschi, 2006). This relationship works in both ways. If 'desirable' individuals consume the brand it instils values of 'luxury' into the brand, and if 'undesirable' individuals consume the brand it has the opposite effect.

This idea of user imagery has led firms to invest in *ideal* users such as sponsored athletes, spokespersons, and people portrayed in advertising to promote the luxury of the brand (Aaker, 1996). The ideal users should not be confused with the target group for the brand, but should rather be seen as a reflection of the image that the firm want to offer the target group (cf. Kapferer, 1994). In contrast to the ideal user who uses a brand because he or she is financially compensated for doing so, the *typical* users are those individuals actually using the brand (Aaker, 1996). In the same way as spokespersons, but arguably even more powerful, these users instil the brand with values by conveying what can be seen as a visual word-of-mouth (cf. Twitchell, 2002; Keller, 2003). The focus in this chapter is on attempts to manage these typical users in order to improve the user imagery.

In essence, user imagery can be used as a tool to create a boundary between 'desirable' and 'undesirable' individuals. Framed in this way, it is clear that user imagery is based on the more general marketing ideal of identifying and targeting certain customer groups. Traditionally, this practice is referred to as positioning which entails segmenting consumers into distinct but homogenous target groups that require similar marketing mixes (e.g., Kapferer, 1994; Aaker, 1996; Keller, 2003). In these positioning strategies, any addition of customers not belonging to the target group is seen as a bonus – a *positive* side effect. However, when applying the user imagery logic additional customers are seen as a *negative* side effect if they are from the 'undesirable' group. Since the consumers are not only perceived as income generators, but also image creators, it is rational for purveyors of luxury to turn away potential consumers if their undesirable characteristics would taint the luxury brand's image. In other words, by employing customer base management to improve brand image, companies sacrifice short term financial gain to create brand meaning. In creating brand meaning, user imagery plays a more central role for luxury products as compared to other product categories, since conventional branding activities are ineffective for luxury products (cf. Baker, 2006). Hence, brand meaning has to be created in alternative ways for luxury products and companies have to rely more on influencing social discourses through tools such as user imagery than traditional activities (cf. Twitchell, 2002).

The boundary creation between 'desirable' and 'undesirable' customers can be expected to affect a person's perception of herself. Several authors have shown that consumption is closely linked to the construction of identities (e.g., Levy, 1959; McCracken, 1986; Belk,

1988), and that this is especially so in consumption of luxury products (Berry, 1994; Vigneron and Johnson, 2004). Hence, by classifying an individual as a 'desirable'/ 'undesirable' consumer, companies influence individuals' identities. As will be shown in the study presented in this chapter, this influence could literally lead to matters of life or death. Despite these corporate responsibility implications, prior research into user imagery has neglected these aspects and solely focused on how firms strategically can employ user imagery to improve the brand personality (e.g., Aaker, 1996). Simultaneously, corporate responsibility research has neglected the research topics of luxury and user imagery, leading to a lack of critical analysis of the implications of this type of corporate practice.

METHOD

To analyse how corporations strive to achieve user imagery through customer base management in luxury products, we make use of a data from a study of Sweden's most luxurious nightclub – The Spy Bar. Data were collected via interviews, observations, and document analysis. The focus in the data collection was on studying the operations of the nightclub in relation to user imagery and customer base management. The Spy Bar is unusual in the sense that individuals from the security firm are the only individuals that the customers interacted with (except for bartenders and DJs). This is true also for the presentation of The Spy Bar on its webpage and in media articles in which the CEO of the security company – rather than the CEO of the nightclub – is the front figure for the nightclub. Hence, the nightclub has outsourced all significant interaction with customers to an independent security company. This has the effect that the head of security at The Spy Bar (also the CEO of the security company) is well known among the general public in Sweden. Given the importance of the security officers, they were the chosen focus in our data collection.

In total, 12 semi-structured interviews (lasting on average one hour) were made with the security officers (including the CEO) working at The Spy Bar. A handful of additional interviews were also made with representatives for The Spy Bar. These interviews were mainly used to provide a background understanding of the directives provided by The Spy Bar management to the security officers. Additionally, 15 semi-structured interviews (lasting on average 30 minutes) were made with customers inside The Spy Bar and potential customers queuing outside the nightclub.

In addition to interviews, observations were conducted during four evenings at the nightclub. During the observation study, the researcher closely followed the security officers' work and interaction with customers. In parts of the observation study, access was granted to the two-way radios used by the security officers. The observation study was focused on two central aspects of the security officers' work – the selection of customers outside the nightclub and the disciplining of customers inside the nightclub.

Finally, written documentations (in the form of web pages and media articles) were used as both input into interviews and as validation of the data received through observations and interviews. There were few inconsistencies between the data obtained in interviews and observations, but some between the data presented in the written documentation and the observations/interviews. In cases of inconsistencies, these were sometimes discussed with the security officers, and we based the below presented descriptions mainly on the data provided

in the interviews and observations since these seemed more reliable than the media articles and web pages.

The collected data were used to construct thick descriptions of the activities of the security officers. To validate the descriptions, they were sent to the CEO of the security company who expressed no critique regarding the descriptions of their work. Based on these descriptions of the security officers' activities and the interviews with customers and The Spy Bar management, a 'typical' nightclub evening was constructed (as presented in the empirical section below). Evidently, there are problems in constructing a 'typical' nightclub evening, since nothing is 'typical' in corporate practice. However, this was perceived as the best way to present the empirical data in order to convey an understanding of a nightclub evening at The Spy Bar to the reader.

Night clubs belong to a specific category of luxury products. As shown by Allères (2005), luxury can be divided into different price levels. There is the inaccessible luxury level of yachts and mansions, the intermediate level of cars, watches, and hotels, and finally the accessible level where although the products are more expensive than their substitutes, most people can afford to buy them should they wish to do so. This level covers, for example, champagne, perfume, and the empirical focus of this chapter: nightclub visits. In focusing on nightclub visits, i.e., on attainable luxury products, the purpose of this chapter is not to discuss the problems related to the first two types of offerings and, hence, to question the excluding nature of prices. Rather, the purpose of this chapter is to analyse those products that are attainable for most individuals. In these cases, the limitation has to be achieved in other ways than through prices, and as is shown in this chapter one way to achieve this is influencing user imagery via customer base management.

A 'Typical' Evening at the Nightclub the Spy Bar

After midnight a regular Friday evening, a large crowd stands outside a small entrance to a nightclub – The Spy Bar – in the city of Stockholm (the capitol of Sweden). Separating the queuing individuals from the nightclub is a red rope and inside the rope numerous security officers dressed in black suits control the queue; carefully selecting who should be allowed to enter the club. The queue is different from the traditional linear queue. It does not even look like a queue; rather, like an unstructured ocean of people. The head of the security officers (also the CEO of the security company) explains that this queue structure is generally referred to as a 'rainbow' queue and that the purpose of the queue is to allow the security officers to freely select who is allowed to enter the nightclub without having to consider how long each individual has waited outside the club. The CEO mainly controls the selection of individuals himself, making him an influential and well-known figure in Swedish nightlife. He has, for example, been offered to go on tours around Sweden as a celebrity security officer.

While the selection procedure is extremely strict at this hour, it was easier to enter the nightclub earlier in the evening. Then, individuals were allowed to enter that now would not even come close to the 'desirability' status of the selected few that are allowed entrance. The security officers explain this by referring to the need for the nightclub to receive revenues throughout the evening, and that they have fewer individuals to select from early on in the evening. At this hour, the possibility to select individuals is seemingly endless. The management of The Spy Bar has defined the characteristics of those that are to be allowed to

enter the nightclub, and the security officers do their best to implement these directives in practice. When asked what they are searching for in a customer, the security officers have difficulties providing a precise answer. Rather, they provide a list of characteristics as to exemplify what they are after. Guests are to be celebrities, over 25 years of age, from the city centre, dressed in Gucci, trendy, financial wealthy, journalists, stock brokers, real estate agents and/or CEOs. While those few with just the 'right' characteristics enter the nightclub quickly, the vast majority of guests wait outside for often over an hour uncertain of if they will be allowed entrance. The length of the wait is also difficult to predict, since the 'rainbow' queue system provides no signals regarding if, and if so when, a person is allowed to enter.

The selection of individuals is a complex and sometimes ruthless process. The security officers establish contact with the visitors through body language and eye contact. Rarely, if ever, is there any verbal communication between the security officers and the visitors other than to inform someone to enter the nightclub or to impolitely answer visitors' attempts to persuade the officers to allow them entrance. Occasionally, the security officers signal (in a hardly noticeable way) to groups of individuals that they are to walk around the block and return without certain members of the group. Hence, the officers force groups to be split into those 'desirable' that will be allowed to enter and those 'undesirable' that will not.

Sporadically, celebrities arrive at the nightclub, walking pass the crowd and straight into the club. This does not seem to surprise anyone. However, sporadically some individuals are allowed to enter the nightclub without fitting the expected characteristics of a Spy Bar customer. The queuing visitors quickly recognise this (they are often highly skilled themselves in judging the likeliness of others entering), and discussions start in the crowd. Some of these unexpected guests wear visible signs indicating that they are part of well-known criminal groups, while other unexpected guests seem to have a close relationship with some of the security officers (most often the CEO). Another surprising event to those in the queue is that some celebrities arrive highly confident of their chances to enter the club, but are denied entrance. This includes famous Swedish actors and Olympic winning sportsmen. Seemingly humiliated these celebrities are forced to leave the queue and continue to another nightclub. Loud discussions start among the other queuing individuals focused on understanding why these celebrities were not allowed to enter. Did the security officers not recognise them? Are the officers incompetent? Are they incapable of making a 'fair' selection?

The answer to why the celebrities were denied access to the nightclub is found inside the club. Here, the security officers are responsible for inducing the 'right' atmosphere to the nightclub. This mainly involves assisting guests and securing that no acts of violence occurs throughout the evening, but it also involves disciplining individuals to behave in a 'correct' way. For instance, visitors standing in certain areas of the nightclub or attempting to climb onto the window-ledges are quickly and harshly reprimanded. If the individuals despite these reprimands do not comply with the 'correct' behaviour, the security officers either make him/her leave the nightclub or restrict the individual's future entrance to the club. Such previous acts of 'incorrectness' (although of more severe nature) were the reasons for denying the above discussed celebrities to enter the nightclub.

In addition to disciplining customers inside the nightclub, the security officers are also responsible for assuring that only 'highly desirable' individuals are allowed entrance into the VIP areas within the club. Hence, The Spy Bar is really two, or even more, nightclubs,

sharing little more than the same entrance. In this way, the security officers' sorting of individuals into categories continues inside the nightclub as well.

About forty-five minutes before closing time, the security officers stop allowing individuals to enter the nightclub. However, this is not signalled to those in the queue, leading many to queue until the nightclub closes. The evening ends with the security officers lining up outside the nightclub making sure that everything runs smoothly when the customers leave the club.

The Role of User Imagery

The conducted study clearly illustrates that the security officers at The Spy Bar use customer base management to influence the user imagery and the nightclub brand in the desired direction. Hence, this study confirms the arguments and results of previous studies that corporations in practice use customer base management to influence user imagery (e.g., Aaker, 1996; Twitchell, 2002). In The Spy Bar case, this practice was explicitly demanded by The Spy Bar management and consciously implemented by the security officers. The security officers even regarded customer base management as one of their most – if not their most – important work task. As the CEO of the security company noted: "Popular nightclubs have strategically organised their activities in order to sort people into an A class and a B class. The entire organisation from the interior to the queue system is designed for this purpose". Furthermore, most security officers did not regard this as problematic or disturbing. Rather, it was seen as the common practice among luxurious nightclubs; a necessary strategy for creating the luxury status of the club.

The Spy Bar's focus on user imagery via customer base management should be seen in the light of that the club had ample opportunities to select customers. Since a nightclub visit is an attainable luxury product (cf. Allères, 2005), most individuals can afford an evening at The Spy Bar and given the perception of the club as the most luxurious club in Sweden numerous individuals attempts to spend an evening at the club. However, the club is limited in size by the building it is occupying, so even if the security officers would have desired to allow all interested individuals to enter the club this would be impossible. Hence, the club is in the rare situation that demand for its product widely exceeds the supply and that the supply capability not easily could be increased.

The security officers used customer base management to influence user imagery in two main ways. First, and most important, when selecting who should be allowed to enter the nightclub. The 'rainbow' queue system at The Spy Bar was an important tool for selecting who is allowed to enter. By creating a crowd of individuals outside the red rope that demarks the division between inside and outside the nightclub, the security officers were able to continuously choose individuals that were perceived as 'desirable'. These 'desirable' individuals included royalties, 'celebrities', wealthy individuals, and 'cool' individuals. Importantly, an individual's spending capability was not the main criterion for the security officers' selections; rather, the officers' attempted to identify an "appearance of luxuriousness". The 'undesirable' individuals, on the other hand, included overweight, poorly dressed, and 'ugly' individuals (especially if these also were immigrants and/or not from the city centre). These individuals were consciously restricted from entering the nightclub, regardless of their spending capability. In addition to the categories 'desirable' and

'undesirable', the security officers also sorted individuals into a 'potentially desirable'/'not undesirable' category. This category filled a central role for the nightclub, since they were to create an as large as possible queue outside the nightclub. Hence, the security officers consciously attempted to maximise the queue outside the club both to create an appearance of popularity, but also to communicate that even the – to an outside observer – seemingly 'cool' and 'desirable' individuals in the queue were not 'desirable' *enough* to enter the nightclub. This practice can be understood as a negative user imagery message: these seemingly desirable individuals are not even qualified to be a 'typical' user of The Spy Bar.

Second, in addition to the queue system, the security officers also used customer base management inside the club. First, in a similar fashion as outside, there were restricted 'VIP' areas within the club only open for especially 'desirable' individuals. Second, the security officers disciplined individuals inside the nightclub that did not act as a 'desirable' individual ought to act. This included evident behaviour such as acts of violence and sexual harassment, but also standing in certain parts of the nightclub and addressing the security officers in the 'wrong' way. Hence, in addition to sorting individuals into 'desirable' and 'undesirable' based on mainly external attributes via different queue systems, individuals were also sorted into 'desirable' and 'undesirable' based on their behaviour inside the nightclub. 'Undesirable' behaviour occasionally led to individuals being forced to leave the club, but more frequently to being restricted in future attempts to enter the club. In this way, the sorting of individuals into 'desirable' and 'undesirable' continued throughout the customers' nightclub visit and effected their future classification. However, since there is not a perfect relation between 'desirable' external attributes and 'desirable' behaviour, some individuals that had 'desirable' external attributes were denied access to the nightclub due to behavioural aspects. For individuals unaware of the behavioural 'problems' of these individuals, this practice sent the message that the security officers were poorly skilled at recognising 'desirability', in turn, potentially threatening the nightclub's user image.

Misery as Corporate Mission

There are several implications of the security officers' classification of individuals into 'desirable' and 'undesirable'. First, the 'undesirable' individuals risk spending their weekend queuing outside the nightclub. It is common that individuals spend hours in the queue outside the nightclub, and still are not allowed entrance. Despite this, they return the next weekend to repeat the procedure. Since the 'rainbow' queue system restricts individuals from contact with the security officers, individuals receive no signals of whether they are to be allowed to enter the club or not. Hence, individuals could – and many in fact do – spend much of their weekend queuing outside The Spy Bar.

Second, and even more important, the classification of individuals into 'desirable' and 'undesirable' not only influence individuals' weekend activities, but also their perception of themselves. Numerous authors have shown that consumption is closely linked to individuals' construction of their identities (e.g., Levy, 1959; McCracken, 1986; Belk, 1988), and that this is especially so in consumption of luxury products (Berry, 1994). Hence, to be classified as 'desirable' or 'undesirable', potentially effects individuals' perception of themselves. The vast majority of visitors to The Spy Bar are uncertain of their status when arriving at the nightclub with only a handful being certain of being allowed to enter the club. Hence, most

individuals are uncertain of their 'desirability', making them susceptible to security officers' classifications. Our study's results also indicate that the security officers' influence the visitors' perception of themselves – both in a positive and negative way. Those few that are allowed to enter seem to experience improved self-confidence (at least temporarily) perceiving themselves as successful individuals. On the other hand, the majority that are restricted from entering seem to experience worsen self-confidence (at least temporarily) perceiving themselves as less successful than they previously had thought. In an era where individuals are increasingly uncertain of their identity and their value (e.g., Gabriel and Lang, 2006), these 'desirability' signals seemingly have important implications for individuals' identities.

Moving from an individual to an organisational level, the links between the security officers' actions and individuals' identities provide an overall understanding of luxurious nightclubs' operations. As much as nightclubs are providing a service in the form of entertainment, they are also providing a service in ranking of individuals. The results of our study indicate that individuals do not mainly visit the nightclub for the music, drinks etc., but rather for the potential to feel 'desirable', 'successful' and 'exclusive'. However, in order for a selected few to feel 'desirable' and 'exclusive', the majority has to be categorised as the opposite as 'undesirable' and 'unsuccessful'. This is achieved through creating a widespread queue of 'undesirable' individuals outside the club – individuals that the few 'desirable' can feel more successful than. Hence, as much as the mission of nightclubs is to create a feeling of 'successfullness' among the selected few, it is also to create a feeling of 'unsuccessfullness' or 'misery' among the vast majority of individuals interested in visiting the club. The nightclubs (and in the Spy Bar case the security officers) have become judges of our times, classifying individuals into an A and a B group while simultaneously promoting that everyone should want to be in the A group.

This categorisation of individuals as 'undesirable' is not always accepted by the 'unacceptables', making them strike back. In the studied case, this resistance mainly took the form of verbal abuse of the security officers, but sometimes it also led to threats and acts of violence. When reflecting on these forms of resistance, the CEO of the security company said that: "In practice, the 'rainbow' queue system leads to increased frustration and disorder among the guests – the opposite of the task of a security officer". Hence, the CEO of the security company was aware of the connections between their practices aimed at creating an exclusive user imagery and the resistance of the 'undesirable'. In extreme cases, the resistance of the 'undesirable' has led to devastating consequences with frustrated 'undesirables' returning after being denied entrance to the nightclub firing into the queues and at the security officers. This has occurred several times in The Spy Bar nightclub area, although not directly at the nightclub itself. Hence, the practice to categorise individuals into 'desirable' and 'undesirable' customers to improve the user imagery could have severe implications not only for the security officers but also for the individuals queuing outside the nightclub.

Cracks in the Façade

So far, the analysis of the role of user imagery at The Spy Bar has focused on the instances where security officers manage the customer base according to the nightclub's mission.

However, there are also instances when this is not the case – when there are cracks in the façade. The most obvious such crack is that the 'desirability' of an individual seems to a related to when the individual attempts to enter the nightclub. A 'desirable' individual at 10-11 p.m. is often an 'undesirable' individual at 1-3 a.m. (not to mention at 4 a.m.). This is due both to that 'desirable' individuals only enter the nightclub scene after midnight, and that it is important for the profitability of the nightclub to receive revenues throughout the evening. This practice can be referred to as a 'geek tax' in the sense that by entering the club early and spending money throughout the evening the otherwise 'undesirable' individuals buy themselves an entrance ticket into the club. However, the consequence of this practice is that 'undesirable' individuals are at the club later in the evening when the 'desirable' individuals arrive. Hence, the 'desirable' individuals are faced with 'undesirable' individuals inside the club, potentially making them doubt the exclusiveness of the club and the 'success factor' of the clientele. Partly, the nightclub solves this by having VIP rooms, protecting highly 'desirable' individuals from mingling with 'undesirable' individuals, but partly the 'problem' remains.

An additional crack in the exclusive user image façade is that the security officers allow some 'undesirable' individuals to enter despite an ample supply of 'desirable' individuals in the queue. This initially puzzling observation is partly explained by some of these 'undesirable' individuals having personal relations with the security officers. The security officers themselves would likely not have been classified as 'desirable' according to their own standards and neither would their friends. However, since decision makers are complex individuals (e.g., Sjöstrand, 1997), as well as bounded rational (e.g., Simon, 1957; Cyert and March, 1963), they make decisions that not necessarily are in-line with the corporate mission. The security officers sometimes prioritised assisting their friends over following the corporate mission, leading to 'undesirable' individuals being allowed to enter the nightclub. In addition to friends, other 'undesirable' individuals that still were allowed entrance belonged to criminal groups and were giving access to the nightclub in order for the security officers and the nightclub to avoid repercussions.

In sum, to enter the nightclub an individual has to either be 'desirable', or 'undesirable' but willing to pay a 'geek tax', or have a personal relationship with the security officers, or belong to a criminal group. Hence, there were several groups of individuals that were, for different reasons, allowed to enter the nightclub and that did not fit the characteristics of a 'desirable' individual. The practice of customer base management to improve user imagery, thus, seems to be somewhat difficult to implement in practice, despite conscious attempts by The Spy Bar management. These cracks in the façade seemed to negatively affect the user imagery with some individuals noting that the nightclub was not as 'exclusive' and 'successful' as they expected. Consequently, the instances of security officers' selection 'failures' negatively affected the nightclub's user imagery.

CONCLUSION

This chapter has shown that corporate responsibility researchers need to broaden their perspective and analyse the intersection between *what* products that are produced and *how* they are produced in order to capture central corporate responsibility issues. It has also shown that marketing researchers are well advised to include aspects of corporate responsibility into

their analyses of user imagery. By addressing these gaps in previous research, this chapter has provided an initial study of the corporate responsibility implications of firms' customer base management strategies aimed at creating an exclusive user imagery. The study's results are distressing, indicating that some companies consciously organise their entire operations in order to sort individuals into 'desirable' and 'undesirable' categories. Furthermore, the employees sorting individuals oftentimes do not perceive this as problematic or unethical, despite being aware of the negative effects of their actions on the 'undesirable' individuals. They are just "doing their job". Based on these results, this chapter has argued that exclusive nightclubs have two sides – one focused on entertaining the selected few and one focused on degenerating the vast majority. This 'enjoyment' and 'misery' of nightclubs are two sides of the same coin with 'enjoyment' being dependent on 'misery' and 'misery' being dependent on 'enjoyment'.

The conducted study has important implications for practitioners interested in altering the situation at exclusive nightclubs. First, the so-called 'rainbow' queue structure could be replaced by a regular queue system. This would shorten the time individuals spend in queues, force the security officers to inform and motivate to each customer why he/she is not welcome, and decrease the frustration induced by the queue system. This fairly simple alteration in the operations of the nightclubs would significantly reduce the problems caused by the strive for an exclusive user image. Second, and more radically, the private security firms could be replaced by police officers, weakening the control of nightclub management on the selection and categorisation of individuals. Such a change would challenge the entire corporate organising for creation of an exclusive user imagery, forcing nightclub management to find alternative (and hopefully less problematic) ways of creating 'exclusiveness'.

Acknowledgment

We gratefully acknowledge the support of Michael Arvidsson, Johan Carlsson, Jacob Jonmyren, and Mattias Magnusson in collecting part of the data for this study.

References

Aaker, D. A. (1996). *Building Strong Brands*. New York, NY: The Free Press.

Allères, D. (2005). *Luxe...: Stratégies, Marketing*. Paris: Economica.

Anner, M., Greer, I., Hauptmeier, M., Lillie, N., & Winchester, N. (2006). The Industrial Determinants of Transnational Solidarity: Global Interunion Politics in Three Sectors. *European Journal of Industrial Relations,* 12(1), 7-27.

Baker, R. (2006). *Top 10 Reasons Why Affluent Life Style Marketing is Essential Today*. Dallas: Premium Knowledge Group.

Balmer, J. M. T., & Gray, E. R. (2000). Corporate Identity and Corporate Communications: Creating a Competitive Advantage. *Industrial & Commercial Training*, 32(6), 256-261.

Belk, R. W. (1988). Possessions and the Extended Self. *Journal of Consumer Research,* 15(2), 139-168.

Berry, C. J. (1994). *The Idea of Luxury: A Conceptual and Historical Investigation*. Cambridge: Cambridge University Press.

Brenkert, G. G. (2000). Social Products Liability: The Case of the Firearms Manufacturers. *Business Ethics Quarterly*, 10(1), 21-32.

Brioschi, A. (2006). Selling Dreams: The Role of Advertising in Shaping Luxury Brand Meaning. In J. E. Schroeder, & M. Salzer-Mörling (Eds.), *Brand Culture* (pp. 198-210). New York, NY: Routledge.

Carley, M. (2005). Global Agreements – State of Play. *European Industrial Relations Review*, 381, 14-18.

Carroll, S. J., & Gannon, M. J. (1997). *Ethical Dimensions of International Management*. Thousand Oaks, CA: Sage.

Cyert, R. M., & March, J. G. (1963). *A Behavioral Theory of the Firm*. Englewood Cliffs, NJ: Prentice-Hall.

De George, R. T. (1990). *Business Ethics*. New York, NY: MacMillan Publishers.

De George, R. T. (1993). *Competing with Integrity in International Business*. New York, NY: Oxford University Press.

Donaldson, T. (1989). *The Ethics of International Business*. New York, NY: Oxford University Press.

Donaldson, T. (1996). Values in Tension: Ethics Away from Home. *Harvard Business Review*, 74(5), 48-62.

Donaldson, T., & Dunfee, T. W. (1994). Towards a Unified Conception of Business Ethics: Integrative Social Contracts Theory. *Academy of Management Review*, 19(2), 252-285.

Dubois, B., & Paternault, C. (1995). Observations: Understanding the World of International Luxury Brands: The "Dream Formula". *Journal of Advertising Research*, 35(4), 69-76.

Egels-Zandén, N. (2007). Suppliers' Compliance with MNCs' Codes of Conduct: Behind the Scenes at Chinese Toy Suppliers. *Journal of Business Ethics,* 75(1), 207-223.

Egels-Zandén, N., & Hyllman, P. (2006). Exploring the Effects of Union-NGO Relationships on Corporate Responsibility: The Case of the Swedish Clean Clothes Campaign. *Journal of Business Ethics,* 64(3), 303-316.

Egels-Zandén, N., & Hyllman, P. (2007). Evaluating Strategies for Negotiating Workers' Rights in Transnational Corporations: The Effects of Codes of Conduct and Global Agreements on Workplace Democracy. *Journal of Business Ethics*, 76(2), 207-223.

Elm, N. (1998). The Business of Unethical Weapons. *Business Ethics: A European Review*, 7(1), 25-29.

Fairbrother, P., & Hammer, N. (2005). Global Unions – Past Efforts and Future Prospects. *Relations Industrielles/Industrial Relations*, 60(3), 405-431.

Frenkel, S. (2001). Globalization, Athletic Footwear Commodity Chains and Employment Relations in China. *Organization Studies,* 22(4), 531-562.

Gabriel, Y., & Lang, T. (2006). *The Unmanageable Consumer*. London: Sage.

Graafland, J. J. (2002). Sourcing Ethics in the Textile Sector: The Case of C&A. *Business Ethics: A European Review,* 11(3), 282-294.

Green, R. M. (2000). Legally Targeting Gun Makers: Lessons for Business Ethics. *Business Ethics Quarterly*, 10(1), 203-210.

Havemann, C. (1998). Hawks or Doves? The Ethics of UK Arms Exports. *Business Ethics: A European Review*, 7(4), 240-244.

Kapferer, J.-N. (1994). *Strategic Brand Management: New Approaches to Creating and Evaluating Brand Equity*. New York, NY: The Free Press.

Keller, K. L. (2000). The Brand Report Card. *Harvard Business Review*, 78(1), 147-157.

Keller, K. L. (2003). *Strategic Brand Management: Building, Measuring, and Managing Brand Equity*. Upper Saddle River, NJ: Prentice Hall, Pearson Education Ltd.

Kinder, P. D., & Domini, A. L. (1997). Social Screening: Paradigms Old and New. *Journal of Investing*, 6(4), 12-19.

Levy, S. J. (1959). Symbols for Sale. *Harvard Business Review*, 37(4), 117-124.

Maitland, G. (1998). The Ethics of the International Arms Trade. *Business Ethics: A European Review*, 7(4), 200-204.

McCracken, G. (1986). Culture and Consumption: A Theoretical Account of the Structure and Movement of the Cultural Meaning of Consumer Goods. *Journal of Consumer Research*, 13(1), 71-84.

McCracken, G. (1989). Who is the Celebrity Endorser? Cultural Foundations of the Endorsement Process. *Journal of Consumer Research*, 16(3), 310-321.

McWilliams, A., & Siegel, D. (2001). Corporate Social Responsibility: A Theory of the Firm Perspective. *Academy of Management Review*, 26(1), 117-127.

Newton, L. (1993). Gambling: A Preliminary Inquiry. *Business Ethics Quarterly*, 3(4), 405-418.

Riisgaard, L. (2005). Industrial Framework Agreements: A New Model of Securing Workers Rights?. *Industrial Relations,* 44(4), 707-737.

Schermerhom, J. R. Jr. (1999). Terms of Global Business Engagement in Ethically Challenging Environments: Applications to Burma. *Business Ethics Quarterly*, 9(3), 485-505.

Schroeder, J. E. (2005). The Artist and the Brand. *European Journal of Marketing*, 39(11/12), 1291-1305.

Simon, H. E. (1957). *Models of Man*. New York, NY: Wiley.

Sjöstrand, S. E. (1997). *The Two Faces of Management: The Janus Factor*. London: Thomson Learning.

Twitchell, J. B. (2002). Living it up: Our Love Affair with Luxury. New York, NY: Columbia University Press.

van Tulder, R., & Kolk, A. (2001). Multinationality and Corporate Ethics: Codes of Conduct in the Sporting Goods Industry. *Journal of International Business Studies,* 32(2), 267-283.

Vigneron, F., & Johnson, L. W. (1999). A Review and a Conceptual Framework of Prestige-Seeking Consumer Behavior. *Academy of Marketing Science Review*, *1999*(1).

Vigneron, F., & Johnson, L. W. (2004). Measuring Perceptions of Brand Luxury. *Brand Management*, 11(6), 484-506.

Wills, J. (2002). Bargaining for the Space to Organize in the Global Economy: A Review of the Accor-IUF Trade Union Rights Agreement. *Review of International Political Economy*, 9(4), 675-700.

Winstanley, D., Clark, J., & Leeson, H. (2002). Approaches to Child Labour in the Supply Chain. *Business Ethics: A European Review,* 11(3), 210-223.

INDEX

A

B

C

D

E

I

J

K

L

M

N

O

P

Q

R

S

T

U

V

W

Y